CAN ROCK & ROLL SAVE THE WORLD?

An Illustrated History of Music and Comics

Ian Shirley

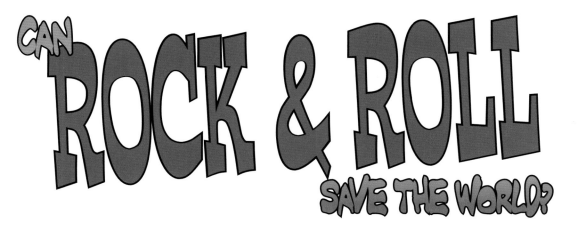

An Illustrated History of
Music and Comics

Ian shirley

saf publishing

saf publishing

First published in 2005 by SAF Publishing

SAF Publishing Ltd.
149 Wakeman Road, London.
NW10 5BH.
ENGLAND

email: info@safpublishing.com
www.safpublishing.com

ISBN 0 946719 80 2

Front cover:	Mike Allred
Back cover:	Top: © Ken Landgraf.
	Middle: Flameboy / © Omnibus Press,
	Bottom: © John Pound. *Bop* published by Kitchen Sink

A CIP catalogue record for this book is available from the British Library

Printed in England by the Cromwell Press, Trowbridge, Wiltshire

Contents

Can Rock & Roll Save the World?

© 2005 Marvel Characters, Inc. Used with permission.

Introduction

Everybody asks me the same question....

"How did you come up with the idea of writing a book about music and comics?"

Well, like all good superheroes the book has a secret origin and that stems from being a bad parent. Let me explain.

When I was a young boy at the beginning of the Seventies I was totally obsessed with Marvel comics. I bought the first issue of the *Mighty World Of Marvel* US reprints in 1972 – complete with iron-on Hulk transfer – and as many of the Marvel comics imported into the UK as I could afford. I built up a vast collection of Marvel and DC comics as well as great titles like *Victor, Warlord, Roy of The Rovers, Action* and *2000AD*.

When I grew older (not up, dear reader!) and started a family, I thought it only proper that my son should become obsessed with Marvel comics. So, when he was old enough to think that Spider-Man was cool he ended up with several Spider-Man action figures and a decent array of villains to pit them against. As for comics, hardcore collectors should avert their eyes because I do not treasure my old comics in the accepted sense. I believe that comics – and my 2,000 vinyl albums for that matter – are like coffee and exist for the sole purpose of stimulating the brain. Thus I wanted my son to get as much coffee as possible, and literally threw old *Spi-der-Man* comics at him to read. One of these was a 1975 UK *Spider-Man* annual. When I gave it to him it was in perfect condition but the attentions of a six year-old boy soon saw the cardboard cover ripped off and the guts of the book face down on the carpet at the end of his bed. Tidying up his room one day I picked it up and opening a page at random – after all this was a cracking story involving Doctor Octopus, The Human Torch and the Spider-Mobile – there was Mary Jane Watson going through boyfriend Peter Parker's record collection and pulling out an Aretha Franklin album. Wow, Spider-Man was a soul fan! Music had become the most important thing in my life after the punk rock explosion and as a music journalist I also thought this would be a great little story for one of the magazines I broke rocks for. A conversation with the editor of *Mojo Collections* saw him suggest I write a feature on the links between music and comics. This was a red rag to a bull and I dredged my subconscious for links recalling Captain America's alter ego, Steve Rogers, discussing the merits of Elvis Costello and Bruce Springsteen, A *Record Mirror* strip depicting a cartoon history of the Sex Pistols, Savage Pencil's *Rock'n'Roll Zoo* strip in *Sounds*, Zenith from *2000AD*, *Punk* magazine, Monkees comics, Kiss comics, Johnny Cash comics and a three ring circus of other references.

That was nearly four years ago and my researches and interviews have taken me high, low and sideways into delightful areas of exploration. There has also been much frustration. As hard as I looked I could never locate the physical evidence that a member of Duran Duran – sadly not Simon Le Bon – appeared as himself in a photo-romance story in a UK girl's teen mag. Saying that, I have tracked down a vast number of examples when the railway tracks of these two brilliant art forms have crossed, or run for some time along parallel lines. Gene Simmons thundering down the phone about Kiss comics, Damon Albarn and Jamie Hewlett talking about the Gorillaz, John Coates recalling the genesis of the Beatles' cartoons, Mort Todd relating the fascinating tale behind Marvel Music, Hugh Cornwell from the Stranglers explaining his early cartoon strip dabbling, Robert Crumb outlining his involvement with music and comics. Every musician I have interviewed as a music journalist has been asked if they had any interest in comics. The responses ranged from Gary Lightbody from Snow Patrol raving about Wolverine to John Cale stating that "I was into high art!" God bless him.

Rather than end up with a book that is nothing more than an exercise in train spotting – listing the ten thousand and one lyrical quotes in comic speech bubbles for example – I have tried to make this book as informative and entertaining as possible. To appeal not only to hardcore comic book readers and hardcore music fans but those who – God forbid! – know nothing about music and comics. Thus I have not written a dense history book that endeavours to cram every fact into the text. I have also avoided making any boring or tenuous comparisons between the two art forms. True, comic books have their big record labels like Marvel and DC, with a vast array of independent labels also releasing fantastic product. It is also true that in the Sixties it took four people to form a band and four people to make a comic. Let's see, Lead Vocals (writer), Lead guitar (penciller), Bass (inker) and Drums (colourist). True you can also throw a keyboard player (Letterer) into the mix! Of course, today although the four-piece group still thrives, music and comics are also created by one person or a small group on a computer in a bedroom studio.

As fascinating as these points are, it is vital to understand that the links between music and comics are fun, entertaining and an important part of popular culture. I can only hope that readers will find that this book shares those traits.

Ian Shirley
London, UK

Acknowledgements

This book could not have happened without the help, encouragement, assistance, connivance and co-operation of the following people. Some gave time to be interviewed face to face, by telephone or by email, whilst others set up these interviews or gave me the benefit of their wisdom, opinions, contacts, expert advice, sold me comics, sold me books, sent me things I could not find, shared insights, gave various approvals or just had their ears chewed off by the author about this insane labour of love.

Firstly, Roger Sabin; thanks for sharing coffee, unstinting support and proofing skills. Dave and Mick at SAF Publishing who agreed to publish this book based on little more than my enthusiasm, and who did not bat an eye when I asked and got the legendary Mike Allred to do the cover art. Mike Allred thanks for a fantastic job! A really big shout to Jay Allen Sanford and Herb Shapiro for their generosity when it came to the Revolutionary Comics story and Bernard MacMahon who stuck his hand into a top hat and pull out one hell of a rabbit for me….

Now for that roll call….

Gary Lightbody, Rick Wakeman, Ken Landgraf, Jon Mikl Thor, Mike Hoffman, John Holmstrom, Peter Bagge, Jaime Hernandez, Gary Panter, Dez Skinn, Gene Colan, Gene Simmons, Spike Steffenhagen, Damon Albarn, Jamie Hewlett, Tom Astor, Nadja Coyne, Peter Noble, Neal Adams, Tony McPhee, Edwin Pouncey, Herb Shapiro, Alan Moore, Alan Lewis, Todd McFarlane, Mike Richardson, Steve Gerber, Joe Quesada, Felix Dennis, Lee Dawson, John Lustig, Trina Robbins, Mile High Comics, Book and Comic Exchange in Notting Hill, Comic Showcase, Robin at the Book Palace, Silver Acre Comics, 30th Century Comics, Gosh Comics, The Mighty World of Comicana, Forbidden Planet, Ebay traders who sold me comics, Peggy Burns, Alex Brewer, Chynna Clugston-Major, Robert Crumb, Denis Kitchen, Gilbert Shelton, Michael English, Nigel Heywood, Ted Owen, Warren Lemming, Ilko Davidov, Mark Andrew Smith, John Pound, Dave Gibbons, Eric Reynolds and Fantagraphics, Scott Kolins, Mike Baron, Storm Thorgston, Nick Mason, Jesse Baggs, Kid Koala, Vezzzzaaaaaaaaa at Ninja Tune, Adrian at Raft, Rob Zombie, Jeffrey Lewis, Flameboy, Barnaby Legge, Jim McCarthy, THE RZA, Peter Milligan, P. Craig Russell, Harvey Pekar, Ian Carney, Mort Todd, Joe Casey, Mike Carey, John Coates, Steve Crompton, Ilko Davidov, Victor Gorelick, Joe at Image, Archie Comics, Rebellion, Ken Meyer Jr, David J, Matt Howarth, Scott Jackson, Steven Morris, Peter Hook, Toby Morris, Hugh Cornwell Tony McPhee, Tony at Knockabout, Matt Degennaro, Callum Laird, Scott Allie, Mark Paytress, DC Comics, Marvel Comics, Dark Horse Comics, Comics International, The Comics Journal, Oni Press, Slave Labor, Richard Sheaf, Bjork, Carol Platt, Amanda Webster, Paul Gravett, Joe Petagno, Freda Dare, Tony Dare, Michelle Urry, Jan Simmons, R.L.Crabb Victor Moscoso, Marcia Terrones Aaron at Apple Corps.

My wife Jennifer, my daughter Charlotte and my son Daniel...

...and the beat goes on.

LAST 💋 KISS

BY JOHN LUSTIG

And now, the event you've all been waiting for...whether you knew it or not! *Last Kiss the Musical!*

To be sung off-key to the tune of any song you don't particularly enjoy!

Systems of Romance

The late Jack Kirby casts a vast shadow over the Marvel universe. How large? Well, anyone familiar with the film *Independence Day* will recall seeing the shadow of an alien spacecraft covering the entire city of Los Angeles as Will Smith comes out of his girlfriend's house. As comparisons go, that will do nicely – especially considering that sibling spaceships also blotted out the sun over Washington and New York. The pencils of Jack Kirby gave physical life and dynamic form to Captain America, The Fantastic Four, Thor, The Silver Surfer, Doctor Doom, The Hulk, The Black Panther, The Watcher, The Inhumans, Galactus and other planetary-sized chunks that make up the Marvel Universe as it exists today. Kirby's genius – let's not quibble here – in the comic book industry is not only generally recognised, but has even spawned an ongoing magazine devoted to the work that he generated between 1935 and his death in 1993. The aptly named *Jack Kirby Collector* is published by TwoMorrows Publishing and celebrates the energy, imagination, vitality, explosive action and stunning attention to detail that Kirby gave all of his work.

What is less well known, is that despite these spacecraft-sized superhero shadows, Jack Kirby also helped launch American romance comics. *Young Romance* started the ball rolling in September/October 1947 and was "designed for the more adult readers of comics". As the title suggests, its 52 pages took the then current vogue for written True Life romance stories and set them to pictures in comic book form. Produced with long-time collaborator Joe Simon – co-creator of Captain America – *Young Romance* was an instant hit and the first printing of 500,000 copies sold out. For the second issue a million comics were printed and sold. Had this been a long-playing album in the Seventies each issue would have achieved platinum status.

The success of *Young Romance* saw the publishers launch further romance comics *Young Love* (1949) and *Young Brides* (1952), although by that time every other comics publisher and their dog had jumped on the bandwagon. As the late Barry White might have sung, they had so much love to give. That the Romance comics of the Fifties and Sixties were written by men and drawn (and inked and coloured) by men, for a mostly female readership did not hurt sales at all!

Music and romance have always gone together and therefore romance comics are fertile soil to begin our investigation. Although many of the American romance comics promoted a very similar theme – true love leads to marriage – writers required plenty of locations and situations to base their stories and this included musical settings. One of these writers was Stan Lee who, along with Kirby, was responsible for the Marvel Universe. Most comic fans imagine Lee typing out

brief plots for the Fantastic Four, The Hulk, Spider-Man or Thor, rather than sitting in a deserted restaurant nodding sympathetically, as a young girl pours out her heart about a broken romance or a love cruelly lost. But before me is a stack of Marvel romance comics from the Seventies containing stories "as narrated to Stan Lee". In fact, women had been narrating to Stan since the early Sixties when Marvel jumped with both feet into the market.

As with other romance comics, it was typical that even in this section of the Marvel Universe, young hearts would be broken or toyed with by musicians. The cover of issue 14 of *Young Love* from November 1971 screams "I came to the festival for LOVE …and MUSIC! No one told me the price of admission would be… a broken heart!" The festival in question was Woodstock, and the female protagonist attends with Rick, her boyfriend of two years standing. As soon as they arrive and pitch their tent, Rick decides that rather than mix with the crowd, he wants to go to sleep. We're not talking a post-coitus nap either, as the story was approved by the comics code, who deemed that a mouth-to-mouth kiss was the nearest artists could get to penetration. Of course, Rick's girl is more interested in exploring the concert site, and walks about on her own when – surprise surprise – she soon meets a cool hippie guy called, ahem, Flowers. By the end of a page that started with her and Rick pitching their tent, she's kissing this new guy.

As for what happens next – step up to the microphone and tell us, girl, "The next two days were like something out of a fairy tale, although I have to admit that I doubt Hans Christian Anderson ever dreamed of using a

© 2005 Marvel Characters, Inc. Used with permission.

setting like Woodstock for one of his tales." As well as spending time with her new stud, she gets to see Janis Joplin, Richie Havens and Country Joe McDonald who are neatly drawn in the comic. As for Rick, after two days alone – or sleeping – he finally finds her and exclaims that he was naturally "worried sick about you!" Does she care? Of course not! She tells Rick that she is love with Flowers and that they are going to New York to get married. Upon hearing this, Flowers acts like any other young guy who has had his fun, and promptly executes an immaculate three-point turn, "Look baby! When I told you I loved you, I really meant it…but not in the way you took it! I mean, I love lots of people…and you're just one of them! Dig?" At that stage she decides that she has been "such a fool" and Rick suggests that they

skip the last day of the festival and go home. What! And miss The Who and Jimi Hendrix help define an era? Yup! At the end of the story they get married, "because I'd had my big romantic adventure and was ready to settle down to being a good, loving wife." All told, a pretty good marriage of music and romance in seven pages. For the record, the other stories in this issue were called 'Jilted', 'With A Boy's Arms Around Me', 'I Stand In Sally's Shadow' and 'A Teen-Ager Can Also Hate'.

You know that I would be untrue, you know that I would be a liar, if I was to say to you, that the vast number of American romance comics that were published from 1947 onwards were chock full of stories based around music. They are the exception rather than the rule, although as the Sixties unfurled there was a definite attempt to reflect the times. No free love, but girls confronted with the dilemma of "His Hair Is Long And I Love Him" or "My Love Wears A Leather Jacket!" John Lustig, who has delightfully de-constructed some old Charlton romance comics by adding new dialogue contends that music, when it did appear in romance comics, was used like perfume to set a mood. "It means that there is romance going on, some kind of gaiety, or it could be rebelliousness. Often when they wanted to show a girl go bad – at least in Charlton comics – they would show her dancing!"

One of the most perverse and amusing stories involving romance, music and dancing appeared in *Love Diary* published by Charlton from January 1967. Entitled "Too Fat To Frug" it relates the tale of a go-go dancer called Sharon who falls in love with the new singer – Bus – at the club where

music and counterculture of the time. It is impossible to find, although I was lucky to get my hands on a photocopy from Trina Robbins, who wrote the excellent overview of women's comics, *From Girls To Grrrlz*.

When we spoke on the telephone Trina captured the intoxication of *Mod Love* perfectly, "That is the most amazing comic I have ever seen in my life. It is gorgeous. The art is totally Peter Max, the *Yellow Submarine*, that whole look and the stories are very sophisticated for a love comic. It is aimed at teenagers but the stories take place in Europe, specifically in Rome and London, and revolve around a fictional rock band. This guy in the band and his girlfriend."

This is all true. The artwork is sumptuous and the stories set in London really reflect the look of contemporary psychedelic bands. The hairstyles and clothing of the groups featured, perfectly capture the look of acts like the Kinks, The Who and early Pink Floyd.

Unlike their American counterparts, English comics have always been published weekly. Being geographically smaller, distribution was not so much of a problem. The production schedule meant that comics, from *Beano* to *Bunty* could be much more responsive to prevailing cultural trends. If an unknown band went top ten in the pop charts one week, you could bet your bottom dollar – or pound – that they would be featured in a comic the following week.

Back in the mists of time when post World War Two rationing was still in force, publications like *Film Fun* and *Radio Fun* had some musical content. One-page strips featured singers like Gracie Fields and the antics of the Beverley Sisters who "in song and fun they act as one." As for the stories, they were

little more than one-joke fare. For example, the Beverley Sisters are going to stay overnight at an inn where Dick Turpin stayed. When they are shown a tired bed in one of the bedrooms, one of them says, "It looks like his horse has slept in it too!" This being 1957, the Beverley Sisters were very much part of the radio-friendly musical establishment, although there was much more exciting fare to be had in other publications.

Launched in 1957, *Valentine* was aimed at young working women or what would soon be known as teenagers. In the first issue, the editor promised that, "every week I will bring you lovely picture stories inspired by the titles of the loveliest tunes in the world, the tunes we hum, that set our feet a dancing – the tunes that bring memories of love and romance, of joy and sweet heartache." When it came to mixing music and comics you could not nail your colours to the mast more firmly than that!

At this time there was a musical sea change underway and *Valentine* tapped into the emerging rock and roll vein with a vengeance. The first romance story was inspired by Elvis Presley's 'Blue Moon', and his 'Love Me Tender' was also the inspiration for the following week's story. Both black and white love stories had more to do with rolling a young lady towards the arms of the man of her dreams, than losing herself to the devil's music. Not so Bill Haley's 'Rock Around The Clock' in issue 7 from March 2, 1957 which had a story totally inspired by music. A trumpeter moves into an upstairs flat and when he begins to practice, the girl downstairs knows the song and sings along. No doubt looking for a husband, she runs upstairs to introduce herself and he quickly suggests that she come

to see his band that night. What is the name of the band, son? "Ron Foster and his Rolling Stones. That's us!" Five years later, Mick Jagger and Brian Jones formed another band by the same name. Returning to the story, the trumpet player gets her to sing with his band and they fall in love. As three-page love stories with a musical theme go, you can't get better than this.

Utilising stories inspired by songs, the publishers of *Valentine* were onto a winner, and the formula went on in this vein for years and years. Only a small number featured music and musicians, but the writers were deft at making sure that the romantic interlude reflected the song title. For example, Elvis Presley's 'Heartbreak Hotel' was about a girl who went on holiday to Spain with her boyfriend. They quickly split up – hence the heartbreak hotel. The poor girl is so lonely that she could cry, but fortunately meets the guy in the next room and true romance blossoms. Over the years, stories were inspired by many artists who are forgotten now, although others like Frank Sinatra, The Who, the Kinks, the Rolling Stones, Cliff Richard and the Beatles are clearly not.

As well as general romance stories, *Valentine* had style and fashion tips combined with excellent pop coverage, and as with today's teen magazines knew they exactly on what side their bread was buttered. When Elvis Presley and Cliff Richard made everybody realise that skiffle really was nothing more than young men playing with washboards, the coverage of the pelvis and his artificial hip (Cliff Richard) was forensic in its intensity. When Elvis made his second feature film *Loving You* in 1957, *Valentine* commissioned an artist to draw the story in comic book form.

Of course, it would be wrong to suggest that the early editions of romance stories in *Valentine* were totally dominated by rock and roll. They were not, and early editions featured stars such as Mel Torme, Perry Como, Aker Bilk, Norman Wisdom, Victor Borge – and even a Gene Kelly romance inspired by *Singin' In The Rain*. *Valentine* also fabricated a first class opportunity to put musical stars in the comic. There was a weekly two-page strip called 'Living Love Stories', each highlighting the love story of how singers, band leaders and the like met their husbands or wives. So readers were able to discover how Vera Lynne was wooed and married by clarinet player Harry Lewis, and skiffle king Lonnie Donegan not only met and wed his wife Maureen, but also signed a recording contract and had his first hit record 'Rock Island Line'. It was a great idea, although it only ran for a year or so, as one can imagine it was pretty tough finding a real life-marriage story in the music business every week, year-in and year-out.

Another Fifties comic that deserves credit for putting music around their pages was *Roxy*. As with *Valentine*, its romance stories were inspired by contemporary popular songs, and like *Valentine*'s 'Living Love Stories' *Roxy* made an effort to actually put the singer inside the story. The front page of the first issue from March 15, 1958, trumpeted

© IPC + Syndication.

that "This Story Is Told To You by Tommy Steele Himself".

Tommy Steele, I should explain, was something of music hall rock and roller, and between October 1956 and March 1958 had chalked up thirteen top-thirty hits in the UK. There were plenty more to come as well. And, on the cover of the first issue of *Roxy* – lo and behold – there was Tommy, about to board a ship, giving a girl his lucky guitar-shaped pin – a replica of which was also conveniently given away free with the magazine. The pin helps her find romance and when later "a certain ship docked and a certain young man with a guitar came ashore", the girl and her new love search out Tommy Steele to tell him that "your guitar pin really brought us luck." Who knows, it might have even been worth half a sixpence!

This mixture of real-life pop singers helping young girls find their ideal man continued every week. A lot of the stars in *Roxy* are long-forgotten now, but the stories are excellent:

"Not long ago Frankie (Vaughan) got a piece of wedding Cake..."

"Marty Wilde felt he had to butt in when he saw a girl and a guy fighting over a guitar",

"It all started one afternoon at a church Bazaar where Tommy Steele had left an old guitar of his to be raffled for charity."

Roxy was only published for four years (1958-1962). One reason for its demise – apart from market forces – was that they expected their readers take a leap of fantasy too far. On March 26, 1960, the title page screamed out, "See Elvis as the boy in the story. You are the girl!" Sadly, in the ensuing pages the boy looked nothing like Elvis at all. It was just an excuse to print a bigger publicity picture of Presley at the beginning of the story. Saying that, there was a possibility of a *ménage-à-trois* with a similar story called 'Passing Strangers' based on the Everley Brothers. "Imagine Don or Phil as the boy, you are the girl!"

Inside the guts of the magazine, *Roxy* contained some excellent music stories. "That New Magic" – which ran for several weeks from June 1958 – manages to totally sum up the musical experience, and even has an undercurrent of sex, drugs and jazz. It revolves around a trumpet player called Dick Merrow, who lacks the 'push' to get ahead. His girlfriend – Cleo Dallons – just wants him to find the 'push' to propose to her. Luckily her brother has just returned after braving three years in the Amazon jungle, where he came across a wonder drug that makes people brave and determined. Cleo doses her boyfriend with the juice hoping that it will give him the required 'push'. It has the opposite effect and gives him the determination to leave town in order to find fame as a trumpet player. He is soon in a band and playing like Chet Baker, Louis Armstrong and Miles Davis combined.

"Gosh!" he gasps between blue notes, "this is the life for me!"

Indeed it is, as Merrow is blowing his brains out in a club full of women who are all screaming "Dick! Dick! Dick!" It would be nice to think they are all offering him backstage fellatio, but I'm probably just letting my imagination run away with me. Anyway, as his confidence is soley based on a drug, his girlfriend worries that he will loose everything when it wears off. Of course it does, and he has to face playing straight without chemicals charging through his veins. He manages not only to pull this off, but also finally marry Cleo. So, a happy ending all round and a cracking music-based story. Certainly better than another *Roxy* story where a relationship nearly flounders due to a boyfriend's obsession with an... accordion player. "We'll hoof it in a minute, Ellie just listen to this guy, he's a wonder on the squeeze box." Like the woman in the song by The Who, Ellie probably wants to demonstrate that she is no slouch in the squeezebox department herself!

It was a logical step to progress to having pop stars appear as themselves in the comics. This started when Adam Faith's biography was serialised in *Roxy*, where his romances and rise to stardom were depicted in comic book form. More inspired fare appeared in the dark story 'The Waiting Hours', where a

Then, under the name of "Mott the Hoople's Rock and Roll Circus", the boys decided on a vaudeville act including jugglers, knife-throwers and comedian Max Wall.

MOTT the HOOPLE'S ROCK'N'ROLL CIRCUS

The circus brought them publicity, but not much else. Fed up, the boys left for Europe.

It was in Switzerland, in Zurich, that they finally felt the end had come.

"WE'RE AS FAR AWAY FROM THE BIG-TIME AS THE TOP OF THESE ALPS!"

"AND WE'RE WORKING OUR-SELVES TO DEATH—AND FOR WHAT?"

But when the news came that Mott the Hoople were breaking up, so did a surprise!

"LOOK, YOU CAN'T GIVE UP NOW. I'VE BEEN LISTENING TO YOUR "WILDLIFE" ALBUM PRACTICALLY EVERY DAY FOR MONTHS. I WANT TO TALK TO YOU. I'M SURE I CAN HELP."

"IMAGINE DAVID BOWIE TAKING AN INTEREST IN US!"

"THIS IS GREAT, DAVID— JUST GREAT!"

Three hours after the 'phone call, David Bowie was with the group, bringing a song he had written for them—"All The Young Dudes". It was to be the big break-through they had been waiting for and soon they were in demand for top TV shows and concerts all over Britain.

MOTT THE HOOPLE
All The Young Dudes

Their autumn tour ended at the most famous home of rock 'n' roll in the country—the Rainbow.

"LOOK AT THOSE QUEUES!"

"BOY, AM I GLAD NOW WE DIDN'T SPLIT UP IN ZURICH!"

In October, 1972, Mott the Hoople were back in the States. At one exciting concert, where they were playing on the same bill as the famous John McLaughlin, a couple of rowdies threw a bottle at Mick's guitar—and the rest of the band set after them!

"WHO WAS IT? I'LL TEACH HIM NOT TO CLOBBER MICK!"

"IT'S OK, LADS— NO HARM DONE!"

MINI TOUR FOR MOTT
A SELL OUT
TOP TEN

1973 opened for Mott with a two-week tour, together with the Alex Harvey Band. It was a huge success.

Mott the Hoople are fond of experimenting. Their single, "Honaloochie Boogie", written by Ian Hunter, has Roxy Music star Andy Mackay on sax, plus a section of cellists.

If you'd like the latest news about Mott the Hoople, write to their fan club—Kris Needs and Caroline Bain, 53 Richmond Road, Aylesbury, Bucks.

SO LONG, FOLKS, 'SBEEN NICE KNOWING YA! C'MON, EL... LET'S GO!

© IPC + Syndication.

couple are abducted and locked in a house by two escaped prisoners. In an act of great fun that would no doubt lead to a legal scrum today, the two escaped convicts are called Frank and El, and were in name and appearance Frank Sinatra and Elvis Presley. Brilliant stuff, and much more entertaining than their duets on Frank's American TV show after Elvis was discharged from the Army.

Roxy and *Valentine* were only two magazines in vast armada of comics aimed at women and girls published in England between the late 1950s and the 1990s. *Bunty, Jackie, Misty, Spellbound, Blue Jeans, Tammy, Jinty, Schoolfriend* and *Pink* are just some that rolled off the presses in their millions, waving jolly hockey sticks into the faces of their readers. Although fashions and attitudes changed, many would contain some form of pop content. Elton John even appeared as a thinly disguised John Eldon in the *Mandy for Girls Annual* in 1978. In the early Seventies, *Judy* came along with a frightening number of stories based in boarding schools – "Bobby Dazzler, the only

girl at Westbury Boarding School for Boys" – contained many excellent two-page histories of pop groups. As a random sample, the Mott The Hoople story from August 1974 is excellent, and even features David Bowie calling the nearly down-and-out band, who conveniently for the artist, were all huddled around the phone, "Look, you can't give up now. I've been listening to your *Wildlife* album practically every day for months. I want to talk to you. I'm sure I can help." And help he does. Three hours later they meet and he gives them a song that kick-starts their success called "All the Young Dudes".

Judy was not alone in running short, two-to-three page pop biographies. From the Sixties to the age of the New Romantics, many UK girls comics ran band stories amidst a forest of colourful pin-ups of teen icons like the Bay City Rollers, Slade, David Essex, Spandau Ballet, Duran Duran and, honest to God your honour, Colin Moulding of XTC! The career of "Mr Stand and Deliver" Adam Ant, was gloriously drawn in *Blue Jeans* and the magazine even gave away a Crazy Cutlass Broach to every reader! Yo ho ho!

Blue Jeans also ran true-life romance stories inspired by pop songs as per the old *Valentine* and *Roxy* formula. Even now, I find it somewhat surreal to see a boy-meets-girl story inspired by "Wondrous Stories" by Yes (30 December, 1977), whilst Queen's "Somebody To Love" and The Darts' "Come Back My Love" and Paul McCartney's "Maybe I'm Amazed" were ideal fodder for true love. And of course, when it came to New Wave bands, there was one song that might have been penned with girls' romance comics in mind, the Buzzcocks "Ever Fallen

In Love (With Someone You Shouldn't've)". (December 30, 1978).

Comics for girls always featured heroines in peril, and in the pages of *Pink* in 1973 the peril did not come any greater than that experienced by top girl singer Tara Boon. She was abducted and imprisoned by a money-mad aristocrat called Lord Bred who was obviously a fan of Phil Spector. Tara is forced to work with a group of four musicians who he kept chained in the dungeon of his castle, under the suitable name of Slave. This strip was top stuff, and the band are forced to live and record in a state-of-the-art dungeon studio with Bred at the controls. When he takes them out on their first tour, the band are lowered onto the stage in a steel cage before being let out to perform. When Tara tries to tell a sold-out crowd that "this is no act! We really are slaves!" she is whipped – yes whipped! – by one of Bred's henchmen live on stage. "What a fantastic act – and the music hasn't even started!" screams one of the audience, who probably considers Alice Cooper tame by comparison. From that point Tara has to try and reveal the plight of the band through song, "Won't somebody help me, I bin shut up so long," she sings

with a misery that would bring tears to Morrissey's eyes, "and these chains are getting tighter." Over the course of the story they get tighter before Slave are freed, but it is masterful stuff with artwork that really does the music and comics synergy justice.

Another top-notch story featuring a fictional rock band appeared in the pages of boys' comic *Eagle* between January and May 1986. D.A.D.D. stood for Dial A Dawn Destructor and followed the exploits of an American band called Dawn Destruction who only play gigs during daylight hours, "because the night is ours! The night is ours – to keep clean!" This does not involve taking showers or washing hands but answering the telephone to help solve "problems the law can't handle". In other words going out and fighting bad guys like King Rat, who runs a gang who operate out of the sewers. As well as enjoying a plethora of excellent adventures the band also play Sand Aid with 200 other acts – not to feed Africa – but to raise money to irrigate the deserts of the world. The only strange thing about D.A.D.D. is that after two adventures lead singer of the band – Missy Troll – turns from a black woman with braids in her hair into a white woman

© IPC + Syndication.

with braids in her hair with no explanation at all!

Look-in was the king of pop content. Launched in 1971, it was not a romance comic, but aimed at both sexes and based stories around popular TV shows like *Kung-Fu*, *The Six Million Dollar Man* and *The Benny Hill Show*. Tapping into popular culture also saw them go to town with pop biographies; Abba, Slik (with Midge Ure), the

Bay City Rollers, the Beatles, the Monkees, David Cassidy, Haircut 100, 5 Star, Bucks Fizz, Flintlock, Madness and Duran Duran to name a few. Even Live Aid was served over three weeks, detailing just how Sir Bob Geldof pulled together the greatest musical event of its time with the intention of Feeding the World. At one stage they even ran a weekly strip called 'When We Were Young' so even Cliff Richard could get a Look-In!

EVERY THURSDAY 14p
I.R. 23p
(Inc. VAT)

POP CONCERT
DENNIS and the DINMAKERS
STARS OF THE SUPER "DENNIS THE MENACE 1985" BOOK NOW ON SALE £2.10

BOOM! BOOM!

If we widen the circle, there is also no keeping *Beano* and the *Dandy* out of the act. The only link that they have with romance is applied to their view of childhood, but as the comics still sell by the bucket-load there is no debating their popularity. Anyway, before they were "Golden Brown", The Stranglers appeared, although as you can imagine the general musical content was more knockabout. There have also been references to Bob Dylan songs like "Highway 61", the Beatles, John Travolta and the disco craze, as well an appearance by Madness. *Dandy*'s Korky The Cat once gave pop star Elvis Stardust a lift in his sportscar before a concert and that original reprobate Dennis the Menace formed a band Dennis and the Dinmakers with Gnasher on drums. When the band

fail to attract fans – apart from Dennis's granny – they decide to explore different musical forms. These include steel band music (banging a dustbin), country music (playing to cows) and reggae (mops on head). Finally they turn to heavy metal (played in a cellar) that is so bad Dennis's dad silences their attempts to be Black Sabbath playing in the coal cellar by putting the manhole cover back in place over the cellar entrance. "This heavy metal cover will silence their row!" At the end of the story the band end up sitting on a wall with Dennis saying, "This is the best sort of pop group to be!" He is of course referring to blowing bubbles from the free bubblegum given away with that week's *Beano*.

And speaking of bubblegum…

2

Cartoons Networked

Believe it or not Frank Sinatra is responsible for one of the most enduring links between music and comics. The sort of link that would lick your face, then swipe a sandwich out of your hand and swallow it in the same movement. No, we're not talking about Jerry Lewis, who shared a comic book with Sinatra's good friend and Rat Pack member Dean Martin between 1952 and 1956. These comics were based on their highly successful films and even when their screen partnership ended, Jerry Lewis continued his comic antics alone. Did Sinatra appear in one of the forty-one issues

of the Martin and Lewis comic book then? No. Did he appear in a Rat Pack special issue with Sammy Davis Jr acting as an additional guest star? Sadly, no. This was before the Rat Pack formed, although Sinatra did make some comic book appearances. Not only the life story in *Junior Miss*, mentioned in the previous chapter, but in *Picture News* (March 1946) where Frank struck a blow with his fists against bigotry in the school yard! A great story drawn from a film appearance, but I am digressing from the point...

It's 1969 and we're two flies on a wall. Not any old wall, but the pressurised inner skin of an aeroplane winging its way towards Los Angeles. Fred Silverman head of daytime scheduling for the mighty CBS Television is below us, embraced by one of the plush seats at the front of the plane. Fred has just had a bad day. He had pitched a programme idea to the Frank Stanton, President of CBS and the idea had been rejected. It was a damn good idea too and perfect for an upcoming Saturday morning slot! A cartoon! Four kids and their dog travelling around America solving mysteries in a van called the Mystery Machine. The working title at this stage was "Mysteries Five" or "Who's Scared?" Okay, okay, not a great title but in this business you can thrash that out such minor details once you get the green light. But there had been no green light, only red – and red meant no go. Fred had to get back to the drawing board....

He's tired. Pitching proposals takes it out of you, and nothing is more draining than rejection. He decides to take his mind off misery and places the in-flight headphones onto his ears. His dark mood improves when a Frank Sinatra song begins to play. Silvermann likes Sinatra. He's a big fan and this track, "Strangers In The Night" is a great tune. So he enjoys it, sipping something cold and alcoholic as Sinatra and some beautiful woman move from "exchanging glances" to "lovers at first sight". Get in there Frank! As the song peaks and reaches for the coda, Sinatra in playful – dare we whisper post-coital – mood, begins to scat: "Dooby Dooby Doo...."

Silverman sits bolt upright as if enjoying the pleasure of an electric chair. We flies on the wall are startled, and, after a swift holding pattern to ensure he is not reaching for

a newspaper, return to our bulkhead perch. "Jesus," thinks Silvermann. "That is it! He literally punches the air. Scooby Doo! Scooby Doo! The dog. Call the dog Scooby Doo and make him the star of the show, not the damned kids! The dog's a great Dane right? We'll make him a BIG Great Dane and make him scared...hey, as scared as his owner – some kid called Shaggy. That would work. The kids would eat it up! A big stupid dog to watch on TV after breakfast on a Saturday morning. Kids love dogs! Bingo! Stewardess, can you ask the pilot if he can turn this damn plane around?"

Thus – with dramatic liberty – this was the inspirational moment that led to the *Adventures of Scooby Doo*. The series hit TV screens in September 1969 and, so it seems to me, has never been off them since. Hell, Scooby recently even made it onto the silver screen and, in the second film of his adventures, gets to pay tribute to the moment of creative epiphany that spawned him by singing "Strangers In The Night"! As you might imagine, he does not sing it as well as Frank, but then again no-one ever has.

Inevitably any discussion about music and comics would eventually spill onto the TV screen and the world of cartoons. After all, quite a few comic book characters have made the transition from the printed page to the small screen and whenever this happens, guitar, bass, drums and music are not far behind. Real bands have also become cartoon characters and enjoyed their own animated adventures.

It is fitting that the world's most famous band spawned a cartoon show. When the Beatles wowed America on the *Ed Sullivan Show* in August 1964, one of the many millions of viewers was Al Brodax, the man responsible for syndicating shows for King Features. "I could help the Beatles!" he screamed down the telephone at Brian Epstein after tracking the Beatles' manager down at his New York hotel. He moved swiftly to portray them on television in cartoon form.

In 1964, television animation was in its infancy and the concept of basing a show around a real-life pop band was a bold gamble. Then again, America had fallen for the Beatles hook, line and sinker and anything to do with the fab four represented a potentially sound business proposition. Brodax quickly found a sponsor to finance *The Beatles* which would run on the ABC-TV network.

Work commenced on the storyboards. Amazingly, when it came to animating the series, Brodax turned to a small company in England called TV Cartoons. Founded by George Dunning and John Coates in 1957, TVC made adverts for fledgling independent television and animated industrial training films. "I think he felt it would be cheaper to do it in England," Coates recalls today, "and maybe he thought that as the Beatles were British, it ought to be done in England." TV Cartoons were initially paid £80,000 to make 26 episodes. The amount of work involved saw them subcontract episodes out to studios as far flung as Canada, Holland and Australia, "as we had never had to do that volume of work before, it was totally new to us." These other studios were given 'model' sheets which dictated how Paul, George, John and Ringo should look.

The Beatles first appeared on ABC at 10.30am on the September 25, 1965 and was an instant hit. The format of each episode was simple. A Beatles song inspired a madcap adventure and this song would be played during the five-and-a-half-minute running time. There would be two 'episodes' per half hour show as well as linking sketches and a singalong introduced by Paul, George or John – with constant interference from Ringo – and the words of that particular song appearing at the bottom of the screen. The Fab Four undertook their adventures in matching uniforms of blue suits and Beatles' boots. John was depicted as the leader of the group, although Ringo, who had been given a cartoon laugh – "Hyuk, hyuk, hyuk, yeah!" – usually stole the show.

Set against today's slick computer-generated animation, *The Beatles* is crude, but there is no denying its charm which literally broke the ground for the live action Monkees show to follow. In every episode the Fab Four get mixed up in some wonderful adventures involving highwaymen, musketeers, Hollywood, villains, animals and all manner of exotic locations around the world. Although aimed at children, the cartoons were, no doubt, also enjoyed by more mature Beatles' fans. Watching from the perspective of the new millennium, what is most striking – apart from a hilarious trip to Greenwich Village to hang out with Beatniks – is how the episodes shadowed the Beatles' musical development.

"We were just handed the music," recalls Coates, "and we made it fit, work and animated to it."

The first series from 1965 drew heavily from albums like *With The Beatles* and *Beatles For Sale*. Therefore, in addition to songs like "Twist and Shout", "A Hard Day's Night", and "She Loves You" there is "Misery", "Roll Over Beethoven" and "Please Mr Postman".

The success of the first series saw further shows being commissioned and songs were culled from seminal albums like *Rubber Soul, Revolver,* and the *Magical Mystery Tour* EP, where the Beatles' musical prowess was increasing at the speed of light. The "Taxman", "Paperback Writer", "Eleanor Rigby", "Strawberry Fields", "I'm Only Sleeping" and "Tomorrow Never Knows" episodes are infused with a growing and knowing psychedelia.

What did the Beatles think of their cartoon alter-egos? Their first impressions were formed when they attended a test screening of two episodes in TV Cartoons' Dean Street offices in 1965.

"The Beatles came to visit the studios at seven o'clock one evening," recalls Coates, "Dean Street was blocked off at either end and they rolled up in blacked-out limousines."

By all accounts the Fab Four enjoyed their comic antics although they were bemused by the accents their characters had been given. This was a matter of political expediency with voice actors Paul Frees and Lance Percival de-scousing the Beatles into a version of English that could be understood by American children. An American comic called *Go-Go* from August 1966 saw fit to include a page of 'Liddypool talk' which allowed readers to understand what the real-life Beatles were talking about. So "plonk" meant "white wine", "the flicks" meant "the cinema" and "To chat up a girl" meant "to talk to a strange girl and try to get to know her."

Although the series was a huge ratings success, Beatles' fans in England never saw the cartoons because of an Epstein embargo. "He would not have the show shown in England," says Coates, "because of the voices. A silly thing because you could have easily put Liverpool accents on them." However, on a business trip to America, Coates did get himself

in front of a colour TV. "They were amazing to watch, especially with all the commercials dotted in. It was jolly exciting!"

What was also exciting for Coates was that *The Beatles* put TVC on the map.

"In the first year's output we lost money, as we did not know how to do a series, the second year we broke even and the third year we did rather well!"

Better still, TVC's next project was the full-length animated *Yellow Submarine* feature film, although if *The Beatles* was a headache to create, *Yellow Submarine* was a migraine.

"The main thing with *Yellow Submarine*," says Coates, "was that it was a nightmare, because when Al Brodax began to talk about doing a feature film we told him that the caricature figures in the series aren't going to make feature films. They weren't strong enough. We needed to rethink the whole thing if we were going to get people to pay money to go to the cinema. I think he could only envisage a lengthening of the series and it was hard to persuade him creatively that we needed something amazing. We arranged a screening of the three minutes we had, be-cause we had no script or story worked out.

We had animated the "Sgt Pepper" song, representing each character as we saw them. We served him (Brodax) lobster and champagne at the Mayfair Hotel cinema. We ran the three minutes and he wasn't expecting it, as he had no idea that we had done it and I'm glad to say that he liked it. It is in the final film but it was done as a test piece."

Unlike the series the TV series, the Beatles themselves gave some input to the film.

"They took a little more interest in *Yellow Submarine*," continues Coates, "because they suddenly realised that it wasn't the simple childish figures in the series. They came to one or two of the screenings, where we showed them sections of the film as we made them."

As with the TV series, actors were used to provide their voices and at one stage over 200 animators were working on the film day and night just to get it finished on time.

The finished results were spectacular and impressed everybody at the time – except, according to Coates, Paul McCartney. "He was the only one who didn't like it. The oth-ers thought it was marvellous. John said that all the good ideas were his (laughs), that we pinched them all off him, but he said that he liked it. George always liked it, and so did Ringo. Paul was saying that it was not what he expected, he wished that it had been more Disney-esque and cuter. I thought, "How could you write those songs and say that they should be Disney-esque? 'Lucy In The Sky' was not something you could do cute Disney to! Odd. I think he has come around to liking it now."

The Beatles TV cartoon series was an im-portant milestone in animation as it paved the way for other cartoon band to follow in its wake. One example featured one of the longest comic book franchises in the world. No, not Superman – but Archie!

"Archie first appeared in *Pep Comics* in 1941," Victor Gorelick proudly tells me, "and not even a year later in 1942, the first Archie comic was published and it has been history ever since."

History indeed. Imagine that, a comic character who started life at the turning point of the Second World War when Hitler's dream of a Thousand Year Reich was defeated by his own decision to invade Russia. The Battles of Moscow, Leningrad, Stalingrad and Kursk aside, Archie has stayed the same ever since enjoying adventures with pals like Jughead

and Reggie and been involved in a bizarre love triangle with two girls called Betty and Veronica. Nothing unsavoury or sexual ever happens of course. Archie is all good clean fun. An apple pie comic.

Archie comics are timeless and in many respects this is the secret behind their success. In personality the Archie of today is hardly different from that of the Fifties. He has not received a Frank Miller retooling and become a character of dark moods prone to robbing Seven-Elevens and asking Veronica and Betty to explore the possibilities of a *ménage á trois*. Even when he met Marvel's Punisher in the Nineties it was good clean fun and nobody got killed.

"It is a style," says Gorelick, who started as an artist on Archie himself in 1958, and when we spoke forty-something years later was Managing Editor. "We try to have the artists follow a certain style with the Archie characters. If you look back at the characters that were drawn in the Forties and Fifties, the artwork has got better. One of the things that keeps Archie contemporary is the fact that we try to keep him up to date with a lot of current fashions, current trends and so forth. That is one of the reasons that Archie has remained popular over the years."

Too true. For generations of American children Archie has been, and remains, the entry level for comic book readers. As Gorelick stated, being a young guy, Archie has always followed fashion and musical trends. The same applies to Jughead, Reggie, Betty and Veronica. It is only natural that a number of famous musicians have graced the pages of titles like *Archie, Betty and Veronica*, *Archie's Pal Jughead* and *Archie and Friends*. In thinly veiled form of course. Elvis Presley appeared as Purley Gates in 1958 singing "Love Me Slender" and "Brown Dog" and Michael Jackson became Michael Jackstone in 1985. Boy George, the Stray Cats, Bruce Springsteen, and of course, the Beatles have also appeared.

"There have always been references to music and musical groups or singers or bands throughout the years," says Gorelick. "It has always been to keep the strip and comic book fresh so that readers will be able to identify with Archie and the fact that Archie likes the same music, likes the same groups and the same singers that our readers find popular."

Archie and his gang have also sailed through Beatlemania, the mod look, psychedelia, punk, disco and even got into break dancing in the Eighties, which just goes to show how flexible this whitest of American white boys can be. Eat your heart out Slim Shady! But what interests us most is Archie's biggest claim to fame. His chart-topping singles and top-rated cartoon show. The boy from Riverdale was once a pop sensation!

There is a brilliant book called *Bubblegum Music Is The Naked Truth* by Kim Cooper and David Smay which I recommend everybody to buy. As the title suggests it takes the reader through the sugar-candied underbelly of this most tasty form of pop music from the Banana Splits via the Bay City Rollers to Britney Spears. There is an illuminating chapter on Don Kirschner. Kirschner was the man responsible for giving the world one of the greatest real-life comic book inventions of all time – the Monkees. Typically he hired the best songwriters and the best session musicians to write and record the songs for the show. Monster hits followed, not only in the charts, but also in the TV ratings. It was then that the Monkees decided that they wanted more freedom than their cage allowed. They wanted to write and perform the songs themselves.

For Kirschner it was an object lesson in ingratitude and ways were parted. Like many a Svengali he thought that if only he did not have to deal with troublesome artists everything would be fine. The next logical step was to create another fictional band that could not answer back, because they would not exist in the first place. So, Kirschner got involved in the process that saw Archie and his pals transformed from comic book characters into a cartoon characters. The group of pals also became a pop band called – drums

please! – the Archies. They had a legendary line-up that read like this; Archie (guitar and vocals), Jughead (drums), Reggie (bass), Veronica (tambourine/vocals) and Betty (keyboards). True, I've seen occasions when Reggie is on drums and Jughead is on keyboards, but I guess this just goes to prove how versatile these guys were! Of course, before they were allowed into the recording studio they had to audition for Kirshner who, despite his problems with those pesky Monkees, was the model of Mr. Nice Guy. "All set. Mister Kirshner!" says Archie after the band have set up their instruments in his recording studio-cum-office. "Okay! Let's hear it!" says Don.

Of course this was visual fiction of the highest order. After all, the Archies did not exist, so as artists slaved over drawings for the animated series *Everything's Archie*, Kirshner began working on the music.

"He had all the music produced for that show and a lot of that music became very popular," recalls Gorelick.

That is an understatement Victor! After minor hits, the Las Vegas jackpot was hit with "Sugar Sugar", probably the most famed bubblegum hit of all time and something that Kirschner had written for the Monkees who rejected it!

Although they were a manufactured band, such was the success of Archies' singles and albums that eventually a band was recruited to go out on tour to play the hits. Meanwhile the Archie cartoon series pulled in viewers and Archie comics flew off the news stands. Of course, fame and fortune did not affect Archie and his gang one bit. In Riverdale they were little more than a garage band who played at weekends, so Archie kept his feet on the ground. More importantly, when

the TV series and the pop group ran out of steam, Archie was free to carry on with his comic book adventures that continue to this day. What Archie thinks of his bubblegum I don't know, but he's into rap now and, at least in Riverdale, giving Eminem a run for his money.

That the Archie cartoon show was so popular was evident by the fact that it spawned another cartoon, in the form of *Josie and the Pussycats*.

"You always try to create a little competition for yourself," says Gorelick. "Josie started out originally just as Josie. The name of the book was *Josie*. It was a book about a girl who was a female Archie, although she was not as clumsy as Archie, she was a little smarter. Nevertheless she had a group of friends and that book ran for a while – quite a number of issues – then when Archie went on television and the Archie group became so popular, the book took a transformation and we developed *Josie and the Pussycats*. We had an all-girl band which was actually one of the first all-girl bands even though they were all cartoons (laughs)."

Any reader who has seen *Josie and the Pussycats* in cartoon or comic form will recall instantly their sexy catsuit costumes. In fact, this was based on a real-life costume that artist Dan DeCarlo invented for his wife Josie, who was the inspiration for the strip.

"Yeah. Yeah. I designed that outfit for Josie maybe in 1963, at a house party," the late DeCarlo told the *Comics Journal* in December 2000. "We were having a costume party. I designed the outfit, and Josie had a friend who was a great dressmaker and made the costume which was later used in *Josie and the Pussycats*. And even later, we went on a cruise

and she used it for a costume party they threw on the ship."

As a cartoon series *Josie and the Pussycats* was just as popular as *Archie* when it began to air in 1970. Not only were they one of the first all-girl groups but they were also racially integrated! Songwriters Danny Janssen and Bobby Hart fought hard to ensure that soul singer Patrice Holloway sung the songs, and as she was black, her character had to be black as well. *Archie* comics, displaying their famed versatility, just went with it.

"We adapted a couple of the characters from the TV show to the book and other ones were written out of the book as we developed Josie and the Pussycats," recalls Gorelick.

When it came to pop chart action Josie and the Pussycats did not score like Archie.

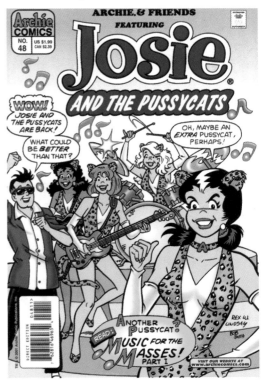

A shame, because the music in *Josie and the Pussycats* is stunning. As with all early-morning cartoon shows, the music was only a small part of the adventure, but as songwriters Janssenn and Hart recruited top soul musicians to provide the funky music, every song they laid down had a groove. I'd like to recommend the soundtrack album from the series, but it has yet to be released on CD. Of course, the soundtrack for the *Josie and the Pussycats* feature film made a few years ago is still out there, but that music is more rock than soul.

The success of the Archies and Josie and the Pussycats spawned a host of other TV cartoons, where every group of teenagers featured had to be in a band. One of the most delicious concepts floating around was an idea to transfer the Beach Boys into cartoon characters. The plan never got off the drawing board, but what was left on it was fascinating; Mike Love, Brian Wilson and the boys transformed into cartoon characters complete with a specially designed car. One imagines the plots would have involved plenty of surfing and tunes written by the Beach Boys themselves.

By the time Neil Armstrong was taking one step for man and a huge step for mankind, they were already making cartoons out of real groups. It shows what a pop phenomenon the Jackson Five was, that Bass-Rankin did a cartoon series on them in 1971. It was pretty good as well, especially the opening sequence of dancing silhouettes that accompanied the track "One Bad Apple". The first story related how the Jackson's met Berry Gordy and Diana Ross and became Motown Superstars. After that, it was straight adventure with episodes like 'Pinestock USA', 'Cinderjackson', 'The Wizard of Soul' and 'Michael In Wonderland' which, no doubt, signposted the way to the latter period of his solo career. In truth, the stories are pretty tame, but this stuff was aimed at children who chewed bubblegum, rather than hardcore music fans and taken on those terms they are highly entertaining. As long as viewers were served up an adventure and a few songs, then everybody was happy. All told 23 episodes were made and broadcast in 1971 and 1972. The Jacksons cartoon was also groundbreaking. After all, after the *Harlem Globetrotters* and *Fat Arthur* and the *Cosby Kids* how many more cartoon shows have since featured an all black cast? The success of the *Jackson Five* series saw Bass-Rankin turn The Osmonds into cartoon characters, and in 1972 seventeen episodes of the adventures of Donny and the Mormons in places like Rio, Transylvania, Australia, Italy and India hit the screens of America and England.

Of course, when push comes to shove, the Archies, the Beatles, the Jackson Five and the Osmonds can't hold a candle to the adventures of Scooby Doo. Although, the members of Mystery Incorporated never found the time to plug in instruments, beneath the veneer of wholesome entertainment there was a subtle whiff of underground counter-culture. With his perpetual quest for 'munchies' Shaggy looked and acted like a classic late-Sixties stoner.

3

Going Underground

"Along with the music of the Sixties and Seventies, it was the comics (or comix as we used to call them) which were responsible for radicalizing an entire generation. In themselves, most of the music and most of the comics will eventually be forgotten, but their force and power helped us shape an entire generation's attiude towards subjects that concern all of us – the necessity for war, the liberation of women from second class citizenship, ecological concerns and constraints placed on freedom of expression following two World Wars within a single generation."

Felix Dennis

None of the five guys in the black and white photograph are smiling. In fact, they stand shoulder-to-shoulder giving the camera a look of intent attitude. This being 1967 and San Francisco, there are no matching suits or hairstyles on display. The clothes they wear reflect a unique style of individuality and flair. Indeed, the guy on the far left has the thumb of his right hand cocked inside the waistband of his trousers and if you peer closely it looks like he has a small badge of his own face attached to the cool black hat he is wearing. Is he a lead guitarist then, or a keyboard player seeking attention? The guy on the far right also wears a hat, although it can hardly contain the frizz bomb of black hair that touches his shoulder. He is also wearing sunglasses and looks meaty enough to throb a bass guitar, or pound a drum-kit into submission. Flanked by two other style-gods with short hair who look at the camera as if it is a full-length mirror, the central figure of the five appears almost scruffy, especially as the kneecap has been ripped out of the left leg of his faded jeans. The blonde hair and beard are offset by dreamy eyes that suggest a singer prone to twisting lyrics around dolphins, surfboards, mystical symbols and the war in Vietnam rather than how to kiss a girl in the back seat of a Pink Cadillac.

But who are these guys? What is their name? Are they one of the psychedelic outfits that supported scene-leaders like Love or the Grateful Dead at the Whisky or Avalon Ballroom? Then again, they might be a *Nuggets*-type garage band who only made it into the studio once to thrash out a clattering proto-punk gem before fading into insignificance with jobs on the factory assembly line or cashiers in secondhand record emporiums. Are they the Nightcrawlers? The Uniques? The Blues Magoos, who even titled an album *The Electric Comic Book*. Or – gasp – the unknown, unheard and until now unseen Guardians of The Ancient Wisdom?

Actually, the five guys in the photograph are not a rock group at all, but representatives of one of the most fascinating links between music and comics that emerged out of the late-Sixties counter culture. Alton Kelly, Victor Moscoso, Rick Griffin, Wes Wilson and Stanley Mouse were the Big Five designers of psychedelic concert posters in the San

Francisco bay area. They lent their unique visual talents to attract music fans to concerts by bands like the Doors, the Byrds, the Grateful Dead, Big Brother and the Holding Company, the Jimi Hendrix Experience, Led Zeppelin and even Chuck Berry! Roll Over Beethoven!

Posters were commissioned by promoters like Chet Helms and Bill Graham for venues like the Avalon Ballroom and the Fillmore Auditorium. As Ted Owen states in *High Art*, his excellent book on the history of the psychedelic poster, "it was through the patronage of these two organisations that the poster developed into a unique, highly creative art form."

Unique and highly creative hits the nail firmly on the head. As long as the artist put the date, place, time, admission cost and name of the bands appearing at the venue they could do what they wanted. And they did. For example, Rick Griffin's work was a fantastic melange of rich symbolic images and eye-popping typography that literally helped brand the Grateful Dead, especially when he progressed to designing their record covers. Typically before becoming a poster God, Griffin was also in an ad hoc band himself – the Jook Savages. On the other hand, Victor Moscoso's style veered from gorgeous fine art motifs, to posters that literally vibrated due to his experiments with colour and tone. Posters from the Big Five and other artists like Gary Grimshaw and Randy Tuten featured a broad range of images from sea liners, trains, Indians and all manner of arresting designs. Ironically it was rare for musicians to appear on the posters and when they did, they were usually drenched in a slurry pit of colour and vibrancy.

Typically, these poster artists lived a life-style similar to that of the bands whose concerts they promoted. Psychedelic drugs, clothes, sex and a total commitment to their art. As Moscoso related in an interview with the *Comics Journal* in September 2002, "Once I started doing the posters, I never paid to go anywhere. I would go to the Fillmore, I'd say, 'I'm Victor Moscoso, poster artist,' at the back door. They let me in. I'd just walk right into the Avalon. I'd walk into the back rooms. I would usually walk into the musicians' room first, or the light booth, where the light-show was. I knew a lot of the light-show people. I knew the musicians. I would say I was thoroughly enmeshed in the counterculture." As was Rick Griffin, who not only became famed for his posters and

surfing designs, but designed the masthead for *Rolling Stone* magazine. As he told interviewer Patrick Rosenkranz in a telephone interview in December 1973, "Yeah, I did the logo, the lettering for the magazine. I did it around 1968 before the magazine actually came out. They came to me and had me design the logo."

Many poster designers moved indirectly into comics. At this time, as well as an underground music scene, there was also an emerging underground comic scene, born when Robert Crumb first published *Zap* and began selling them out of a pram on a corner of San Francisco's famed Haight-Ashbury district. Moscoso and Griffin were then asked to contribute, along with other artists like Robert Williams, S Clay Wilson and Spain. Subsequent issues of *Zap* have little to do with music and it would be wrong to state otherwise. But they are informed by a counterculture of which drugs and music were the bread and water of Holy Communion. Some of the work of Griffin and Moscoso expressed acid trips better than any singer from this period could, even if their artwork was printed in black and white.

One underground comic that was inspired by music was *Snuk*, a collaboration between a campaigning Chicago band called Wilderness Road and Skip Williamson. Singer and guitarist Warren Lemming had arranged for a show of Williamson's art at a venue where the band played and things developed from there.

"I then had an idea for a comic book," Lemming recalls today. "I thought, why not push it further and become characters in a comic

WILDERNESS ROAD AND FLIPPY SKIPPY WILLIAMSON PRESENT

SNUK comix

book. Skip would illustrate it and we would also contribute some material."

The comic was drawn, given to a local underground printer called Joe Land to press up – and then things ground to a halt.

Lemming takes up the story: "He had the material, the comic had been printed but it had not been collated because Joe, was an incredible speed freak and nothing was happening. This went on for months! Finally, we were sitting around one night and I said,

'Fuck it! We are going around there and I am going to liberate the comic books!' So, we ran over to his loft the next day, but could not get in because he was not answering the phone or the door. So I climbed up the face of this two-story building, saw the comics stacked on the floor, and swung in through the window. And as I swing in through the window there is Joe with a shotgun cocked in my face! I was thinking, 'Fuck this! Art for art's sake but not murder for art's sake!'

I thought that if he freaked out enough he is going to blow my fucking head off, but I just kicked the gun out of the way and said, 'What the hell is going on? Where are the comics?'"

The comics were duly liberated and taken back to the band's rehearsal space where they were collated and hand-stapled together. This comic was then given away at concerts in 1970/71 and is now a rare and collectable item amongst underground collectors. Although Wilderness Road's career only extended to two excellent albums, Lemming remains proud of their foray into comics.

"I do not know of any other band who did it back then. There were comics like the *Fabulous Freak Brothers* and what Crumb was doing that involved rock bands, but I do not know of any direct relationship between a band and an artist. Quicksilver Messenger Service and the Dead in Frisco had local artists who had done posters and album covers for them, but nobody had done a comic book."

Across the Atlantic Ocean in England, there had been a similar poster explosion in the late-Sixties. The English scene emerged out of the UFO Club spearheaded by the house band, Pink Floyd. Posters for these events were designed by Hapshash and The Coloured Coat, whose work was so stunning that people literally began peeling them off the walls and stealing them. Hapshash was the combined talents of Michael English and Nigel Weymouth. Weymouth was a partner in the famed boutique, Granny Takes A Trip, whilst English went to art school with Pete Townshend from the Who and began his career by designing and making hand painted

Union Jack sunglasses which he sold to other emerging trendy boutiques.

Originally, it was English alone who did the UFO club posters, but when he was introduced to Weymouth, a vital collaboration was born, or as English described it to me, "my talent and his combined created a very interesting melange of visual delights." Such visual delights were applied to posters drumming up audiences for Pink Floyd, the Crazy World of Arthur Brown, the Fifth Dimension and the Move. Crucially English and Weymouth's artistic collaborations drew upon a wide range of influences from Art Nouveau, Aubrey Beardsley and general popular culture. Both perceived their poster work as art, and like modern-day graffiti artists "felt sidelined by the art establishment, the art world and the galleries, so we thought that we would make the streets our gallery and the poster is the perfect medium to do that."

As Hapshash posters were being ripped off walls, it was a logical step for the printers to run off more copies and sell them at selected retail outlets like Mr Freedom in Carnaby Street. Even then there was little money in it for English and Weymouth. Of course, money meant little when they were at the heart of the scene that embraced music, fashion and art. English and Weymouth hung out with rock aristocrats like Eric Clapton, Paul McCartney and Brian Jones of the Rolling Stones.

"When I first knew, say Eric Clapton, he was a struggling guitarist," recalls Weymouth, "He was well known, but he was living in the Pheasantry in the Kings Road with another poster artist Martin Sharp before he became a huge success."

It was almost inevitable then, that Hapshash would end up making an album, and the medium used to contact the other side was Guy Stevens.

In music circles the late Guy Stevens is one of those producers who are usually filed under genius, although the word 'erratic' usually comes first. During the Sixties he was cresting his personal wave of success as one of the faces and prime movers on the scene. In this day and age where any song can be downloaded on the internet, it is amazing to think that back then he was one of the few people in London who had a vast collection of American soul and rhythm and blues singles and albums. As a DJ at the Scene Club in London, he introduced the emerging Mod movement to the sounds of early Motown.

Indeed, the nascent Who and Small Faces learned their rhythm and blues cover versions from a compilation tape of Stevens' records. Working with Chris Blackwell at Island Records, Stevens was instrumental in ensuring that records by the likes of Elmore James, Bobby Bland and James Brown were released through the Sue label. He also began to produce albums, and fascinated by the vibrant posters of English and Weymouth suggested that they go into the recording studio with some musicians he was working with and lay down some tracks.

"It was a surprise to us in a way – Michael and I – because we had no musical ambitions at all," recalls Weymouth. "We were artists. We wanted to visualise things and put them down on posters."

Of course, Stevens was persuasive: "He came up with this concept idea of inviting all these people down to the recording studio, a general mish-mash and it was his idea

that this first album be crazy and anarchic. I'm not sure if he was pissed off with Chris Blackwell at the time or what. It was his way of producing a record in a way that was almost Dadaistic. Crazy. Then we did the album cover which is much more famous than the music – obviously."

Actually, this first Hapshash album released in 1967 – on red vinyl no less! – is a charming document of the time, although it hardly broke any sales records. Saying that, English still thinks that it influenced a certain supergroup.

"The Stones brought out an album just after the Hapshash album (*Their Satanic Majesties Request*, November 1967)," he recalls, "and there is one track on it that was really naughty. Mick had heard what we had done before it came out, because we had gone around to see him and stupidly played it to him. Anyway," he laughs, "it doesn't matter. Who cares? Everything is free anyway."

Ironically it was music that led to the ending of the Hapshash partnership. The Hapshash band was supposed to move from the recording studio into the live arena, although after a disastrous gig in Amsterdam, English and Weymouth went their separate ways. Although Weymouth toyed again with the loins of rock as lead vocalist for the second Hapshash album *Western Flyer*, (1969) both went on to enjoy fine art careers. English even spent time drawing an unpublished comic book, "I did it in 1968 or 1969. The plot and the whole adventure happened during an orgasm." A pretty short comic then, Michael? "Not if you package the time space smaller; it becomes long. It is just a matter of how you see time. So during that (orgasm) the hero went right out to the edge of the universe, where he created what became a new star in the universe. It was called Amen."

One other hero who went out to the edge of the universe and beyond during the late Sixties was Dr Strange. Although underground comics like *Zap*, *Mom's Homemade Comics*, *Insect Fear*, *Illuminations*, *Slow Death* and *Feds 'N' Heads* were part of the scene and sold in alternative outlets like head shops, Marvel Comics were also in on the psychedelic revolution. Characters like Doctor Strange and Jack Kirby's Silver Surfer were perfect counterculture icons. With his vast cloak and amulet, this Strange master of the mystic art would have blended in perfectly with the hip audiences in San Francisco's

© 2005 Marvel Characters, Inc. Used with permission.

Avalon Ballroom, Fillmore Auditorium or London's UFO Club.

"He actually smoked as well in some early issues," recalls Dez Skinn who helmed *Comix The Underground Revolution*, "and I remember having earnest conversations with friends over exactly what he was smoking. There seemed to be too much smoke billowing out for it to be a normal cigarette!"

In fact, Pink Floyd may have had these conversations, and if Strange and his stunning girlfriend Clea (who naturally came from another dimension) had dropped into the UFO Club, the Floyd would probably have introduced themselves to the good Doctor. According to graphic designer and Floyd collaborator Storm Thorgerson, they were great fans of his adventures and a section of a page from a Doctor Strange comic (*Strange Tales*, 158, July 1967) is incorporated in the montage cover of Pink Floyd's *A Saucerful Of Secrets* album in 1968.

"It appeared as part of a collection of ephemera that was associated with our youthful upbringing," recalls Storm. "It is two things basically. It is a collection, a box of chocolates, a collection of items and things that pertained to our interests. The second more important thing was the way that they were put together. They were put together as superimposed objects, they did not have edges and there were no boundaries between the photos, they were more merged, more like the music and the thinking and the philosophy and the drugs – oops I never said that!"

The Floyd also name-checked the Sorcerer Supreme in the song "Cymbaline" – "Doctor Strange is always changing size." The fascination with Strange extended to space rockers

© 1974 H Bunch Associates Ltd. Used with permission.

Hawkwind, with sax player Nik Turner having a picture of the character Eternity painted on his clothes in 1972. The Hawkwind song "Brainstorm" also inspired the underground comic of the same name, and in a nice act of synergy the band took out an advert in the first issue published in 1975. This was an outstanding British comic featuring Bryan Talbot's "psychedelic alchemist" Chester P. Hackenbush and his talking Hash pipe: "Any human being is not really a free agent – what he does he is compelled to do by the very nature and structure of the universe."

Whilst on the subject of British underground comics, the red carpet should be rolled out for the two issues of *Rock'n'Roll Madness* published by Cozmic Comics in 1973 and 1974. These excellent publications contained great stories with rock and roll themes, including some of the first printed work by famed *Watchmen* artist Dave Gibbons.

"There was one I did about the making of an album, set in a recording studio," he recalls. "Then there was another called the 'Vince Eugene Story', a sort of spoof Elvis Presley biography written by Mick Farren actually."

Both of Gibbons stories are brilliant, although the best must be Petagno's take on glam rock featuring the leader of "America's latest hard cock band FAG," who might dress up and pretend that he is gay, but at the end of the day declares, "SHIT! I ain't no fuckin homo, I do it FOR THE PROMO!!"

Getting back to Floyd, according to Thorgerson, Marvel comics were one of the flavours that wafted before his young eyes and those of his equally famous associates.

"Our gang, us kids, we were thinking late-teens. We all met and hob-nobbed heavily in Cambridge; me, the Floyd, Syd and others. A large and very active peer group, quite a gang in a way, mostly boys, some girls but mostly boys. We became very thick, probably in more ways than one (laughs). Very connected to each other, and spent a lot of time hanging out. Cambridge was a great place to be. So out of this cauldron of testosterone appeared us lot. One of our many interests were Marvel comics, particularly Doctor Strange but also the Hulk; even the Fab Four, the Fantastic Four because they were stretchy. Also Spider-Man because he had psychological defects if I remember rightly. He was paranoid wasn't he? Not Daredevil so much. Not some of the others so much. The Silver Surfer we liked. Some of the stories were quite neat and some of the drawings were

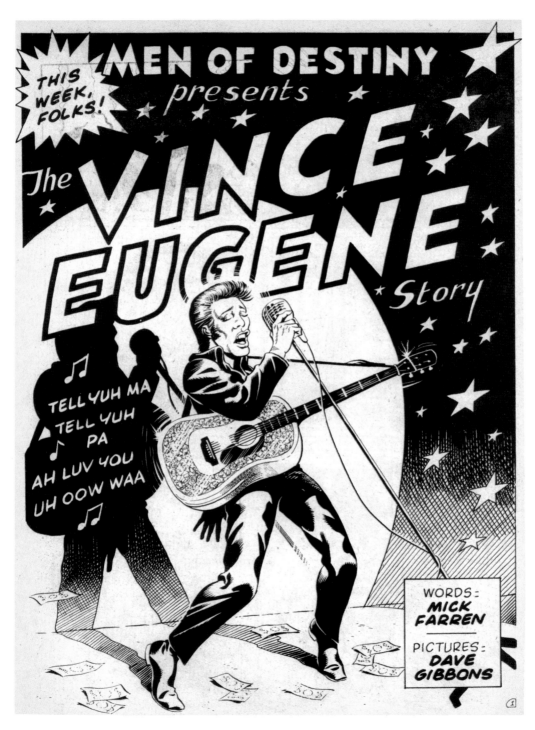

Art © Dave Gibbons.

good too, so there was reason to like them."

According to Storm, this Marvel connection not only extended to a comic book programme he drew for Floyd's 1974 world tour, but nearly set the controls for the heart of the sun.

"We also tried the Silver Surfer for the *Dark Side of the Moon*. I wanted to use the Silver Surfer because we liked him. I wanted to use him, literally, on one of those huge great rollers in Hawaii, a guy sprayed or body clad in silver. I thought that would be really cool; it would look like a comic character come to life and he would be able to really surf – obviously the real Silver Surfer could surf anyway – if I remember his board was telekenetic, magic, hovering like it was a hovercraft. But the only place that a surfer could easily surf, would be snow or in water, and the image of the big curling wave has been used often. In fact, it was used by the Floyd in a film for "The Great Gig In The Sky". They used the crystal voyager, but I had the idea to use it in a way that would represent the MAGNITUDE of the Floyd sound. The Silver Surfer would have represented something more precise, acute, particular and focussed. BUT THEY TURNED IT DOWN!"

The Silver Surfer had to be content appearing on the cover of Joe Satriani's *Surfing With The Alien* album in 1987, and although he is a great guitarist, Pink Floyd he ain't!

As we have seen earlier, Rick Griffin not only designed poster concerts for the Grateful Dead, but also album covers. Robert Crumb did album covers, most famously for Big Brother and the Holding Company – "how many times have I told THIS story?" – although his passion for old jazz and blues has seen his splendid artwork adorn a vast

number of reissues, along with his own band the Cheap Suit Serenaders. Famed English poster artist Martin Sharp did fabulous work on Cream's *Disraeli Gears* and *Wheels of Fire* but as he was sharing digs with Eric Clapton at the time he also wrote the lyrics for "Tales of Brave Ulysses" on the *Disraeli* album. Back across the Atlantic, *Freak Brothers*' creator, Gilbert Shelton did a Grateful Dead album cover for *Shakedown Street* that appeared in 1978.

"When I did that album cover for them," he recalls, "I went down to a couple of recording sessions and said to some of the guys, 'do you have any suggestions, any ideas?' They said, 'No.' Then Bob Weir or someone just said, 'Just don't put any skulls on it!' It's one of the few that does not have any skulls on it!"

A vast number of underground comic artists have designed album covers and the list is too extensive to go into here. One of the most controversial was when Guns 'N Roses used one of Robert Williams graphic paintings called *Appetite For Destruction* to grace their debut album from 1987. In typical rock and underground style, it offended many people and had to be changed.

Of course, by this time underground comics had changed their spots. Indeed, by the mid-Seventies the golden age had ended, although artists continued to work in the medium for small independent publishers on a no compromise basis. The work of Peter Bagge and the Hernandez brothers was in some respects underground, as it dealt with adult themes and was huge fun to read. The link between underground comics and music strengthened in 1990 in what was, on paper, a marriage made in heaven. The

Grateful Dead were without doubt the greatest underground band in the world whose devoted entourage of 'deadheads' had followed them across the Sixties, Seventies and Eighties. Main creative force Jerry Garcia was a huge comic book fan – legend has it when he received his first royalty cheque he went out and bought a complete set of classic EC horror comics.

"Basically, I knew Lucy Wilson, the head of licensing for Lucas Films Licensing, which is George Lucas," recalls Denis Kitchen who set up underground publishing house Kitchen Sink in 1969, and kept pumping out a compelling selection of comics through thick and considerable thin for over twenty five years. "I knew her socially, and we talked about a number of projects that were not right for Kitchen Sink, like *Star Wars*. Somehow, and I think it was for geographic reasons, Lucas came to represent the Grateful Dead – I think they lived in the same area – so at a certain point the Grateful Dead gave Lucas the right to license their merchandise. She contacted me and said, 'Look, you do underground comics, isn't this right for you?'"

Although not a big Grateful Dead fan himself – "I enjoy some of their music" – the more Kitchen thought about the idea, the more it appealed to him. Not only would Kitchen Sink be able sell the comics through their usual distribution channels, but would also be able to sell comic books at venues where the Grateful Dead played concerts.

"I thought, if anything this would be a big expansion of our distribution. That is how it began on paper, it sounded great but it turned out not to be that great."

Kitchen Sink had to pay the band a licensing fee to produce the comic, as well as royalties on each copy sold. So, in effect each comic was to be treated like an album unit. As Garcia himself was the main driving force behind getting the comic produced, it was arranged for Kitchen to meet with him prior to a Dead concert in Chicago, spending an afternoon going through ideas for the comic. One sticking point arose immediately with the Dead insisting that they would own the material, and where the artists were concerned it would be work for hire.

"My preference, as you probably know or surmise," recalls Kitchen, "was that underground comics were based on a very fundamental premise that the creator owned what he created, and as a publisher I had certain rights for a period of time and what I did with them – under contract – I had to pay for. Any ancillary use, adaptations, merchandise or whatever had to be spelled out and ultimately controlled by the creator. They (the Dead) came from the music industry where the publishers own everything and they would not compromise on that at all."

Kitchen knew that this approach would eliminate many of the finest underground artists who would not undertake work for hire as a point of principle. Robert Crumb may have designed an album cover that explored the roots of the Grateful Dead's influences, but was he the kind of guy who would work for hire? No way!

When it came to the stories inside the comics, Garcia told Kitchen that his favourite book at that moment was *The Killing Joke*. This is a classic Batman and Joker confrontation written by Alan Moore and illustrated by Brian Bolland, whose attention to detail as an artist is legendary, giving this meeting between these two arch-enemies a great feel.

Of course, the thought of Alan Moore writing a story about the adventures of a superhero based on Jerry Garcia is mind-boggling, especially drawn by Bolland. Not only was Garcia too big to skin into spandex, but even after a visit to a tailor it was hard to imagine Garciaman despatching super-villains with shots from a gun that squirted portions of Ben and Jerry's ice-cream.

"I said that I'm not sure that stories like *The Killing Joke* are going to translate," recalls Kitchen treading deftly through the tulips. Of course, Moore and Bolland were also top-dollar creators who "would command certain rates that were going to be tough for us, because the circulation base probably would not be there." So, no *Killing Joke*, then.

Then Garcia floated the idea of basing stories around real events that happened during the Grateful Dead's long career.

"I said that would be wonderful," says Kitchen. "I think true stories that are exclusive, that are illustrated that is perfect."

There was also talk of artists drawing stories based upon their interpretations of Grateful Dead lyrics. Again, this was an interesting premise.

Because he thought that a Grateful Dead comic would broaden the appeal of Kitchen Sink, Kitchen went ahead with the project and employed artists like Randy Holmes, Dan Steffan, Tim Trueman and others who agreed to work for hire terms. They were also big fans of the band and delighted to be working on the comic. The first Grateful Dead comic was published in 1990 selling around 50,000 copies through the direct market. More copies were sold through the Grateful Dead's merchandising company, although because of stern business terms,

Kitchen Sink saw little money from this relationship. The first three issues of *Grateful Dead Comix* were well-received by fans and contained a mixture of Grateful Dead tales, like an eight-page affair relating the events behind a free concert the band played in Lille in 1972.

However as time progressed, Kitchen hit a brick wall as far as co-operation went.

"It was tough getting stuff out of them," he recalls, "that first meeting I probably spent three hours with Jerry in a hotel room. His publicist was there and it was a great conversation, he was sober and was very forthcoming promising access which was never forthcoming after that. He led me to believe that periodically he would call or I could reach him and we could chat about some of these editorial issues. He would be involved, which the fans would love, and it would also be great for us. But it never happened. So his publicist became the conduit and he was tough to pull stuff out of, frankly because he had trouble pulling it out of Jerry and the band."

With little material forthcoming for artists to work with, subsequent issues turned to illustrating more song lyrics like "Ripple", "Truckin", "St Stephen" and "The Golden Road", as well as stories from the perspective of Grateful Dead fans which usually entailed getting to a concert come rain or shine. A third source was Robert Hunter.

"He was the lyricist for the band and he had created something like an epic rock opera," recalls Kitchen. "It was a science fiction story basically, and one of our artists – Tim Truman – had heard about it and wanted to know if he could interpret it. Well, they put us in touch with Robert Hunter and he was

© 1991 Grateful Dead
Productions.

thrilled to have it interpreted as a graphic novel and that ended up being serialised throughout the series." This was called "Eagle Mall".

Although they knew little of the politics behind the creation of the *Grateful Dead Comix*, the fans of the band generally appreciated and enjoyed the bi-monthly offering. Kitchen thought that as the series progressed, problems regarding work for hire and oner-ous distribution deals at concert locations would be ironed out. Perhaps, even the stipulation that the band insisted upon approving stories before publication would be lifted.

"They were such control freaks – at least Jerry was – they insisted upon approval for every single story before it was published. So we had to send stuff to them in proof form and wait. For the most part they did approve

it, but they took forever, so they were holding up our deadlines. I think Jerry was the only one who cared and Jerry was not paying attention to business. Perhaps the novelty had worn off after the first couple of issues."

Perhaps this was the case, although Garcia was photographed proudly clutching a copy of *Grateful Dead Comix 1* on the back cover of *Grateful Dead 2*.

Ironically, when it came to approval there was one area that the Grateful Dead's legal team insisted was a total no go area – drugs.

"Everybody knows there is a drug association with the Grateful Dead," says Kitchen who still sounds somewhat exasperated, "You go to their concert and even if you don't smoke you are going to get high, because of the cloud of marijuana smoke – not to mention hallucinogenics. That is a given – conventional wisdom. However, for legal purposes they insisted we could not depict any of that. We could not even have an innocuous somebody at a concert taking a toke of something like that, and God forbid, suggest that the band did. They were legally afraid that it would come back to bite them, and if somebody was busted and they denied something, the prosecutor would wave a comic book and say, 'In your own authorised comic books you are shown using drugs aren't you, Mr Garcia?' Their lawyers were paranoid about that and again unrealistically tied the hands of these underground cartoonists who were used to absolute freedom."

So, no drugs and few original stories directly from the band. As each bi-montly issue came out sales began to decline.

"It dropped to 42,000, 37,000, 33,000 and 27,000. A colour comic book under the best circumstances needs to sell at least 20,000 copies to meet costs. At the end we were there or about break even."

Matters were not helped by the fact that although he had an exclusive licence from the band, in 1992 Kitchen was faced with competition. Revolutionary Comics, who produced black and white "unauthorised and proud of it" comic biographies of bands, began to publish their own three-part series on the Grateful Dead. Kitchen crossed swords – by fax – with Revolutionary publisher Todd Loren over these comics. Worst of all, apart from a "cease and desist" letter from their lawyers, the Dead did nothing.

"Here I was paying a licensing fee to the Grateful Dead, when he was doing a Grateful Dead comic without a licensing fee," recalls Kitchen. "When I brought it up with the Grateful Dead's attorneys, they said, 'Well, we don't know if we can sue him and we don't know if we want to spend the money to sue him.'"

In order to keep the comic going, Kitchen changed the format from a magazine style to a normal comic style with issue 8 (or volume 2, No 1) in 1993. Even so, with sales falling the writing was on the wall and Kitchen made an appeal to Dead fans: "Despite the enthusiasm evidenced in each issue's letter column, sales figures just aren't high enough to justify continued publication. What we do next depends on you: if sales go up for the issue you hold in your hands, we can consider continuing the series; if not, then

What kind of person reads Grateful Dead Comix?

© 1991 Grateful Dead Productions.

we may have played our final note. So, it's up to you, the fans of the world's most popular rock group – can you recruit enough of your fellow Deadheads to lend support to this title?"

Some support was forthcoming, but after one final issue the Dead were laid to rest. At least Grateful Dead Comix went out with a two-issue bang. Number 8 contained a fantastic story relating the Dead's performance at the 1967 Monterey Rock Festival. Written by James Vance and drawn by Ray Fehrenback, it is tremendous, especially the part where we read, "and then it was Sunday, the big finale. The Dead were sandwiched between a couple of British acts we'd never heard of." These acts happened to be The Who and, er, Jimi Hendrix whose intense performances are expertly conveyed in two panels that show Pete Townshend trashing a guitar and Keith Moon raging away banging the drums before we see Hendrix in iconic guitar-burning mode. Of course, this comic

55

Permission by Interlicense Ltd. on behalf of the author and copyright holder, Gilbert Shelton.

is about the Dead, so when it came to their performance, "what is as clear as yesterday was the charge that ran through the crowd when the Dead took the stage." The band also insisted that those outside the event get in for free to enjoy the last night of the concert.

Looking back, Kitchen remains proud of his *Grateful Dead Comix*, although they never got the distribution in record shops and concert venues that he had hoped. "At the end of the day we had to rely upon the comic shop audience and the truth is, the overlap of

Deadheads and comic fans was not as large as we thought."

Although the Grateful Dead are the prime example of an underground band being featured in an underground comic, there were fellow travellers – although not based on real bands. As an underground artist, Gilbert Shelton is famed for his creation of the *Fabulous Furry Freak Brothers*, Fat Freddie, Phineas and Freewheelin' Frank whose adventures in trying to get and keep stoned are legendary. What has made these stories evergreen for over thirty years is the comic brilliance.

Although music hardly features in the stories, it takes but a little leap to imagine the boys laying around stoned listening to the Doors, the Grateful Dead or the Byrds. In fact, as their adventures continued down the years the Freak Brothers, lured by the thought of "The fame! The glamour! The sex! The DOPE!" formed their own punk band – the Freaks – in 1981. Typically unable to play their instruments – "nowadays the worse the Better!" states Fat Freddy – they played a one-off gig that, through poor sound engineering, microwaves the entire audience of on-looking punks.

Shelton also decided to invent a fictional rock band called Not Quite Dead, "I used to know many musicians and everything," he told me, "and I thought that I would be able to collect a lot of funny stories." The first issue was published in 1993 and in the opening editorial Shelton set the scene, "the name of this band is Not Quite Dead, and they're nothing if not the world's most experienced rock band, if you count the combined playing experience of all thirty full and part time members which would total up to six hundred years."

The core membership of the band is Cat Whittington (vocals and monostring bass), Elephant Fingers, (lead guitar and backing vocals), Felonious Punk (keyboards), Sweaty Eddie (tenor Sax), Thor (drums) and Gnarley Charlie (tambourine).

So far, Shelton and his collaborator Pic have issued five copies of the adventures of *Not Quite Dead*, the reason for this slow output according to Shelton is because, "I did

not get as many funny musician stories as I thought. The funniest ones are about jazz musicians and I started out (the band) with a blues-rock type of image, so the jazz jokes did not work so well. Occasionally I used them. It was also a bit of a mistake to have six main characters, which makes it difficult for character development." Still, *Not Quite Dead* is a fun and enjoyable read.

Another fictional band to emerge out of the underground was published by Rip Off Press. R. L Crabb invented *Rockers*, who hailed from Cedar Flatt, a small rural community in the foothills of California Sierra, Nevada. Unlike Shelton, who played *Not Quite Dead* for laughs, Crabb turned his mind to the serious business of a band working hard for success based on his own

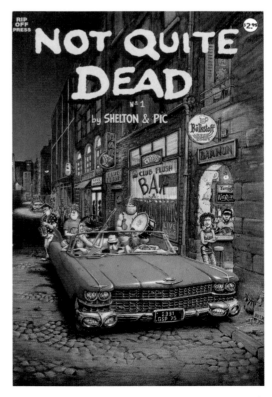

© R.L. Crabb.

experiences as a musician, "I was the lyricist for a band called Carrie Nation back in the Seventies and a lot of the stories were loosely based on those times."

Therefore Rockers have to negotiate the traps, hurdles and pitfalls of the music business and the attendant lifestyle. This being an underground comic, there was plenty, of sex and drugs mixed in with the rock and roll – all based on truth.

"Drugs were everywhere when I was in the music biz," Crabb told me. "It was a fact of life, like it or not."

The drugs angle was well played with the lead singer – Rocky – swiftly sliding down the slippery slope of addiction. Indeed, at one stage there was so much drug use in the comic that a reader – who was in a band – wrote in to complain!

"There's only one thing that bothers me, and that is the Rockers doing coke. Now, I'm a drugger myself. I love to smoke pot, get drunk and trip on acid, but I've seen too many good friends go down because of coke. This may seem hypocritical, but I don't believe it is. Coke is a different thing, and I believe the glorification of it is wrong."

Of course, the coke was very much part of the ongoing plot and after one particular intense cocaine, tequila and alcohol binge. Rocky's dreams take him into a nightmare world of dead rock stars. Not only does he meet Buddy Holly, Keith Moon, The Big Bopper and Janis Joplin, but his tour guide is none other than Sid Vicious.

"The legion of dead rock stars was something I had been toying with for some time," Crabb recalls, "it was a hoot to write."

It's superb stuff, especially when he meets the master of this nightmare, who proves to be Las Vegas-period Elvis Presley. "Find the Blue Suede Shoes! They're your ticket back to reality, if that's what you want!" Those who might groan at this somewhat pithy line should be quiet. When Rocky goes to Disgraceland Fair he gets a monkey on his back. This metaphor for addiction has been with music since jazz times and this monkey is no different, demanding Quaaludes, seconal and speed and threatening trouble if he does not get them. Rocky finds the courage to rip the monkey off his back and destroy it in a one-page spread that hits home hard about the lifestyle choices that have destroyed the career of famous rock, jazz and pop stars, as well as musicians who only got to lay a foundation stone at the base of their career pyramid.

This fight against drugs takes two issues to resolve, before the band plunge headfirst into their career, although not before Rocky gets married to his pregnant girlfriend. The wedding is in some style, with the cover of this issue depicting the happy couple, the band and wedding guests in a parody of the Beatles' *Sgt Peppers Lonely Hearts Club Band* album. Once married, Rocky is flown to Los Angeles where he meets up with April Fool – "Queen of Crotch Rock" – and helps her re-record a track called 'World of Hurt'. As he is re-recording his vocals at four in the morning, April keeps him awake by giving him an expert blow job. Shades of Jim Morrison, although unlike the Doors' frontman, Rocky's wife is giving birth in hospital at the same time as Rocky's rocket is receiving a spring-cleaning. What made *Rockers* work – and it still does – is the obvious love of mu-

sic. This extended to regular 'rock oddities' profiles that included the likes of Joe Meek and Syd Barrett.

At the core of underground comics was the ideal of unfettered content, as well as self-publishing. In many respects although his work began to appear in publications like *Heavy Metal* in the Seventies, artist Matt Howarth is very much an underground artist. Either handled by underground publishers like the Rip Off Press, or his own company, comics like *Particle Dreams, Savage Henry* and *Connie and Czu* are chock full of musical references.

"It's not really a matter of choice," he told me via email, "music is a vital work tool for me. Besides constantly listening to music while I work (isolated away in my attic studio with headphones clamped to my head) I find that the work is fundamentally influenced by whatever I'm listening to."

Howarth recalls that as his family upbringing was devoid of music, one part of his teenage rebellion involved investigating music. Finding little of interest in the general pop arena, he spread his net.

"I originally discovered bands like Tangerine Dream and Can because of the weird cover art of their albums in the early Seventies. Once I hit on something I liked, I found ways of searching out other like-strangeness. Once such patterns were established, it became a passion to hunt for music that was relatively uncommercial, since I found more active creativity in those 'uncommercial' regions."

One of Howarth's most enduring comic book creations is Savage Henry, who not only fronts a band called the Bulldaggers, but enjoys kosmiche adventures involving

from SAVAGE HENRY 27 ©1993 Matt Howarth

space, time and the monsters of H.P Love-craft. Many issues of Savage Henry feature guest musicians ranging from the members of English art rock band Wire to electro pop funsters Yello.

"Each guest in the Savage Henry comic book happened for different reasons, but obviously such guest appearances were incited by my personal interest in the bands' music. The decision to invite them to appear as guest stars was a welcome escalation of my desire to blend comics and music, mixing reality with fiction. Since Savage Henry is a guitarist whose inter-dimensional travels can take him anywhere, each guest's story could be designed to tailor-fit the band's eccentricities or musical style. The Residents got to be sonic wizards with a thousand different faces. Moby got to explore an artificially induced dreamscape. Hawkwind got to explore the galaxy."

One of the most amusing examples appears in *Savage Henry* 27 from 1993. In a record shop Henry encounters a fan that not only collects musical artefacts – "Syd Barrett's invisible guitar, a pillow that Karlheinz Stockhausen drooled on in his sleep," – but musicians themselves. He has imprisoned Teutonic keyboard wizard Klaus Schulze in a universe devoted to Space Music. Naturally during the comic, Henry frees him. This story was approved by Schulze's manager who had related to Howarth – after a T-Shirt commission – how tired Schulze had grown of being typecast as a Space Music musician by many of his devoted fans. Thus this story served as metaphor.

Howarth's desire to mix music and comics also took a left turn into comic strip album reviews. These began to appear in *Heavy Metal* magazine and evolved into 'Sonic Curiosities', where Howarth would review music as diverse as George Clinton, the Residents, Miles Davis, Hawkwind, Thelonious Monk, Tangerine Dream, Ministry and Skinny Puppy.

"Originally the 'Sonic Curiosity' comic strip was done for a newspaper (the Quakertown Free Press). Although the editor was entirely receptive to my *outré* tastes, the publisher would frequently put pressure on him to pressure me to review more 'accessible' music. I resisted with intense passion, citing that there was no point in reviewing a new Madonna album when the audience could

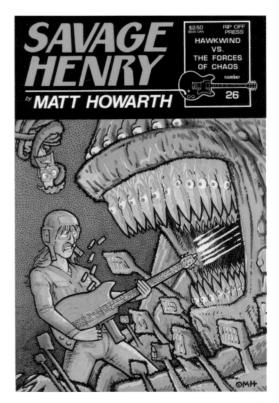

Left and right:© Matt Howarth.

SONIC CURIOSITY

© MATT HOWARTH

turn on the radio and hear it for themselves. I was more interested in reviewing the music the public might not have known about otherwise."

Although he enjoyed illustrating these reviews, there were restrictions imposed by the one, two, three or four panel form.

"There simply isn't adequate space to delve into describing anything when you have to fit it all into a few word balloons in a tiny comic strip, leaving space for some kind of comic punchline," he recalls. "This forced me to compress my remarks, highlighting impact more integrally than substance. In recent years (it's been ages since I did any new 'Sonic Curiosity' music reviews in comic strip format) I've found more freedom doing text reviews of music, which are posted weekly on my Sonic Curiosity Website (www.soniccuri osity.com)."

Howarth continues to slave away with a passion in his attic on a number of comics and music-related projects: "I've moved to a fourth level, in which I'm creating projects directly in collaboration with musicians." Like those posters to promote concerts back in the late-Sixties, the link between music and comics over and underground still remains strong.

Robert Crumb

Listen to me..... Robert Crumb is not an "underground cartoonist". He is a great artist whose work is an important – indeed vital – part of our contemporary culture.

Setting aside his eye-catching, mind blowing, side-splitting incisive confessional work, his long-standing passion for music has found expression as a record collector, a live performer, a recording artist and, of course, through the medium of his glorious art.

I was fortunate enough – through that other medium, Denis Kitchen – to be able to submit some questions to Robert about his love of music and music-related activities. He took my typed questions, stuck them on pieces of paper and wrote out his answers in pencil. Rather than transcribe his answers for this book we have reprinted the letter as it stands.

Word processors, Microsoft Word and PDFs were vital in getting this book published but only Robert Crumb's pencil can convey the full flavour of his fervour for, involvement in and opinions on music.

Ian Shirley

MR. SHIRLEY:

RECEIVED YOUR TWENTY QUESTIONS. I WILL TRY TO GIVE THOUGHTFUL ANSWERS WITHOUT SPENDING A WEEK ON IT, WHICH I EASILY COULD. I THINK THEY ARE GOOD QUESTIONS FOR THE MOST PART, SO HERE GOES——

MUSIC

1. Could you tell me a little bit about how you 'got into' the music that you love. I have read letters from your early years and this suggests a voyage of constant discovery as you found old blues and Jazz records. Does this voyage continue?

THE MUSIC THAT I WAS SUBJECTED TO AS A KID IN THE LATE 1940S— EARLY '50S WAS MOSTLY MAINSTREAM POP, NOVELTY SONGS AND BIG BAND SWING. MY MOTHER LIKED PERRY COMO, MARIO LANZA, EDDIE FISHER, DORIS DAY, FRANK SINATRA, ROSEMARY CLOONEY, THAT SORT OF THING. MY PARENTS WATCHED THE LAWRENCE WELK T.V. SHOW EVERY SATURDAY NIGHT. I WAS NEVER THRILLED BY ANY OF THIS POST-WAR AMERICAN POPULAR MUSIC, TO SAY THE LEAST. OFTEN IT GAVE ME A BLEAK FEELING INSIDE.... SOMETHING ABOUT IT. ONCE IN A WHILE I WAS EXPOSED TO COUNTRY & WESTERN, OR POLKA MUSIC, OR THE OCCASIONAL RHYTHM & BLUES, BUT NONE OF THIS GRABBED ME ESPECIALLY EITHER. THE FIRST MUSIC I HEARD THAT I REALLY LIKED AS A KID WAS THE SOUNDTRACKS OF OLD 1930S ANIMATED CARTOONS, AND ESPECIALLY THE BACKGROUND MUSIC OF THE HAL ROACH COMEDIES OF THE EARLY 1930S; LAUREL & HARDY AND "THE LITTLE RASCALS". WE WATCHED THESE ON AFTERNOON T.V. KIDDIE SHOWS.

WHEN ROCK AND ROLL GOT GOING STRONG AROUND 1955, '56, WHEN I WAS ELEVEN, TWELVE YEARS OLD, IT WAS A REFRESHING CHANGE. ELVIS, JERRY LEE LEWIS, CHUCK BERRY AND LOTS OF LESSER-KNOWN GROUPS SEEMED TO BREAK THROUGH TO SOMETHING MORE PRIMAL, A KIND OF MUSIC WITH MORE RAW POW- ER THAN THE DREARY POP AND SMOOTHED-OUT COUNTRY-WESTERN, THE SILLINESS OF LEROY ANDERSON, RAY CONIFF AND ALL THAT CRAP. I WAS ATTRACTED ES- PECIALLY TO ROCK-A-BILLY, AND AT AGE 13-14 I WOULD SEARCH THE RADIO DIAL FOR STATIONS THAT PLAYED THIS TYPE OF MUSIC. IT BECAME INCREASINGLY HARD TO FIND TOWARDS THE END OF THE FIFTIES, AND FINALLY SEEMED TO VANISH AL- TOGETHER FROM THE AIRWAVES, THAT ROCKABILLY.

IN MY MIDTEENS I BEGAN LOOKING IN MUSIC STORES FOR RECORDS - CURRENT 33⅓ ALBUMS, FOR MUSIC THAT I HOPED WOULD SOUND LIKE THOSE HAL ROACH SOUNDTRACKS. I TRIED SOME DIXIELAND JAZZ, BUT THIS GENRE WAS COMPLETELY UNSATISFYING. I BOUGHT SOME ALBUMS BY THE ENOCH LIGHT ORCHESTRA IMITATING THE DANCE-ORCHESTRA SOUNDS OF "THE ROARING TWENTIES" BUT IT WAS INAUTHENTIC, A BASTARDIZED, HOKED UP VERSION. IT DID NOT SOUND LIKE THE MUSIC I HEARD IN THE BACKGROUND OF EARLY TALKIES AND THE HAL ROACH COMEDIES. IRONICALLY, DECADES LATER I FOUND OLD 78S MADE IN 1927 IN PARIS BY ENOCH LIGHT AND HIS GAUMONT PALACE ORCHESTRA, FINE EXAMPLES OF THE AMERICAN STYLE JAZZ/DANCE ORCHESTRAS OF THE PERIOD (THE GAUMONT PALACE WAS A BIG MOVIE THEATRE IN PARIS). MR. LIGHT SHOULD'VE KNOWN BETTER IN THE LATE '50S!

THEN, AROUND THE AGE OF 15 OR 16, I DISCOVERED OLD 78S. I WAS ALREADY ADDICTED TO COLLECTING COMIC BOOKS, AND IN MY SNOOPINGS THROUGH SECOND-HAND STORES I NOTICED LOTS OF OLD RECORDS. THIS WAS RIGHT EXACTLY AT THE MOMENT WHEN THE 78 RPM RECORD WAS BEING PHASED OUT. SALVATION ARMY STORES HAD HUGE STACKS OF THESE OLD RECORDS. THE PRICE WAS USUALLY FIVE OR TEN CENTS APIECE, SOMETIMES 25 CENTS. ONE DAY I DECIDED TO SEE WHAT THESE WERE ABOUT AND BOUGHT SOME FROM AN OLD PREACHER MAN WHO SOLD OLD CLOTHING, BOOKS AND RECORDS AT A LOCAL FARMER'S MARKET (FLEA MARKETS AS SUCH DID NOT YET EXIST IN THE U.S., AS FAR AS I CAN RECALL).

— 2 —

I WAS ABSOLUTELY THRILLED TO DISCOVER THAT SOME OF THESE OLD 78S HAD JUST THE MUSIC I HAD BEEN LOOKING FOR. THIS WAS THE REAL THING, THE AUTHENTIC SOUND THAT SEEMED SOMEHOW BURIED, OR CORRUPTED, IN THE CURRENT POPULAR MUSIC. I REMEMBER THAT MOMENT WELL, IN THE SUMMER OF 1959. IT WAS ONE OF THOSE "DEFINING MOMENTS." I KNEW INSTANTLY THAT I WAS GOING TO BE AN AVID COLLECTOR OF OLD RECORDS. I KNEW NOTHING ABOUT THIS MUSIC, NOTHING OF THE HISTORY OF JAZZ, OR BLUES, OR ANY OF IT. I BEGAN MY OWN PERSONAL RESEARCH. THERE WERE A COUPLE OF BOOKS ON THE HISTORY OF JAZZ, NOTHING YET ON THE BLUES AT ALL. PEOPLE DIDN'T START WRITING ABOUT THE BLUES UNTIL A FEW YEARS LATER, IN THE '60S. AND NOTHING WAS WRITTEN ABOUT EARLY COUNTRY MUSIC UNTIL MUCH LATER.. THERE STILL IS NOT A THOROUGH, COMPREHENSIVE TOME ON THE SUBJECT OF OLD-TIME AMERICAN COUNTRY MUSIC.

AT FIRST I WAS MAINLY DRAWN TO THE JAZZ AND DANCE ORCHESTRAS OF THE 'TWENTIES. ONCE I STARTED SERIOUSLY COLLECTING, I FOUND TO MY AMAZEMENT A VAST, FORGOTTEN CULTURE OF DANCE MUSIC, SO LOST AND OBSCURE IT MIGHT AS WELL HAVE BEEN FROM THE 13TH CENTURY, WHEN IN FACT IT WAS, AT THE TIME WHEN I DISCOVERED IT, ONLY 30 TO 35 YEARS IN THE PAST. THE MUSIC INDUSTRY HAD GROWN SO MONOLITHIC BY THE 1950S, HAD PUSHED AND PUSHED ITS PRODUCT SO HARD, SO AGGRESSIVELY, THROUGH THE '30S '40S & '50S, THAT THIS MUSIC OF THE '20S ALREADY SOUNDED COMPLETELY ANTIQUE, QUAINT, SOMETHING FROM A LOST WORLD. BUT TO ME IT WAS INFINITELY MORE VIBRANT AND ALIVE THAN THE CURRENT STUFF. ALL THESE NAMES ON THE LABELS THAT I COULD FIND NO REFERENCE TO IN ANY BOOK ON THE HISTORY OF JAZZ. WHO WAS "TINY" PARHAM? WHO WAS CHARLIE FRY? LOUIS DUMAINE? FRANCIS CRAIG? THERE WAS NO INFORMATION ANYWHERE. NOTHING.

I BEGAN DISCOVERING OLD BLUES RECORDS, SCARCER THAN THE JAZZ AND DANCE ORCHESTRAS, AND VERY STRANGE TO MY EAR AT FIRST. AGAIN, WHO WERE THESE PEOPLE? WHO WAS JOE EVANS? THE "FAMOUS HOKUM BOYS"? 'BIG BILL"? LUCILLE BOGAN? BLIND ROOSEVELT GRAVES?

OVER THE ENSUING YEARS, I DISCOVERED MORE. I GOT INTO OLD COUNTRY MUSIC, WHICH AT FIRST I REJECTED, ASSOCIATING IT WITH MODERN COUNTRY-WESTERN AND BLUE-GRASS, WHICH I DISLIKED. I FOUND OLD 78S BY GID TANNER & HIS SKILLET-LICKERS, CHARLIE POOLE WITH THE NORTH CAROLINA RAMBLERS, THE BLUE RIDGE HIGHBALLERS, BINKLEY BROTHERS' DIXIE CLODHOPPERS. BY THIS TIME I WAS PICKING UP ANY 78 RECORD THAT LOOKED PROMISING, WHICH MEANT THAT IT HAD TO BE FROM THE '20S OR EARLY '30S. I FOUND THAT THERE WASN'T MUCH THAT INTERESTED ME AFTER ABOUT 1935-36. FOR JAZZ AND DANCE ORCHESTRAS, THE CUT-OFF POINT WAS AROUND 1932. FOR COUNTRY MUSIC AND BLUES, A FEW YEARS LATER. AFTER THAT, IT ALL STARTS TO SOUND TOO SLICK, TOO SMOOTHED OUT. I BEGAN BUYING 'ETHNIC' RECORDS FROM THE '20S-EARLY '30S, AND DISCOVERED THE WORLD OF OLD-TIME IRISH FIDDLING, EASTERN-EUROPEAN POLKA MUSIC, EARLY TEX-MEX, GREEK, ITALIAN, FRENCH CANADIAN... AND NOW, OVER HERE IN FRANCE, I'VE GOTTEN DEEPLY INTO OLD FRENCH 78S, ARAB AND AFRICAN 78S, AND MANY OTHER INCREDIBLY OBSCURE AND BURIED GENRES OF MUSIC. YES, INDEED, IT IS STILL A VOYAGE OF CONSTANT DISCOVERY! A VAST BURIED TREASURE OF LOST MUSIC, RECORDED IN MY GRANDPARENTS' TIME.

2. Did you enjoy compiling the 'That's What I Call Sweet Music' CD?

I HAD BEEN MAKING TAPES FOR PEOPLE FROM MY 78 RECORDS FOR YEARS. I HAVE A SORT OF EVANGELISTIC SPIRIT ABOUT OLD MUSIC. I LIKE TO TURN PEOPLE ONTO IT, IF I CAN. OFTEN IT CAN BE DISAPPOINTING. ALOT OF PEOPLE DON'T GET IT. THEY DON'T APPRECIATE IT AS MUCH AS I THINK THEY SHOULD. ADMITTEDLY IT TAKES A CERTAIN AMOUNT OF ORIENTATION, GETTING USED TO. IT'S SO FAR BACK IN TIME NOW, IT SOUNDS STRANGELY FOREIGN TO THE EARS OF PEOPLE WHO HAVE NEVER HEARD IT BEFORE. BUT ONCE IN A WHILE, YOU MEET SOMEONE WHO, FOR WHATEVER QUIRKY REASONS, LOVES THIS OLD MUSIC. SO, FOR SUCH LIKE PEOPLE, IT'S A PLEASURE TO MAKE TAPES FROM THE OLD 78S. NOW I MAKE C.D.'S. "THAT'S WHAT I CALL SWEET MUSIC" WAS JUST AN EX-TENSION OF THAT, MAKING MY OWN PROGRAM OF OLD FAVORITES FROM MY COLLECTION, BUT WITH ALOT OF FANCY ARTWORK AND SOME NOTES THROWN IN.

I DID ANOTHER COMMERCIAL C.D. RECENTLY FROM MY 78 COLLECTION, CALLED "HOT WOMEN", WOMEN SINGERS FROM THE TORRID REGIONS OF THE WORLD." I DID ALOT OF RESEARCH FOR THIS, TRYING TO GET ANY INFORMATION I COULD ON THESE OLD-TIME WOMEN SINGERS FROM AROUND THE WORLD, PLACES SUCH AS BRAZIL, INDIA, ALGERIA, GREECE, CUBA, VIETNAM. I COULD FIND NOTHING ON SOME OF THEM, EVEN WITH THE INTERNET BEING THE AMAZING RESOURCE THAT IT IS. THIS C.D. TURNED OUT TO BE A HUGE AMOUNT OF WORK, WHAT WITH WRITING THE NOTES, DOING ALOT OF ARTWORK, GETTING THE RECORDS REMASTERED... I'LL NEVER DO IT AGAIN.

MUSIC AND COMICS

3 Was it natural that your love of music crossed over into your work?

YEAH, I GUESS SO, SINCE THE OLD MUSIC MOVES ME SO PROFOUNDLY AND OCCUPIES SO MUCH OF MY ATTENTION, AND HAS SUCH A GOSHDARNED ROMANTIC AURA AROUND IT, IT'S NATURAL THAT I WOULD APPLY MY ARTISTIC SKILLS TO EXPRESSING THIS DEVOTION, THIS ENTHUSIASM. PLUS, I WANT TO TELL THE WORLD ABOUT IT, WANNA SHARE THIS WEALTH WITH OTHER PEOPLE. I SEE THEM AS CULTURALLY DEPRIVED, CUT OFF FROM THEIR MUSICAL HERITAGE. THEY DON'T KNOW! THE POOR LOST SOULS! I MUST ENLIGHTEN THEM!

4 Your biographical stories of people like Charley Patton, Jelly Roll Morton and others not only educate readers but also convey your love of their music. Was that their intention?

I GUESS I HAVE ANSWERED QUESTION ✕4 UNDER QUESTION ✕3. I WILL ADD, THOUGH, THAT IN THE CASE OF THE PATTON STORY, I AM NOW EMBARRASSED BY IT, SINCE THE BIOGRAPHICAL SOURCE WHICH I USED AT THE TIME TURNED OUT TO BE FULL OF UNFOUNDED RUMORS AND ASSUMPTIONS, PROVEN FALSE BY A LATER, MORE THOROUGH TEAM OF RESEARCHERS, GALE WARDLOW AND STEPHEN CALT. CALT HAS WRITTEN THE BEST BOOKS ON THE SUBJECT OF THE BLUES YET IN PRINT, IN MY NOT-SO-HUMBLE OPINION.

5 Does this also apply to the cards on blues, country and Jazz artists/greats that you have produced?.

IN DOING THOSE CARD SETS, EXAMINING MY MOTIVES, I REALIZE THAT PART OF IT WAS A CONTRARY STREAK IN ME. I WAS DELIBERATELY SINGING THE PRAISES OF THE FORGOTTEN, THE OBSCURE—A SORT OF ANTIDOTE AGAINST THE RELENTLESS ONSLAUGHT, THE FURIOUS DELUGE, OF MODERN MASS MEDIA. I MADE IMAGES OF

— 4 —

GREAT MUSICIANS AND SINGERS WHO LOOK NOTHING LIKE MODERN CELEBRITIES... THEY ARE ORDINARY LOOKING PEOPLE, MOSTLY, DRESSED IN SUITS AND TIES, GAZING AMATEURISHLY AT THE VIEWER, AWKWARD, STIFF,... AS MOST PEOPLE WERE WHEN HAVING THEIR PICTURE TAKEN. THEIR NAMES ARE UNKNOWN, EVEN THEIR RECORDED LEGACY IS LITTLE KNOWN OR APPRECIATED. ALL THOSE PERFORMERS CAME FROM A TIME BEFORE MUSIC WAS THE HUGE MONOLITHIC BUSINESS IT IS NOW. THEIR MUSIC HAS AN AUTHENTICITY THAT IS LARGELY LOST TODAY. IT WAS THE REAL MUSIC OF ORDINARY PEOPLE, HOME-SPUN, DEEPLY EMBEDDED IN LOCAL CULTURES. WELL, I COULD GO ON AND ON. I GUESS I TRIED TO GET THIS MESSAGE ACROSS IN THE MAKING OF THOSE CARD SETS, SINCE, ON THE WHOLE, I TRULY DESPISE WHAT MUSIC HAS BECOME IN THE PAST SEVERAL DECADES, AS A RESULT OF THE RISE OF ELECTRONIC MASS MEDIA CULTURE.

6 Sorry, old question. How did the album cover for the Big Brother and the Holding company album sleeve come about?

HOW MANY TIMES HAVE I TOLD *THIS* STORY?! JANIS JOPLIN AND ALL THE OTHER MEMBERS OF HER BAND LIVED AROUND THE HAIGHT-ASHBURY NEIGHBORHOOD, WHERE I WAS ALSO LIVING THEN, IN 1968-'69. JANIS HAD SEEN MY ZAP COMICS AND LIKED THEM DIRECTLY — OR WAS IT DAVE GOETZ?- DON'T RE-MEMBER EXACTLY — MAYBE THEY BOTH CAME TO SEE ME TOGETHER. I WAS FLAT-TERED, AND I NEEDED THE MONEY, SO I DID IT. SIMPLE AS THAT. OF COURSE THEY NEEDED IT, LIKE, THE NEXT DAY, SO I TOOK SOME SPEED AND WORKED ALL NIGHT ON IT, FINISHING IN THE MORNING. ORIGINALLY I DID A FRONT AND A BACK COVER. THEY DECIDED THAT THEY DIDN'T LIKE MY FRONT COVER DESIGN AND ENDED UP USING THE BACK COVER FOR THE FRONT. I GOT PAID $600 FROM C.B.S. RE-CORDS. SOMEONE AT C.B.S. KEPT THE ARTWORK. 25 OR SO YEARS LATER, THAT COVER ART SOLD AT SOTHEBY'S FOR $21,000. I DON'T KNOW WHO GOT THE MONEY. I CERTAINLY DIDN'T. I DON'T KNOW WHAT BECAME OF MY ORIGINAL FRONT COVER. I NEVER SAW IT AGAIN AFTER I HANDED IT OVER TO JANIS AND DAVE GOETZ.

DID I LIKE THEIR MUSIC? NO, NOT VERY MUCH. I THOUGHT IT WAS RATHER SILLY, ALTHOUGH IT WAS OBVIOUS THAT JANIS WAS A TALENTED SINGER WITH A POWERFUL VOICE. I HEARD A TAPE OF HER MADE IN TEXAS AROUND 1965-66, ON WHICH SHE WAS SINGING OLD-TIME BLUES SONGS AND MAYBE PLAYING A GUITAR, DON'T REMEMBER EXACTLY. IT WAS, I THOUGHT, MUCH BETTER — MUCH BETTER — THAN WHAT SHE DID LATER, ALL THAT PYROTECHNIC SCREAMING. ON THE EARLY TAPE, SHE WAS MUCH MORE RELAXED, LAID-BACK, A NATURAL-BORN WHITE-OKIE BLUES SINGER. SHE LEARNED TO PANDER TO THE AUDIENCE, WHICH LOVES TO WATCH PERFORMERS THRASH ABOUT ON STAGE AND SHRIEK AND BELLOW AND SWEAT BLOOD. I THINK SHE ALSO FELT PRESSURED, TOWARDS THE END, TO TRY TO SOUND MORE AND MORE BLACK, WHICH WAS — STILL IS, LARGELY — CONSIDERED SUPERIOR TO AND MORE GET-DOWN NITTY-GRITTY HIP THAN ANY WHITE MUSIC. SHE ENDED UP TRYING TOO HARD, AND WAS KILLING HER VOCAL CHORDS, AND THEN SHE JUST KILLED HERSELF. FAME DID HER IN. I WATCHED IT HAPPEN. FAME CAN KILL YOU.

I read somewhere that when you first met Janis Joplin you squeezed here breast. A wonderful story. I'm being cheeky here, but could you elaborate?

WHERE DID YOU READ THAT?? I MIGHT'VE SQUEEZED HER BREAST. IT'S SOME-THING I WOULD'VE DONE IN THOSE DAYS. IT WAS THE FIRST FLUSH OF MY FAME, WHICH GREATLY EMBOLDENED ME WITH WOMEN. I QUICKLY DISCOVERED THAT FAME ALLOWED ME TO GET AWAY WITH OUTRAGEOUS BEHAVIOR...SOMETIMES, NOT ALWAYS.... I WAS A BAD BOY THROUGH THAT EARLY FAME PERIOD — ABOUT THE FIRST TEN YEARS OR SO — OR MAYBE THE FIRST 20 OR 30 YEARS, I DUNNO. I WENT AROUND CRUDELY MAULING ATTRACTIVE WOMEN. I WAS ALWAYS, AND STILL AM, BASICALLY A VERY SHY PERSON. I NEVER DEVELOPED A SMOOTH LINE WITH WOMEN. I WAS TONGUE-TIED IN FRONT OF THEM. INSTEAD I WOULD JUST MAUL, HUMP, GRAB, OR EVEN LEAP UP ON THEM. ONCE I JUMPED ON A GIRL'S BACK AND SHE CALMLY OBSERVED, "ROBERT, YOU DON'T COP A FEEL, YOU COP A RIDE." YES, I WAS BAD. I'M BETTER NOW — I THINK... A LITTLE... MY SEX DRIVE HAS GONE DOWN SOME IN RECENT YEARS, ANYWAY. SO I'M

— 5 —

7 You have done other album covers. Do you enjoy employing skills to help package music that you like? Do you still get requests to illustrate others?

SURE, I ENJOY USING MY SKILLS FOR ALBUM COVERS. I LOVE GOOD PACKAGE DESIGNS — ANOTHER LOST ART. I LOVE GOOD LETTERING AND LAY-OUT. THE "GOLDEN AGE" OF COMMERCIAL ART WAS THE 1920S THROUGH THE '40S. IT STARTS TO DECLINE IN THE '50S AND GOES INTO A SHARP NOSE-DIVE BY 1960. NOW IT'S UNBELIEVABLY BAD. JUST WHEN YOU THINK IT CANT GET ANY WORSE, THEY COME UP WITH YET ANOTHER NEW TECHNOLOGY THAT ALLOWS THESE PUNKS IN "ART" DEPARTMENTS AND DESIGN STUDIOS TO CREATE EVEN MORE APPALLINGLY UGLY GRAPHICS. IT'S TRULY UNBELIEVABLE HOW BAD COMMERCIAL GRAPHICS HAVE BECOME. BY COMPARISON, ALMOST EVERY MANUFACTURED OBJECT CIRCA 1930 WAS ATTRACTIVELY DESIGNED, FROM THE MOST COMMON HOUSEHOLD PRODUCTS — A CAN OF PEAS, A CARD OF BUTTONS, A BOTTLE OF HEAD-ACHE PILLS — TO THE MOST GRANDIOSE — A SKYSCRAPER, A MOVIE PALACE, LOCOMOTIVES,...,

WHAT WENT WRONG ?? I ASK YOU !

I STILL GET MANY REQUESTS TO DO C.D. COVERS. SOMETIMES I CONSENT, BUT I HAVE TO LIKE THE MUSIC. THE MUSIC HAS TO INSPIRE ME, WHETHER IT'S OLD OR NEW. IF IT'S NEW, IT HAS TO SOUND AUTHENTIC, SOMEHOW. 99 PERCENT OF THE TIME, IT JUST SOUNDS LIKE MODERN MOVIE SOUNDTRACK MUSIC. HATE IT.

8 There is much playfulness in your treatment of music that is not your cup of tea - like Hendrix 'Purple Haze' - as well as peoples desire to dance. Do you get inspiration from the way that music affects different people in different ways?

ONCE IN AWHILE I HAVE NEEDED TO VENT MY SPLEEN AGAINST MODERN POPULAR MUSIC, SINCE IT IS FORCED ON ME EVERYWHERE I GO. IT'S HARD TO GET AWAY FROM IT. ONE HEARS THE SAME CRAP OVER AND OVER UNTIL ONE IS THOROUGHLY SICK OF IT. I HATE JIMI HENDRIX, JIM MORRISON, VAN MORRISON,..., I HAVE TO STOP — I COULD FILL PAGES WITH THE NAMES OF OBNOXIOUS POPULAR PERFORMERS THAT I HAVE BEEN FORCED TO LISTEN TO OVER THE DECADES. I REMEMBER HOW MUCH I HATED HAVING TO HEAR JOHNNY MATHIS' MOST BELOVED SONGS — "CHANCES ARE", ETC. THE THING IS, YOU HEAR THESE TUNES ENOUGH AND THEY BECOME PERMANENTLY STUCK IN YOUR HEAD AND YOU HAVE TO DEAL WITH THEM SPONTANEOUSLY BUBBLING UP FROM YOUR MEMORY. OFTEN I CATCH MYSELF WITH SOME INANE POP TUNE FROM MY CHILDHOOD, BY FRANKIE LAINE OR WHOEVER, GOING THROUGH MY HEAD, OR SOME HATEFUL HIT FROM THE '70S, OR WHITNEY HOUSTON SINGING "I WILL ALWAYS LOVE YOU," BECAUSE IT IS BRANDED ON MY BRAIN FROM HEARING IT IN SUPERMARKETS,..., HORRIBLE.

TO ANSWER THE SECOND PART OF YOUR QUESTION, I S'POSE I'VE GOTTEN INSPIRATION FROM HOW MUSIC HAS AFFECTED ME PERSONALLY, AND ALSO FROM HOW VARIOUS CULTURES HAVE EXPRESSED THEMSELVES MUSICALLY, WHAT SORT OF MOOD OR FEELING IS EXPRESSED BY DIFFERENT MUSICAL CULTURES, AND HOW THAT REVEALS OR REFLECTS THE WAY OF LIFE THAT PRODUCED THE MUSIC, STUFF LIKE THAT, SORTA, KINDA.

9 Your art depicts you as intolerant of music that you don't like. Is this true or an artistic amplification?

I AM EXTREMELY INTOLERANT OF MUSIC THAT I DONT LIKE. THAT'S THE OTHER SIDE OF DERIVING SUCH PROFOUND PLEASURE, SUCH ECSTASY, FROM MUSIC THAT I LOVE. WHEN I'M AT THE SUPERMARKET WITH MY WIFE ALINE AND THERE'S SOME BAD POP MUSIC BLARING OVER THE P.A. SYSTEM, I'LL START RANTING ABOUT HOW HORRIBLE IT IS. ALINE ALWAYS SAYS, "JESUS, JUST TUNE IT OUT." BUT I CANT. IT PUTS ME IN A BAD MOOD. I WANT TO SHOOT AT THE SPEAKERS. I CANT TUNE IT OUT!! WISH I COULD.

68

— 6 —

10 Do you have any interest in bands like the 'White Stripes' whose music and attitude have helped modern young music fans go back to listen to some of the blues artists that you like?

"WHITE STRIPES"?? NEVER HEARD OF THEM.... I AM SO STEEPED IN THE MUSIC OF THE 1920S AND '30S, I RARELY EVEN TAKE THE TIME TO LOOK AT WHAT'S BEING PRODUCED CURRENTLY. PEOPLE SOMETIMES SEND ME C.D.S OF CONTEMPORARY BANDS, SINGERS, MUSICIANS. USUALLY BECAUSE THEY WANT ME TO DO SOME ARTWORK FOR THEM. I WILL GIVE THESE C.D.S A CURSORY LISTEN. RARELY EVER DO I LIKE WHAT I HEAR. MOST OF IT IS SO JIVE, SO CONTRIVED. LIKE I SAID, IT ALL SOUNDS LIKE MOVIE SOUNDTRACKS. THERE ARE EXCEPTIONS, BUT THESE ARE FEW AND FAR BETWEEN, WHEN SOME NEW MUSIC SOUNDS GENIUNE TO ME, DOWN-TO-EARTH, TRUE ... AUTHENTIC ... I'M ALWAYS AMAZED WHEN IT DOES.

YOUR OWN MUSIC

11 Can you tell me when you learned to play the banjo and why?

I STARTED OUT PLAYING A PLASTIC UKULELE AT AGE 12. I HAD A MINDLESS, INSTINCTIVE URGE TO PLAY MUSIC. IT WAS IN MY BLOOD. MY MOTHER'S FATHER, JOE HALL, WAS A MUSICIAN, A PLAYER OF POPULAR MUSIC ON STRINGED INSTRUMENTS: GUITAR, MANDOLIN, BANJO. HE DIED WHEN I WAS A YEAR OLD, SO HE WAS NOT A DIRECT SOURCE OF MUSICAL INFLUENCE ON ME. I GRADUATED TO A PLASTIC BANJO AT AGE 13. BUT I NEVER LEARNED PROPERLY, NEVER HAD A TEACHER. I NEVER BECAME A VERY GOOD MUSICIAN. TOO SPASTIC... EYE-HAND COORDINATION NOT GOOD. I ALWAYS HAD A GOOD EAR FOR TUNES AND CHORDS, THOUGH. I REMEMBER THOUSANDS OF MELODIES. I JUST CANT PLAY THEM VERY WELL.

12 When did you first start to play before an audience. Was it daunting, or a real pleasure?

MY FIRST PAYING 'GIG' IN FRONT OF A CROWD WAS IN THE SPRING OF 1972, WITH ROBT. ARMSTRONG AND AL DODGE, IN ASPEN, COLORADO, FOR THE END-OF-SEASON BEER BASH OF THE ASPEN SKI PATROL. THEY HATED OUR LITTLE STRING BAND, OUR LITTLE PLUNKETY-PLUNK OLD-TIMEY TUNES, THEY WANTED TO BOOGIE DOWN HARD. IT WAS A TRAUMATIC EXPERIENCE. PLAYING BEFORE AUDIENCES WAS ALWAYS DAUNTING FOR ME, NOT WHAT YOU'D CALL A REAL PLEASURE. I ENJOYED THE MUSIC, BUT IN FRONT OF AN AUDIENCE, I ALWAYS, INVARIABLY, GOT VERY NERVOUS, WOULD SCREW UP ALOT, LOSE ALL MY WELL-REHEARSED CHOPS... EACH TUNE WAS AN ORDEAL TO GET THROUGH. REALLY! THE BEST GIGS, FOR ME, WERE WEDDINGS, OR SIMILAR SOCIAL EVENTS, WHERE THE CROWD DIDNT PAY THAT CLOSE ATTENTION TO THE BAND. YOU WERE JUST IN THE BACKGROUND. THAT WAS MUCH MORE RELAXING FOR ME, AND I ALWAYS PLAYED BETTER IN SUCH CIRCUMSTANCES. OUR BAND DIDNT HAVE MUCH OF AN ACT. WE JUST SAT THERE AND PLAYED THE TUNES. NOT MUCH RAPPORT WITH THE AUDIENCE. I MOSTLY LOOKED DOWN AT MY INSTRUMENT, CONCENTRATING REAL HARD NOT TO MAKE MISTAKES. LACKING IN CHARISMATIC PRESENSE, WE HAD ONLY OUR MUSIC TO PUT US ACROSS. IF THEY DIDNT DIG THE TUNES, WE WERE DOOMED UP THERE... DEAD MEAT.

14 What prompted you to go into the recording studio and record?

RECORDING WAS A HARROWING, NERVE-GRINDING ORDEAL. THERE WAS ALOT OF PRESSURE TO MAKE AN ALBUM, AND ARMSTRONG AND DODGE WERE BOTH VERY ENTHUSIASTIC ABOUT THE IDEA. I ALREADY HAD MY WAY OF GETTING ALL THE PUBLIC ATTENTION I EVER WANTED THROUGH THE COMICS, SO I WAS NOT HIGHLY MOTIVATED TO MAKE RECORDS, BUT I LET MYSELF BE CARRIED ALONG BY THE GENERAL TIDE. FIRST WE MADE TWO 78 RPM RECORDS. I LIKED THAT IDEA, REVIVING THE 78. BUT THOSE TWO 78S DID NOT SELL WELL. WE HAD OVERLOOKED THE FACT THAT, BY 1972, ALMOST NOBODY POSSESSED HI-FIS WITH 78 SPEED ON THE TURNTABLE ANYMORE!

— 7 —

15 Was it fun to have your very own 78 record when you first recorded with the 'Keep on Truckin' orchestra?

YEAH, WE WERE THRILLED WHEN THAT FIRST 78 CAME OUT, PRODUCED BY DENIS KITCHEN. THEN WE IMPETUOUSLY PRODUCED A SECOND 78. IT WAS FUN TO DESIGN THE LABELS AND THE SLEEVES, INSPIRED BY THE GRAPHICS ON THE OLD RECORDS OF THE '20S AND '30S THAT WE LOVED. HOW TOUCHINGLY NAÏVE WE WERE! STILL, THOSE TWO 78S ARE CERTAINLY ECCENTRIC ARTIFACTS OF 1970S AMERICA, COMPLETELY OUT OF STEP WITH THEIR OWN TIME!

16 Could you tell me how the Cheap Suit Serenaders came about?

WE WERE ALL JUST GEEKS WITH SIMILAR MUSICAL TASTES WHO MANAGED TO FIND EACH OTHER. WE ALL HAD A COMMON INTEREST IN THE MUSIC OF OUR GRANDPARENTS' GENERATION — THE 1920S, MOSTLY. ROBERT ARMSTRONG AND AL DODGE HAD KNOWN EACH OTHER SINCE THEIR TEENS AND HAD PLAYED MUSIC TO- GETHER IN ECCENTRIC LITTLE BANDS IN THE L.A. AREA. TERRY ZWIGOFF CAME IN LATER. WE NEEDED A BASS, AND HE HAD TO LEARN TO PLAY 'CELLO FROM THE GROUND UP. LATER, OTHER MUSICIANS WERE DRAWN IN, GUYS WHO LIKED THAT OLD MUSIC, LIKE TOM MARION AND BOB BROZMAN AND TONY MARCUS. ACTUALLY, THE BAND GOT BETTER, MUSICALLY SPEAKING, AFTER THE PERIOD IN WHICH WE MADE OUR THREE L.P.S, IN THE 1970S. WE WERE MUCH BETTER MUSICIANS IN THE '80S & '90S.

16 Do you recall what it was like the first time you recorded? Was it daunting, a pleasure or real hard work? Did you like what you heard during playback?

THE RECORDING STUDIO IS A BRUTAL SITUATION. IT CAUSES NERVOUS BREAK- DOWNS AND BANDS TO BREAK UP. IT IS REAL HARD WORK. IT CAN BE DEVAS- TATING TO HEAR YOURSELF DURING PLAYBACK. THE ENGINEER WILL ISOLATE YOUR PART AND TURN THE VOLUME WAY UP FOR ALL TO SCRUTINIZE. ALSO, MOST OF THE RECORDING ENGINEERS WE HAD TO WORK WITH DID NOT SEEM TO UNDER- STAND HOW TO RECORD A GROUP OF ACOUSTIC STRING PLAYERS. THEY ALWAYS WANTED TO PUT A MICROPHONE RIGHT UP AGAINST YOUR INSTRUMENT, WHICH PRODUCED AN AWFUL, UNNATURAL SOUND. IT TOOK US YEARS OF BITTER EXPERIENCE WITH THESE LORDLY FELLOWS WITH THEIR BIG SOUNDBOARDS, TO HAVE THE CON- FIDENCE TO ARGUE WITH THEM AND CONVINCE THEM TO LET US RECORD WITH JUST ONE OR TWO MICROPHONES PLACED SEVERAL FEET AWAY FROM US, WHICH PRO- DUCED A MUCH MORE NATURAL AND PLEASING SOUND. IT WAS AMAZING TO GRADUALLY REALIZE THAT, WITH ALL THEIR FANCY MULTI-TRACK EQUIPMENT, THEY DID NOT GRASP THIS SIMPLE EQUATION ABOUT STRINGBAND MUSIC,
I STILL HEAR THIS BADLY RECORDED ACOUSTIC STRING MUSIC ON A LOT OF C.D.S, WHERE THE MICROPHONE HAS OBVIOUSLY BEEN SHOVED RIGHT UP AGAINST THE INSTRU- MENT. THEY STILL DONT GET IT, THOSE ENGINEERS, BUT I'M OUTA THERE. 'S NOT MY PROBLEM ANYMORE. I'M THROUGH WITH ALL THAT.

17 You actually went on tour as a musician at one stage. Looking back was that an enjoyable experience? (Did you enjoy the long journeys, worry about getting decent food and hotels with soft pliant pillows!)

IT WAS ALWAYS KIND OF FUN TRAVELING WITH THE CHEAP SUITS. THEY WERE A WACKY AND INTERESTING BUNCH OF ECCENTRICS. WE HAD A FEW EGO PROBLEMS BUT SO IT GOES IN THE BAND BUSINESS. DECENT FOOD?? SOFT PILLOWS?? HA HA... THOSE GUYS WOULD EAT ANYTHING — DONUTS, HOT DOGS, WHATEVER. AND WE SLEPT ANYWHERE, UNDER A KITCHEN TABLE, IN A HALLWAY... WE WERE YOUNG, AND OUR "TOURS" WERE ANYTHING BUT DELUXE AFFAIRS... BUT, YEAH, IT WAS AN ADVEN- TURE, FREE OF RESPONSIBILITIES. A GOOD WAY TO MEET GIRLS, OF COURSE, ONLY THE TRULY ODD AND CRAZY FEMALES WERE ATTRACTED TO US. WE HAD NO GROUPIES, BUT THERE WAS THE OCCASIONAL ODD-BALL GIRL THAT WOULD TAKE UP WITH US, OR ONE OF US, I GOT MY SHARE. I CANT COMPLAIN.

— 8 —

18 I interviewed Peter Bagge about the time he was in a band – The Action Suits - and he told me that it annoyed him when he was playing the drums, people in the audience having a good time would distract him. Do you get the same feeling when playing or do you love playing before an audience?

WELL, THE MAIN THING TO WORRY ABOUT WHEN PLAYING MUSIC FOR AN AUDIENCE IS IF THEY'RE BORED ... YOU HOPE THAT THEY'RE ENJOYING THE MUSIC. THAT'S WHY THE CONCERT-TYPE GIG WAS ALWAYS THE MOST NERVE-WRACKING TO GET THROUGH. THEY'RE ALL SITTING THERE JUST WATCHING YOU. THAT'S THEIR WHOLE REASON FOR BEING THERE. IN OTHER TYPES OF GIGS, SUCH AS WEDDINGS, PARTIES, OR EVEN IN BARS, THE PEOPLE HAVE OTHER THINGS TO DO BESIDES JUST LOOK AT THE BAND. THEY'RE GATHERED TOGETHER TO CELEBRATE, OR AT LEAST TO DRINK AND CHAT AMONG THEMSELVES. THE BEST IS WHEN THEY GET UP AND DANCE. A CROWD OF DANCING PEOPLE IS VERY INSPIRING TO A GROUP OF MUSICIANS. BANDS PLAY THEIR MOST GENIUNELY SPIRITED MUSIC FOR PEOPLE DANCING. THAT WAS MY EXPERIENCE. BUT WHEN YOU'RE FACING AN AUDIENCE OF PEOPLE WHO ARE JUST SITTING THERE ALL FACING YOU, ALL THERE SOLELY TO BE ENTERTAINED BY YOU, YOUR MUSIC, YOUR PERSONALITY, YOUR INTERACTION WITH THEM— HO BOY, THAT'S TOUGH, THAT'S A LONG HAUL, A LONG COUPLE OF 45-MINUTE SETS OR WHATEVER. THAT'S WHEN IT'S GOOD IF YOU HAVE A FEW JOKES, A LITTLE CLOWNING AROUND BETWEEN BAND MEMBERS, SOMETHING TO GET A LAUGH OUT OF THEM, SOMETHING TO PENETRATE THAT VAST, SCAREY SILENCE OUT THERE, THAT HEAVY, PALPABLE SEA OF EXPEC- TATION THAT'S SITTING OUT THERE. I REMEMBER SO OFTEN SITTING UP THERE ON A STAGE IN FRONT OF A DARKENED AUDITORIUM FULL OF PEOPLE, FEELING THE WEIGHT OF THEIR COLLECTIVE SCRUTINY ON US — US PUNY FOUR OR FIVE MUSICIANS UP THERE, SITTING IN OUR CHAIRS LINED UP SIDE BY SIDE FACING THEM, HOLDING OUR LITTLE RINKY-DINK INSTRUMENTS; BANJO, GUITAR, MANDOLIN, FIDDLE, ZWIGOFF WITH HIS 'CELLO... WE SEEMED SMALL, WEAK, INSUBSTANTIAL, FACING THAT AUDIENCE, EVEN IF WE HAD A SOUND SYSTEM BETWEEN US AND THEM; MICROPHONES, SPEAKERS, ETC. OFTEN I WAS REQUIRED TO ADDRESS THE AUDIENCE. "UHH, HELLO FOLKS, WE'RE GOING TO START OFF WITH AN OLD TUNE FROM WAY BACK WHEN CALLED 'CREOLE BELLES'. IT'S WHAT WAS KNOWN AS A CAKE-WALK, WHICH CAME BEFORE RAG-TIME, SORTA, AND, UHH...WELL, HERE GOES..." YEAH, IT WAS ROUGH... SHON 812... HOW'D I EVER GET MYSELF INVOLVED IN THAT?? I'M A SHY PERSON, I AM VERY UNCOMFORTABLE IN ANY SITUATION IN WHICH ALOT OF PEOPLE ARE LOOKING AT ME. I LIKE BEING ANONYMOUS IN PUBLIC, THE OBSERVER, RATHER THAN THE OBSERVED...

ANYWAY, CONTRARY TO PETER BAGGE'S REACTION, I FOUND WHEN PLAYING BEFORE AN AUDIENCE THAT, IF THEY WERE HAVING A GOOD TIME, IT WAS INSPIRING TO THE MUSICIANS. WE TENDED TO PLAY WITH MORE RELAXED ENTHUSIASM FOR A CROWD WHO WERE OBVIOUSLY ENJOYING THEMSELVES THAT NIGHT.

AND THAT'S WHY YOUR BIG-TIME PROFESSIONAL ENTERTAINERS, ROCK BANDS, ALL OF THEM, KEEP ALL THEIR BITS OF BUSINESS COMING AT THE AUDIENCE SO THICK AND FAST—ALL THAT HISTRIONIC EMOTING, ALL THAT JUMPING AND LEAPING AROUND, AGONIZED GYRATIONS, SWEATING AND STRAINING, AND THAT MASSIVE, EAR-SPLITING TIDAL WAVE OF ELECTRIC-INDUSTRIAL NOISE THEY CALL MUSIC... IT'S ALL TO KEEP THE AUDIENCE AMUSED EVERY SECOND—EVERY NANO-SECOND, SO THERE'S NOT ONE HAIR'S BREADTH IN WHICH THEY MIGHT POSSIBLY EVEN CONSIDER BEING BORED. IT'S CERTAINLY NOT ABOUT MUSIC. IT'S ABOUT OVERPOWERING THE MEDIA-JADED MODERN AUDIENCE, BURY- ING THEM IN AN AVALANCHE OF SENSATION THAT GIVES NO QUARTER, TAKES NO PRISONERS. BUT IT SURE AS SHITIN' ISNT ABOUT MUSIC — OR EVEN ABOUT DANCING AS DANCING WAS ALWAYS KNOWN BEFORE...

19 Do you listen to music when you work? Everyone goes on about your vast collection of 78's but I imagine you listen to CD's now.

I CAN'T LISTEN TO MUSIC WHILE I WORK. I EITHER LISTEN TO MUSIC OR I WORK. CAN'T DO BOTH AT ONCE. I'M SO FUCKIN' SELECTIVE ABOUT WHAT I LISTEN TO, I HAVE TO GIVE IT MY FULL ATTENTION, AND THEN I CAN DEEPLY EN- JOY IT, CATCH ALL THE, YOU KNOW, NUANCES 'N' STUFF,

— 9 —

EVERYONE GOES ON ABOUT MY VAST COLLECTION OF 78S?? DO THEY REALLY? WHO GOES ON ABOUT IT? WHERE?? IT'S TRUE, I DO HAVE A SPLENDID COLLECTION OF 78S, AN EMBARRASSMENT OF MUSICAL RICHES HERE IN MY ROOM TO LISTEN TO. I ALSO LISTEN TO C.D.S, BUT AGAIN, ONLY SELECTIVELY. I WILL PICK OUT A TRACK I WANT TO HEAR, AND WHEN IT'S FINISHED I WILL USUALLY STOP IT AND THEN PICK OUT ANOTHER TRACK, JUST AS IF I'M PLAYING SOME OLD THREE-MINUTE 78S. I ALMOST NEVER PUT A C.D. ON AND JUST LET IT PLAY THROUGH. AND MOSTLY I STILL PLAY THE OLD 78S THEMSELVES. I ENJOY THE WHOLE RITUAL, PICKING OUT A DIFFERENT RECORD TO PLAY EACH TIME.

NOWADAYS, THOUGH, THERE ARE ALOT OF REISSUES ON C.D. OF OLD MUSIC THAT ARE SO WELL REMASTERED, THE SOUND QUALITY IS SO GOOD, IT SEEMS REALLY CRAZY TO HANG ONTO THE OLD SCRATCHY SHELLAC RECORDS. I THINK I SHOULD GET RID OF THE TONS OF 78S AND JUST LISTEN TO C.D. REISSUES, WHICH TAKE UP SO MUCH LESS ROOM AND DON'T REQUIRE A BUNCH OF ESOTERIC ANTIQUE EQUIPMENT TO PLAY THEM. STILL, THOUGH, THERE'S PLENTY OF GREAT OLD MUSIC THAT HAS YET TO BE REISSUED FROM THE OLD 78S. NOW, SINCE LIVING IN FRANCE, I'VE COLLECTED HUNDREDS OF GREAT OLD RECORDS OF FRENCH DANCE MUSIC, MOSTLY ACCORDION-LED SMALL GROUPS OF THE '20S AND '30S, BEAUTIFUL MUSIC, THAT HAS YET TO BE REISSUED TO ANY EXTENT. THIS OLD DANCE MUSIC IS LARGELY BURIED AND FORGOTTEN HERE.

C.D.S ARE BETTER THAN THE OLD 33⅓ L.P.S., TECHNICALLY. BETTER SOUND QUALITY AS FAR AS REMASTERING OF OLD 78S GOES, AND LESS FRAGILE. THE VYNAL 33⅓ MICROGROOVE WAS A PROBLEMATIC FORMAT FOR A NUMBER OF REASONS. TOO FRAGILE, FOR ONE THING.

20 Finally, what are your views on the relationship between music and comics?

MY VIEWS ON THE RELATIONSHIP BETWEEN MUSIC AND COMICS?? UHH, LET ME THINK, DO I HAVE ANY VIEWS ON THE RELATIONSHIP BETWEEN MUSIC AND COMICS?? UHH, WELL, HM..., I NEVER THOUGHT MUCH ABOUT IT. IT SEEMS THAT MOST OF THE GUYS I'VE PLAYED OLD MUSIC WITH OVER THE YEARS WERE ALSO HEAVILY INTO COMICS. ROBERT ARMSTRONG MADE COMICS HIMSELF, VERY GOOD ONES AT THAT. MAYBE THERE'S A CONNECTION BETWEEN THESE LOW POPULAR FORMS OF ENTERTAINMENT. COMICS WERE ALWAYS A LOW-BROW ART FORM FOR THE COMMON PEOPLE, AS WAS VIRTUALLY ALL THE OLD MUSIC THAT I AND THESE OTHER OLD-TIMEY MUSICIANS LIKED: JAZZ, BLUES, COUNTRY MUSIC. THESE WERE ALL VERY DEMOCRATIC ARTFORMS, ACCESSABLE TO EVERYONE, PROLETARIAN, UNPRETENTIOUS, NOT REQUIRING ALOT OF EDUCATION OR A HIGH DEGREE OF CEREBRAL EFFORT TO APPRECIATE, AND ALSO, YOU COULD DO THEM IF YOU WANTED TO WITHOUT HAVING TO FIGHT YOUR WAY INTO A HIGHLY PROFESSIONALIZED, ELITE. YOU COULD DRAW CARTOONS, YOU COULD PLAY SIMPLE TUNES ON A GUITAR OR BANJO IF YOU WANTED TO, AND YOU COULD TAKE IT AS FAR AS YOU WANTED TO. YOU COULD BECOME A MASTER VIRTUOSO OR YOU COULD REMAIN AN AMATEUR, IT'S STILL A POPULAR ART FORM, A "LOW" ART FORM. MAYBE THAT'S THE CONNECTION. NOT SURE, REALLY.

CHRIST, THIS HAS TAKEN ME TWO SOLID WORKING DAYS TO GET THROUGH! HOW I DO PRATTLE ON....EMBARRASSING..., ENOUGH ALREADY. SHUT UP!

LET ME KNOW WHEN YOU NEED A PIECE OF MUSIC FOR THE C.D. COMPILATION. I WILL SEND YOU SOMETHING, HOPEFULLY FROM A MORE RECENT PERFORMANCE OF THE CHEAP SUIT SERENADERS (OUR LAST "TOUR" IN 1998), OR AN EVEN MORE RECENT CONCERT BY ME AND MY DAUGHTER SOPHIE, EARLIER THIS YEAR, JUST HER AND ME. SO LET ME KNOW HOW SOON YOU NEED THAT.

— R. CRUMB

5

Pop Goes The Easel

As you might imagine, with his profile elevated so high by the *Osbournes* TV series, there have been several biographical comics on the life and wild times of Ozzy Osbourne. Or to be more truthful the life and antics of a man who once bit the head off a live bat on stage, pissed on that American shrine the Alamo, and generally abused his body with drugs and alcohol. The impressive thing about the Ozzy Osbourne comics is that they were all published before he became a compelling staple on MTV. Revolutionary Comics, Personality Comics, Rock-It Comix and Image all drew from the waters of the Osbourne well in the Nineties. They concentrated upon the Ozzy of Black Sabbath and an eventful solo career that won and retained a legion of world-wide, fans long before they saw him struggle with the control box of a satellite TV system. Of course, bat chewing, the Alamo as urinal and the substance abuse added some great seasoning to the pen and ink stories.

When it comes to biographies of rock bands in comics most companies – fly-by-night or long-in-the-tooth – have concentrated upon the blue chip stocks. The Beatles, the Rolling Stones, Pink Floyd, The Who, Led Zeppelin and Kiss are whips that have been cracked time and time again. The reasoning behind such choices is commercial. The glut of music comics published in the early-Nineties were knocked out by small independent companies whose comics had to sell in order that they might survive. These bands had a large, loyal and established fanbase that had crossed two three – or in the case of the Beatles and Stones – four generation gaps. Therefore publishers aimed at the hardcore fans that had bought every album on vinyl and CD and also wanted every piece of memorabilia – printed or otherwise – about their beloved band. With comics retailing at a few dollars each, sales were – it was hoped – guaranteed. Anybody who argued with the publishers of, say Personality Comics, producing yet another comic biography of the Fab Four would simply be directed to the music sections of book stores where casual browsers would usually find several written biographies or picture book on the band.

Also, most of the comic publishers who became involved in publishing rock biographical comics were American, so the range of bands featured were going to be bands who appealed to Americans. You and I (I hope) know that Kraftwerk are the Godfathers of Techno, House and electronic pop music in general, but no American publisher – not even Revolutionary – was going to stick their neck out and publish a comic on them with a backup story on the Human League. A shame, as turning Ralf and Florian into German ninjas would have gone down a storm with the Hip Hop, Rap and dance acts who were sampling albums like *Man Machine* and *Computer World* to death. In fact, as with the New Wave, electronic music took a

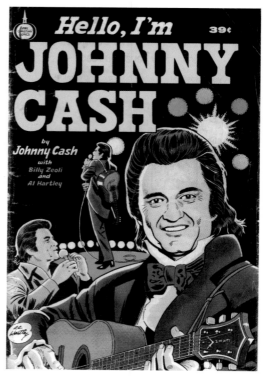

© Spire Christian comics.

while to take effect on white Americans. On the other hand, that the Cure have spawned two biographical comics – Revolutionary and Personality – just shows the impact that Robert Smith and his Goth chic had upon America in the 1990s. Although as far as the alternative market went, REM and Nirvana were as far left as the crosshairs went. So we got no Smiths, New Order, Oasis, Blur or Morrissey comics. Come to think of it no Clash comics either.

As for content, most music biographies are like the missionary position in sex, pretty straight-ahead affairs, with some sort of flashback history. So the curtains of Revolutionary's Bob Dylan biography part to say, "In his early teens, Bob Zimmerman can already plunk a few tunes on the piano." Ironically the 1976 Christian biographical comic *Hello, I'm Johnny Cash* was a firecracker of a read. This was in large part due to the fact that it not only charts how he walked the line to fame, but also his path back towards redemption through Jesus Christ. So it's totally frank about his addiction to pills, "I was hooked now! The pills took over my life!!! White Pills! Green pills! Red Pills! Pills to lift me up! Pills to put me to sleep! They promised to put it all together, but tore it all apart!" When Johnny finds salvation after spending time in a cave, he manages to overcome his addiction and, inspired by Jesus, finds more spiritual and musical fulfilment. Great stuff! At the other end of the scale, in 1977 Cash appeared in the monthly French magazine *Metal Hurlant* in a four-part story called 'Tueur De Fous' as a hitman whose victims included actor Charles Bronson shot in a desert near Reno, one imagines, "just to see him die."

Things got kinky when bands or individuals found themselves at the centre of horror or science fiction stories. Top marks in this department are awarded to Aerosmith, who appeared in a comic called *Shadowman* in

November 1993. Like fried chicken, the plot was delicious, with a devoted fan selling his soul in return for an opportunity to become Steve Tyler and front the band. Of course, Michael Jackson outdid everybody by starring in two 3D comics based on the *Moonwalker* film and the *Adventures of Captain Eo,* a short film directed by George Lucas. Despite his current problems, it must be said that both Jackson comics were superb and feature guest appearances by his original nose. Current international superstar Justin Timberlake has yet to have his own comic book, but when still a member of N'Synch he appeared in a crowd scene in *Wolverine* 168 (November 2001). The most down and dirty stuff appears in porn comics where the likes of John Lennon – or at least his head – have made a casual appearance. 'Come Together' indeed. Sorry Major Tom, but no sordid details following…

On the subject of the man in a tin can considering his impact upon music, it is amazing that David Bowie has only spawned one comic, a black and white biography published by Revolutionary in 1993. It was excellent fare and crams his entire history into

Shadowman © Acclaim Entertainment.

32-pages, including his love of Columbia's most famous export.

"David Bowie's coke period has everything to do with everything he did in the mid- to late-Seventies," says writer Jay Allen Sanford. "His stage act, his marriage – everything. It had a lot to do with the coke use – even the movies he was doing – so it had to be a major part of the story."

Attention should also be drawn to a 1974 offering published in the UK, *It's Only Rock & Roll But We Like It,* where Bowie was mercilessly parodied by the artist Petagno in the five-page story 'The Rise And Fall Of Lippy Fartdust And The Syphilis From Mars'.

Like all good satire, it is viciously amusing, including targets such as Lou Reed, Mick Jagger and Elton John as well as Bowie. "It was just a lark, all these 'rock stars' that started taking themselves just so seriously in the dollar-concious Seventies rock environment," recalls Petagno.

Cocaine aside, musically, during the Seventies Bowie was – bar none – the most significant and important solo rock artist in the world. From 1967 in a series of twelve albums Bowie raised the bar as to the infinite possibilities open to a solo artist. He was, in effect, the original human sampler, taking elements of his favourite musicians, culture, art and literature and blending them into something that was unique and compelling. *The Rise and Fall of Ziggy Stardust and the Spiders from Mars* was easy to parody by Petagno, and the album from 1972, the vibrant tours which famously included fellatio of guitarist Mick Ronson's guitar, took Bowie to the mountain peaks of pop stardom.

From that point he licked his own decals, exploring the worlds of *Aladdin Sane,* soul on *Young Americans,* and even Germanic experimental electronic textures on *Low* and *Heroes.* He returned to pop perfection with *Let's Dance* in 1983 which even got America

Page from Bowie's Revolutionary Comics biography.© Infinite One.

eating out of his hands again. Not only was the music as Bowie passed from station to station good – but even more enticingly, each album was accompanied by a different image or persona. The impact of *Ziggy* back in 1972 is hard to imagine now, but it was shocking, camp and highly arousing for boys, girls, men and women. The number of punk and new wave musicians ranging from Bauhaus to the Human League who either got into music or were inspired to make music by Bowie's appearance on *Top of The Pops* playing 'Starman' was legion. Bowie also branched out into film, theatre, singing with

"LIPPY PLAYED A STAR, FLAMING GOOD, WHILE LOOKING SILLY.

Bing Crosby and even narrating a children's story.

Despite falling back to Earth in the Eighties and Nineties, when his work lost some of its compelling nature, there was more than enough material for some great comics here. *Ziggy Stardust* or *Aladdin Sane* had the look, image, and even the costumes to transfer with ease into the shell of a superhero. Indeed it is interesting to speculate if Bowie was indirectly inspired by superheroes himself. Original American comics began to

flow into England from January 1960, and as an avid follower of culture, fashion and music, did Bowie dip his nose into the Marvel, DC, Dell and Charlton comic imports coming into the United Kingdom? It would be wrong to push this link too strongly, although it is a matter of record that when Bowie put together one of his early solo bands in 1970 – The Hype – Tony Visconti played bass dressed in superhero costume with a big H sewed onto his chest – Hypeman. Other band members were called Rainbowman, Gangsterman and Cowboyman. This band was short-lived; when the bass and superhero chores failed to bring in the bacon, Visconti moved into production, being vital to the musical development of Marc Bolan – who was a massive Marvel comics fan – as well as Bowie.

That there have been no Bowie comics is easily explained. Although a pop darling in England, and along with Bolan and Roxy Music responsible for igniting the touchpaper of the Glam Rock movement, Bowie was generally perceived by Americans as "that faggy English guy with the red hair". So he was unlikely to be a guest star, or even name-checked in 1970s editions of the *Fantastic Four*, *Batman*, *Superman*, *Spider-Man*, *Iron Man* or *The Beano* or *Dandy* for that matter. One could also not imagine Robert Crumb or the underground fraternity embracing Bowie as a suitable subject for their skills.

Of course, there have been proposals to get Bowie onto the drawing board. Scott Allie who is a respected editor at Dark Horse Comics recalls fantasizing about Bowie as a young boy – although not in a sexual way.

"When I was a teenager I used to adapt my favourite songs into comics. I did 'Five Years'

by Bowie. I adapted that one. If you have music that is really visual like Bowie it makes a certain amount of sense."

Even today, Allie will not let the dream of a Bowie comic go away.

"One of my dreams used to be a graphic novel adaptation of the whole of *Ziggy Stardust and the Spiders from Mars*. Take that album and just make a graphic novel out of it, which I think would work perfectly well. That is something that I have wanted to do – forever! But how many other musicians give you that kind of material to work with that is do-able?"

Allie has a point. As well as Bowie, acclaimed songwriters like Bob Dylan, Lennon, McCartney, Bruce Springsteen, Lou Reed and Thom Yorke are all famed for their ability to create pictures and feelings in the listener's imagination with their lyrics. For example, *Revolver* is generally perceived as one of the greatest albums of all time – and

rightfully so – but would it really translate well into a four-colour comic adaptation? The same applies to *Sgt Peppers*. Mr Kite, Lovely Rita and Sgt Pepper himself, are all characters of lyrical imagination that are best perceived inside the head, or peered at through the prism of the *Yellow Submarine* cartoon feature film. On the other hand Bruce Springsteen's 'Born In The USA' could serve as an excellent springboard for the imagination of a gifted artist.

Indeed, in 1992 the album *Freak Show* by famed San Francisco musicians and multimedia artists the Residents was turned into a comic book published by Dark Horse. Gifted artists like Brian Bolland, Dave McKean, Savage Pencil, John Bolton, Matt Howarth, Les Dorscheid and Richard Sala each illustrating a story based on an album track about a particular freak. Inspired stuff.

Illustrating songs as comic strips is an obvious step and several of Dave Mustaine's song

lyrics were adapted as comic stories in the lush *Cryptic Writings of Megadeth* published by Chaos Comics in 1998 which, as far as the style went, was a colourful melange of sex, death and blood. Eye-catching, but not a patch on Serge Clerc's 'Rock Fantasies' that appeared in *Metal Hurlant*. Here, the classic Doors' song "LA Woman" was wonderfully transformed into comic form, but was probably beaten in October 1977 by a strip featuring a comic-book Lou Reed, based around the Velvet Underground's "I'm Waiting For The Man". – "Hey! Le blanc, qu'est que tu fous ici?!" (Hey white boy, what you doing downtown?)

Unlike Bowie, Springsteen, Reed and Dylan, musical artists who have had their own four-colour comics usually come from the sweeter end of the pop market. These comics are more often than not one-off affairs, such as Ricky Nelson (1959 and 1961) and the Lennon Sisters (1958 and 1959) who were both given outings in wholesome adventures. Indeed, dance craze The Twist made such an impact that it was awarded a one-off comic by Dell in 1962.

Such was the cultural impact that the Beatles had on America when they arrived in August 1964, that their aroma was swiftly baked into comics. In September 1964, Superman's pal Jimmy Olsen went back in time – 1000BC – and ended up making Beatles' wigs and selling them to make money. He also played a ram's horn (don't ask) with such skill that he starts a Beatles' fad. In March 1965, Marvel Comics 'The Thing and The Human Torch Meet The Beatles' in *Strange Tales* 130, and as well as bumping into the band, both try out Beatles' wigs. Archie comics – always with their fingers on the musical pulse – featured a visual gag with the Beatles on the front cover of *Laugh* 166 in January 1965. Charlton's *My Little Margie* in November 1964, also featured the Beatles on the front cover.

Best of all was – of course – the official *Complete Life Stories of the Beatles* published by Dell in September to November 1964. This 64-page beauty contained no adverts and depicted the life and early career of the Beatles, as well as also featuring seven full-colour pin-ups. For the record, the two pages where Brian Epstein discovers the Beatles are excellent, depicting a procession of young girls coming into one of the Epstein family-owned stores trying to buy their records. "Yes, there is something about them that's different! Their enthusiasm, their

SURPRISED AT HOW CLOSE HE WAS TO THE QUARTET, BRIAN EPSTEIN TOOK OFF AT LUNCH TIME TO CHECK THE CAVERN! THE MATHEW STREET CLUB WASN'T EASY TO ENTER! THE VAULTED CATACOMBS OF THE CLUB WERE PACKED WITH STOMPING, ROCKING TEEN-AGERS, WHO WERE TWISTING TO THE BEAT...

BRIAN'S FIRST TEMPTATION AFTER SEEING THE RATHER ENERGETIC BUT SCRAGGILY YOUNGSTERS IN THEIR JEANS WAS TO FIGHT HIS WAY OUT FOR A BREATH OF FRESH AIR ...

BUT HE STAYED! HE FORGOT THE JACKETS AND SCRUFFY HAIR STYLES; HE LINGERED AND LISTENED...

YES, THERE IS SOMETHING ABOUT THEM THAT'S DIFFERENT! THEIR ENTHUSIASM, THEIR STYLE -- THEY HAVE TALENT!

Opposite: Dell Comics.
Above: © 2005 Marvel Characters, Inc. Used with permission.

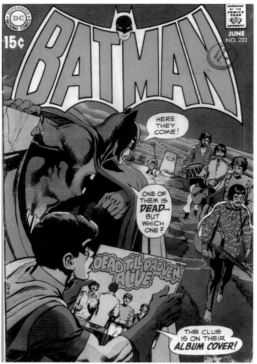

© DC Comics.

(February 1968) must run it a close second. This four-page extravaganza not only parodied the album cover better than Frank Zappa's *We're Only In It For The Money*, but also included lyrics to seven of Sgt Fury's 'songs'. As I know you are gagging for a sample, here it is:

"It was twenty years ago today
That Sgt Fury taught the band to fight
They've been whipping Nazis just for fun
And sinking Hirohito's rising sun
So let me introduce to you
The squad you've known for all these years
Sgt. Fury's Lonely Hearts Club band!"

DC Comics also got in on the 'psychedelic' Beatles act, most famously in *Batman* 222 in June 1970. Although the 16-page mystery story 'Dead Till Proven Alive!' features a fictional band – The Twists – they look very much like the Beatles. The band members are depicted on the cover drawn by Neal Adams in classic *Abbey Road* and *Magical Mystery Tour* poses.

"We did the Beatles on the cover," he recalls "but one of them was missing. The story was about the missing Beatle, but it was not the Beatles, it was somebody else, but I did the Beatles on the cover. Because everybody did the Beatles…"

The Beatles phenomenon also inspired another DC title called *Swing With Scooter* which began publication in June/July 1966. It featured a famous English singing star called Scooter, who leaves England to get away from hysterical female fans, only to discover that in America he attracts hysterical female fans! With his Beatles-style haircut, motorbike, mod clothes and guitar strapped

style – they have talent!" Epstein thinks after catching the Fab Four at the Cavern club in Liverpool.

Over the next few years, with the popularity and influence of the Beatles becoming even more pronounced, there were a multitude of appearances in American monthly comics. This ranged from the romance field – *Summer Love* October 1966, 'The Beatles Saved My Romance' – to *Jerry Lewis* number 93, where Ringo, Paul, George and John appear as babies. My personal favourite must be Ringo – who because of his big nose was cartoonists' favourite Beatle – appearing as a window cleaner in Marvel parody title *Not Brand Echh* 7 in April 1968. Saying that, the glorious parody of *Sgt Pepper's* album – *Sgt Fury's Lonely Hearts Club Band* – in issue 12 to his back at all times, Scooter was the British invasion in comic-book form. Indeed, by February 1967 this phenomenon was even producing villains for American superheroes to fight, with the Teen Titans having to take on the Mad Mod of Carnaby Street who smuggles "chemicals" around the world in the fabric of suits he makes for rock stars like Holly Hip.

Although the Beatles made a multitude of 'guest appearances' in American comics, they never had their own monthly comic book. The one-off 1968 Gold Key, *Yellow Submarine* offering based on the film does not count! Typically though, the most famous band inspired by the Beatles did have their own comic. Between July 1967 and December 1968 Dell comics published seventeen issues of a monthly Monkees comic. The reason for the existence of the comic was due to what we now call synergy. As a band, the Monkees were manufactured for a TV show which would follow the trials and tribulations of a fictional musical group. Michael Nesmith (guitar), Peter Tork (bass), Michael Dolenz (drums) and Davey Jones (vocals) were the lucky boys selected to play the parts although – vocals aside – the original music for the show was written by seasoned songwriters and performed by session musicians. For example, Neil Diamond wrote 'I'm A Believer', a song so evergreen that it even appeared in the first *Shrek* film, although even in his wildest dreams Diamond would never have imagined it being performed by a singing computer-generated donkey.

As for the Monkees, the show was first broadcast in America in September 1966, quickly picking up a large audience. Such was the success of the group that hit singles,

© Dell Comics.

albums and all manner of merchandise ranging from toy cars to Monkees shirts appeared. Like live-action donkeys being asked to bear too-heavy-a-load, the actors rebelled – both Nesmith and Tork were real musicians – and the fictional TV band transformed into a real band that began to play their own instruments in the studio, wrote their own songs and went out on tour. Unlike Minni Vanilli – who lip-synched in live performance until their backing tape broke live on camera – from the *Headquarters* album (1967) onwards, the Monkees did it for real.

At some stage in early 1967, someone at Dell comics did the math and worked out that a comic devoted to the Monkees would sell like American flags in the week before Independence Day. After all, what better ad-

vertising was there than a weekly TV show? Dell were well-known for their film and TV tie-in comics and a deal was struck. Fictional TV characters became comic book characters. *The Monkees* first issue was published in June 1967, selling great guns across America, mostly to teenage and female fans of the band. Each comic usually contained about three stories that placed Davy, Michael, Peter and Micky in amusing situations. An example would be 'The Ad Men' from *Monkees* 9 (February 1968) where the boys tired of

never having enough money, throw away their instruments and go out looking for real work. They want to get into advertising and meet Oscar, a hot dog vendor who "ain't had any business for eight and a half days." They decide that if they can drum up business for him, "we can save Oscar here, and establish a name for ourselves at the same time."

Over the next few pages the Monkees do everything possible to pass on through word of mouth how good Oscar's hot dogs are. This extends to skywriting, writing on an orbiting satellite, putting articles in newspapers and broadcasting on TV. The end result is that about ten thousand people end up crowding around his stand eager to buy a hot dog from him. When the boys ask him for his opinion on their sterling work he retorts, "Business is so good I'm thinking of putting in live entertainment. You boys wouldn't know of a good combo that might like the job would you?" The story ends with the Monkees at the city rubbish dump trying to find the instruments that they threw away. Although to hardened pop fans this story might sound pretty weak, it should be remembered that Monkees comics were aimed mainly at young teenage and pre-teen girls who had a crush on the band, and young boys who just thought it was all good fun. The writers of the comics were also – no doubt – trying to translate the zany humour featured in the TV shows onto the printed page.

The artwork in the *Monkees* comics was pretty workmanlike, although to be fair to the artists involved, they did manage to capture the likeness of the band quite well. What drove the sales were the covers, as each comic featured a black and white or full colour photo of the band taken from the TV show.

The economics of the *Monkees* comic mirrored the band's fortunes. The final episode of the series was broadcast in America in March 1968, although the comic ran until November 1968. By the time the publishers got around to this issue either the money had run out, or sales were so low that they decided to simply reprint the first comic – photo cover and artwork and all – and slap the number 17 on the inside cover! Typically, this issue is now a rare and collectable

treasure. *Monkees* comics are now collected by fans as essential items of memorabilia and one fan was lucky enough to stumble across some of the original artwork.

"When you collect Monkees stuff," the fan told me, "you go for the neat stuff if you can find it, and I just came across the art accidentally by looking at a friends' (selling) list in the Midwest almost ten years ago. None of that art had popped up before and he had two books – which was 32 pages! I went 'Wooaaahhhhh! Monkees art!' I'd never seen anything like it!" He paid $1,500 for the 32 pages, "which at that time was a pretty good deal."

As to whether the band got a good deal and received any money from the comics is unknown. Then again, perhaps the producers who made the show simply received a flat fee from Dell to produce the comic. It should be mentioned that due to the power of television, the Monkees phenomenon even reached England. There were not only the hit records, but the Dell comics were imported and sold on newsstands alongside Marvel and DC's superhero comics. In England the Monkees enjoyed further adventures in weekly comic books like *Lady Penelope*. This 1967 spin-off from Gerry Anderson's Century 21 *Thunderbirds/Stingray/Joe 90* empire, was tabloid in size with artwork that was far superior to that in the American stories, and explored a similar zany formula.

One example from the 1968 *Century 21 Annual* has aliens landing in the Monkees' back yard. The four aliens are blue, have eyes on the end of stalks and – unusually for aliens – wear plaid kilts complete with sporrans. Like the Monkees they are also a rock group called 'The Earthmen', and for the boys' pleasure belt out their best song, 'Hey Hey We're The Earthmen" in the hope that they can get them some club dates.

The following day, the Monkees take The Earthmen to the Freak Out Club where they are next scheduled to play. The Flower Power audience find the Monkees too tame for their taste, although lap up The Earthmen who are "Like psychedelic! How does that grab you?" As the dispirited Monkees pack up their gear out back and prepare to leave, the aliens run out of the club, jump into their saucer and fly away. "We thought it was great when those chicks went crazy over us," one of them says, "but when that bunch of guys started after us we decided it was better back home!" The punchline being that The Earthmen had confused the long-haired male hippies with the girls. Something of a stereotype I agree but the strip was aimed at teenagers! One wonders if the uncredited artist was a member of the English underground scene, or at least culturally aware, as one of the hippies is wearing a pair of hand-painted Union Jack sunglasses that Hapshash poster artist Michael English originally designed and sold a small number of emerging hip London boutiques.

In this multimedia age The Monkees music, TV show and reputation have worn well. It's hard to hate guys who actually insisted that Jimi Hendrix opened for them when they toured America in 1967. Even their psychedelic film – *Head* – which baffled their teenage audience when it was first released is now perceived as a valued piece of cinematic work.

This crossover from music TV programmes into comics was not only limited to the Monkees. Charlton comics published

a comic featuring The Partridge Family that ran for twenty-one issues between March 1971 and December 1973. For those unfamiliar with the name, this TV programme began airing in America in September 1970 and featured a fictional family pop group. The show was inspired by the real-life family pop group The Cowsills who scored impressive hits in 1967 with 'The Rain, The Park and Other Things' and 'We Can Fly'. And yes, the Cowsills did have their own one-off comic published by Harvey Comics in October 1968, which as well as stories, lyrics and interviews also featured some pretty groovy psychedelic pin-ups of the band.

As for The Partridge Family, their shows were wholesome entertainment, which seemed to preach the message that, "the family that plays together stays together." Never to be confused, of course, with Robert Crumb's "the family that lays together stays together" or – come to think of it – Rob Zombie's "the family that slays together stays together." As there were songs featured in the show, this led to real-life top twenty hits in America and England with 'I Think I Love You', 'Breaking Up Is Hard To Do' and 'Looking Thru The Eyes Of Love'. The TV show and hit records no doubt helped shift a comic or two. To be fair, the Charlton comics were pretty good. As with the *Monkees*, the four or five stories in each comic featured the family as a unit or individually enjoying wholesome adventures. There were also song lyrics and in most issues several pages specifically devoted to the guitar playing and singing star of the family – David Cassidy.

The Partridge Family helped Cassidy launch a solo career as a teen idol. It helped that – unlike Archie – he actually sung on their

hit records. Charlton were quick to give Cassidy his own comic, and between February 1972 and September 1973 fourteen editions chock full of his adventures were published. Some of them were quite fun, especially 'The Red-Headed Runaway' in number 11 from March 1973. At the beginning of the story we discover that "one of the things David liked least was posing for publicity pictures, but it was a necessary part of show business – so he went along with it!" Yeah, sure. Cassidy's flame burned so brightly that he was not only a teen idol in England, but even enjoyed more graphic comic book adventures in magazines like *Look-In*.

© Harvey Comics.

Looking back, it is amazing that there were no Jackson Five or Osmonds comics, as both sets of brothers had their own TV shows in the early Seventies. Granted they were cartoons, but did no-one think that there was a buck to be made in printed four-colour adventures? Then again, one supposes that the Osmonds would have presented problems, especially if they insisted that all fathers shown in the book be Mormons and were to have more than one wife. The Osmonds and the Jackson Five did make one comic book appearance together in a story inside Marvel's *Spoof* 3 from January 1973. They were in good company on the cover with David Cassidy being sworn in as President by John Lennon, as the rest of the ex-Beatles, the Rolling Stones, Elvis Presley, Bob Dylan and Richard Nixon look on.

When it came to serious bucks being made out of teen sensations in comics, let us fast-forward to 1990 and look at New Kids on the Block. Apparently the New Kids were paid $100,000 by Harvey Comics for the rights to print and publish comics on the band. Harvey – this is what I heard – made all of this money back on the first New Kids comic that was published! Wow! The presses ran hot and heavy for the next year with over a dozen comics being published some specifically for live tours, summer specials, Christmas specials, *Valentine* specials and comic signing tours. Of course, as teen sensations are always ripe for satire, alongside this New Kids comic industry was an unauthorised comic biography of the band published by San Diego's Revolutionary Comics. When the New Kids' management went after them with lawyers there was a court case. When the fallout of the subsequent agreement settled, Revolutionary brought out another New Kids comic which gleefully depicted the New Kids fall from grace, embracing the sex and stimulants part of the teen-dream equation.

There are a vast number of examples of pop and teen stars being parodied in cartoon strips and magazines. *Mad*, for example, are masters of this particular mystic art and throughout their fifty-plus year history, have delighted in poking fun at all types of music and pop sensations that have passed like water beneath the bridge. The Beatles, the Jacksons, Bruce Springsteen, Vanilla Ice, Guns 'N Roses, Prince, Boy George, Sting, Madonna, Cyndi Lauder, New Kids on the Block, Michael Jackson, The Who, the Rolling Stones. Jerry Garcia and Eminem are a few stars to feel the whip of satire on their back. Musical movements like punk, rap and especially disco were flayed with delight. *Mad*'s black and white stories about 'Disco Owner Of The Year' and 'Saturday Night Feeble' remain great fun to read.

Short-lived rival satire titles like *Crazy* and *Cracked* also mined a similar vein. One of the most biting satires I came across when researching this book was Drew Friedman's depiction of Natalie Cole singing a duet with her late father Nat King Cole. Friedman is an artist whose black and white stipple style gives the people he draws a delightful, almost photographic realism and his work featuring musicians is compelling. The drawing of Cole and Cole appeared in 1991 in a music trade publication called *Radio and Records* and showed Nat King Cole as a skeleton wearing headphones and Natalie saying, "Dad, you're stepping on my lines again…on the next take, could you drop it an octave?" This was referring to the (unforgettable or unforgivable) practice of Cole re-recording her voice over some of her father's old songs. "It's sort of the equivalent of Paloma Picasso painting over her father's paintings," Friedman related to the *Comics Journal* in July 1992. "How would people feel if Julian Lennon sang over his father's Beatles' recordings? People would be a little outraged." People were more than a little outraged at Friedman's cartoon, which saw him lose his contract with the publication, who correspondingly lost a lot of advertising from record companies – Cole's no doubt. Still, it was a brilliant piece of satire.

The Spice Girls were also on the receiving end of a similar comic blunderbuss. In this instance it was not one cartoon – although there are loads out there – but an entire comic dedicated to sending them up conceived at a time when they went totally champagne supernova in England and America. This broadside was masterminded by Peter Bagge.

"*Spice Capades*?" said the artist when I raised the subject. "How that came about is that a friend of mine, Jennifer Nixon, who also has a pen name of Queen Itchie was a really big Spice Girls' fan when they came out. Like a lot of people in the Nineties she used to put out her own fanzine publications by just Xeroxing them off. She came up with the idea of a Spice Girls fanzine, but no-one knew when it would come out because she had to save up her pennies to pay for twenty copies at Kinkos (an American photocopy chain)."

Of course, at the time that the Spice Girls were cresting their wave – 1996/7 – Bagge was the poster boy of underground comic book artists. Okay, okay the postcard boy of underground comics. His *Hate* series, following the ups and downs of Seattle-based music-loving slacker Buddy Bradley, was compelling and hilarious. At one stage there was serious talk about it becoming a TV cartoon series. Therefore, after sitting down with Nixon he went to his publishers with a proposal for a Spice Girls comic. As publishers went, Fantagraphics were not exactly in the business of printing comics about teen sensations. Fantagraphics were – and thankfully still are – an organisation who perceive comics as art, and the artists they encourage through publication and republication of their work have been vital in conveying the message that comics in America are not all about superheroes.

© Peter Bagge.

Initially, they were resistant to the idea about a Spice Girls parody comic, "but we just wore them down and bugged them relentlessly about publishing it," recalls Bagge.

Of course whilst negotiations between Bagge, Nixon and Fantagraphics were ongoing, the Spice Girls' career was peaking. I don't speak from experience, but I hear it's all downhill after pop stars make their first feature film, although that did not ruin U2 or Eminem.

"Anyway," recalls Bagge, "by the time Fantagraphics agreed to publish the thing and my friend was able to get it all together, Geri had already quit and the Spice Girls phenomenon was gone! If we had only got the thing out six months earlier it would have sold a whole lot better (laughs). It is funny, but I really felt bad for my publisher, because we browbeat them into publishing this thing

about a group that they loathed and then they don't even make any money out of it! (laughs). They try to exploit the Spice Girls and they don't even make a dime! (laughs uproariously)".

Although Bagge feels bad that Fantagraphics took a bath on the deal, the *Spice Capades* book published in Spring 1999 is excellent. Nixon pulled together a mouth-watering selection of artists to give their take on the Spice Girls mythos including Mort Todd, Gilbert Hernandez and even Robert Crumb. The artist Kaz drew a page of rejected Spice Girls, that included White Power Spice, Pregnant Spice and Slovenly Spice. David and Kevin Sclazo take the girls back in a time machine to 1984 to meet Lady Diana and Mike Gorman's 'Momma Had Girl Power' features Ed Gein and Norman Bates ending a two-page strip dressed in the skin of their victims as Scary Spice Girls. All told a great read, although what a teenage die-hard Spice girls fan – or the girls themselves – made of it is open to question. For the record, Pete Bagge drew the cover and also a story about what it was like to attend a Spice Girls' concert. Like the Beatles' *Magical Mystery Tour* he reported that a splendid time was guaranteed for all.

Of course, the Spice Girls came from England, where there have been all manner of teenage heart-throbs depicted in comics. As publications hit the newsagents every week, there was greater scope to feature the flavour of the month, week or even year. As you might imagine the Beatles were everywhere in the Sixties, especially in the vast armada of teen magazines and girls comics. Special mention should also go to a comic called *Judy* in the Seventies which along with typical teen fair featured two-page biographies of bands like Slade, Mott the Hoople, Electric Light Orchestra, Steeleye Span and others. The best comic coverage – outside of music magazines – of teen bands probably went to *Look-In*, which featured regular artist-drawn biographical stories of bands like Duran Duran, Adam Ant, Madness, Haircut 100, Abba, The Monkees, Slade, Culture Club, The Beatles, Bucks Fizz, Slik and even the Bob Geldof Live Aid experience.

One of the most amazing pop music and comic crossovers occurred in the pages of *Roy of the Rovers*. As the title suggests, Roy Race played for the football club Melchester Rovers and his flirtation with promotion, relegation, football politics and a regular flow of goals captivated boys throughout the Fifties, Sixties, Seventies and Eighties. Although famed for his thunderbolt left foot, Roy had

a lot in common with pop stars. Despite his forty-year career, he never looked a day over thirty and his blonde hair was always immaculate. Moving into the shark-infested waters of becoming a player manager in September 1985, he made two of the most audacious signings in football history. No, no, no! not Bob Wilson (former Arsenal goalkeeper) and the late Emlyn Hughes (former Liverpool legend and unfortunate knitwear advocate). He signed Martin Kemp and Steve Norman from the chart-topping pop group Spandau Ballet, who not only spearheaded the New Romantic movement, but had monster hits with songs like 'True' which, as great tunes go, is as evergreen as green paint on a green door.

Norman (saxophone/good looks) and Kemp (good looks/good looks/bass) played against Melchester in a charity match and Roy was so impressed with the boys that he decided to draft them into his team. When there is unrest in the squad over these new faces and their seriously dangerous highlighted hairstyles Roy calls the team together and lays it on the line, "No-one is guaranteed a place in the senior squad… not even me! You've got to fight to get into it and fight to stay there! And that goes for Martin Kemp and Steve Norman! I signed them because I think they can make the grade…not because they are pop stars…"

And make the grade they do, turning in some stellar performances for Melchester, even when rain flattens their blow-dried hair and mud soils their pop star knees. Of course, Spandau Ballet are more than happy to play charity performances for Melchester Rovers. They even act as a backing band behind Roy at the club Christmas party although he wisely decides to sing the classic football

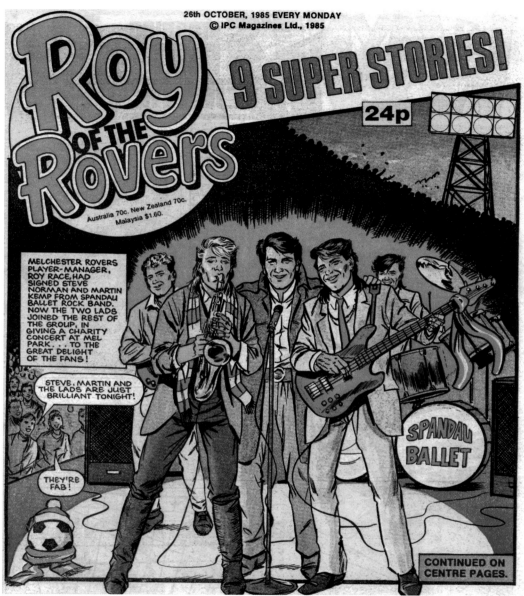

26th OCTOBER, 1985 EVERY MONDAY
© IPC Magazines Ltd., 1985

Roy OF THE Rovers

9 SUPER STORIES!

24p

Australia 70c. New Zealand 70c.
Malaysia $1.60.

MELCHESTER ROVERS PLAYER-MANAGER, ROY RACE, HAD SIGNED STEVE NORMAN AND MARTIN KEMP FROM SPANDAU BALLET ROCK BAND. NOW THE TWO LADS JOINED THE REST OF THE GROUP, IN GIVING A CHARITY CONCERT AT MEL PARK... TO THE GREAT DELIGHT OF THE FANS!

STEVE, MARTIN AND THE LADS ARE JUST BRILLIANT TONIGHT!

THEY'RE FAB!

SPANDAU BALLET

CONTINUED ON CENTRE PAGES.

song 'Walk On' rather than 'To Cut A Long Story Short', 'Chant No 1' or 'Communication'. Before we leave the subject of music and comics and football, a special mention must got to the *Viz* cartoon strip 'Billy the Fish' which at one time featured Shakin' Stevens and Simply Red's Mick Hucknall in the Fulchester Rovers line-up.

At Christmas in England there have always been hard-backed Annuals of weekly comics.

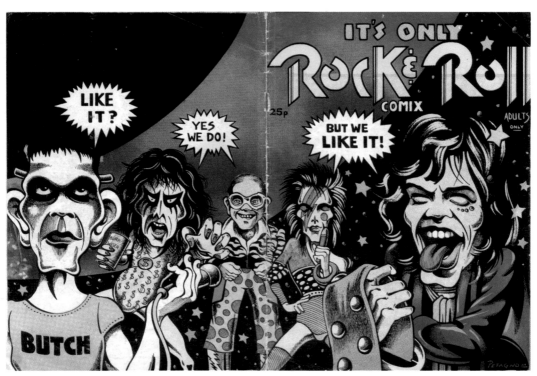

© Joe Petagno. Used with permission.

From the Fifties to today, these publications were *de-rigueur* items to be placed under the Christmas tree for young children and teenagers. Pop stars who made it really big in the singles' charts were often awarded their very own annual. So, the Bay City Rollers were under Christmas trees for a couple of years in the mid-Seventies, as was Gary Glitter in 1975. Along with photos of the tinfoil turkey there was also – because he was a stout lad – an article on slimming food! "As far as I'm concerned I eat plenty of lean meat and maybe a little salad with it," he confides.

There were two six-page artist-drawn comic stories of how he became successful and the genesis of his hit singles like 'Rock and Roll' and 'Do You Wanna Touch Me (Oh Yeah!)'.

"Seems like a good song," ponders Mr Glitter, as he sits with writing partner Mike Leander, "wonder if I'll have another hit." A sample of other pop stars deemed worthy of annuals over the years include Adam and the Ants (1983), Madonna (1987), Oasis (1998) and Take That (1994, 1995 and 1996). More recently Eminem has got in there, although his best Christmas appearance came in the 2003 *Viz* annual in a *Beano*-inspired spoof strip called 'Eminem The Menace'!

So, David Bowie never got his own annual in the Seventies did he? Nope! So we're still waiting for the Starman which, as all Bowie fans will know, is a little White Light reflected – (with thanks).

6

Jazz, Blues and Opera Into Comics Will Go... On Occasion.

It would be nice to report that there are a vast array of references to jazz, blues, classical music and opera in comics. Well, there are – and there are not. Maybe I am looking under the wrong rocks and stones, but these forms of music have received less coverage in comics than good old rock and roll, pop music and rap.

However, the shopping trolley is not totally empty. There have been, for example, excellent graphic novels on portions of the life and times of both Billie Holiday and Louis Armstrong, although these have been written and drawn in more recent times rather than during their illustrious careers. Hardly surprising you might say, for between the Twenties and Fifties when jazz was the music of the discerning listener, the comics industry was in its infancy. At a time when 'Strange Fruit' was still swinging from the trees, it was hardly going to turn colour pages over to coloured artists like Lester Young, Charlie Parker, Coleman Hawkins, Miles Davis, Count Basie, Art Tatum, Sonny Rollins, Errol Garner or John Coltrane.

But it was not all doom and gloom on the music front. There was an excellent five-page biography of bandleader Glenn Miller who got America 'In The Mood' during World War Two. This appeared in *Real Fact Comics* 9, published in 1947 and even showed Miller playing for the Queen of England, "Major Miller, I've listened to you often on the wireless," she purrs, "Will you play 'St Louis Blues?'" And so he does.

A sister publication – *Real Fact Comics* – covered the life of George Gershwin and Bing Crosby, although I have not been able to get my mitts on a copy of either, as they are as rare as hen's teeth.

In 1946 *Sweet Sixteen* printed the life story of singer Rose Marie Lombardo – whoever she was! Better than this – although I have not been able to get my hands on this one either – is a comic called *Taffy* from 1946, that featured the legendary composer and bandleader Duke Ellington. Was it a comic strip examination of his career or just a photo and some text? Answers on an electronic postcard please to ijshirl@hotmail.com. In England, the pages of the weekly *Valentine* magazine in the late-'50s covered some jazz, especially the trad output of Aker Bilk. Indeed, the magazine got so carried away that they even sent a journalist on the road with him to cover a string of gigs between London and Norwich!

When rock and roll hit the beaches in the late-Fifties, comics also began to get into their stride. Although rock and roll began to pick up some coverage, jazz references were few and far between. God, I'd give anything to find a strip which features a guest appearance from Miles Davis, or a two-page comic book story that covers his career from his days as a sideman with Charlie Parker to *Kind of Blue* (1959) and *In A Silent Way* (1969). Saying that, the artwork of the *On*

The Corner album from 1972 had an element of comic book art about it, although I suppose the same can be said for Funkadelic's *Hardcore Jollies*.

Although during their careers there was little coverage of jazz and blues artists in comic books, it must be said that reparations have been made. Artist Justin Green began to contribute regular 'Musical Legends' biographies to Tower Records' *Pulse* magazine from March 1992. Over the years these included strips like Fats Waller breaking the colour bar when being asked to play 'Honeysuckle Rose' on the organ at a baseball game at the New York Yankees stadium in 1932. Lil Hardin, Armstrong, Dinah Washington, Anita O' Day and even Captain Beefheart were covered in these excellent and informative strips.

Underground cartoonist Robert Crumb is well-known for his deep love of early jazz and blues, and this has informed his work. He delighted in drawing biographical strips like Jelly Roll Morton's 'Voodoo Curse' (1984), six pages of brilliance. It puts into visual form Morton's own belief, as related to Alan Lomax of the Library of Congress, that the decline of his career was all down to a former business partner who once cheated him. When caught, he told the jazz man that "Jelly Roll Morton, you will lose everything you have!!!" Morton is convinced – and finds evidence – that the man has put a curse on him. Some of Crumb's work in this field has been collected into *R. Crumb Draws The Blues*, a slim Fantagraphics volume but well worth the investment.

Also worth tracking down, now that they are being reprinted by Kitchen Sink, are Crumb's Jazz, Blues and Country music

PULSE! *Presents* **Musical Legends** by JUSTIN GREEN

FATS & BABE

By 1932, the composer, organist, pianist, bandleader, vocalist and clown Thomas Wright ("Fats") Waller's star was rising to the zenith of swing music. But the "Sultan of Swat" had already peaked, and was on a downward spiral. On a summer Sunday of that year, their brief meeting made baseball history.

WALLER

RUTH

THE DAY BEGAN LIKE ANY OTHER FOR WALLER. HE TOOK HIS "LIQUID HAM AND EGGS" (i.e., FOUR FINGERS OF STRAIGHT GIN).

HOW YA DOIN'?

JUS' FINE!

EDDIE CONDON, A JAZZ GUITARIST ASSIGNED BY THE VICTOR LABEL TO MAKE SURE THAT WALLER SHOWED UP FOR AN IMMINENT RECORDING DATE, PAID A SURPRISE VISIT TO THE ROTUND TUNESMITH.

TOP O' THE MORNIN', THOMAS! FREE PASSES TO YANKEE STADIUM COMPLIMENTS OF VICTOR.

AWREET! WE GONNA SEE THE BAMBINO SWING!

IT WAS UNUSUAL TO SEE A MAN OF WALLER'S SIZE AND COLOR IN A PREMIER BOX SEAT, WHICH WAS SITUATED JUST BEHIND THE HOME TEAM DUGOUT.

GEEZ, WOULD YA LOOK AT THAT?

HOW COULD I NOT LOOK? THE GUY IS BLOCKIN' MY VIEW.

GREAT SEATS!

WORD SPREAD LIKE WILD-FIRE THAT THE CELEBRATED JAZZMAN WAS IN THE CROWD. HIS SATIRICAL SEND-UPS OF INNOCUOUS SHOW TUNES WERE A POWERFUL ANTIDOTE TO THE MORIBUND DEPRESSION ERA.

IT'S FATS WALLER!

I THOUGHT HE WAS STILL IN FRANCE.

RUTH HIMSELF STEPPED OUT OF THE DUGOUT AND DOFFED HIS CAP TO THE MAESTRO. WALLER RETURNED THE COMPLIMENT BY STANDING UP AND PALMING DOWN A HOT DOG BABE-STYLE.

I'LL SWAT 'EM! YOU CAN SWING 'EM!

DOWN THE HATCH IN ONE BITE!

YANKEE MANAGEMENT SENT AN EMISSARY INTO THE STANDS, WHO SUMMONED WALLER.

JUST ONE MORE FLIGHT.

DURING THE SEVENTH INNING STRETCH, WALLER MANNED THE MIGHTY WURLITZER. AFTER A FLAWLESS BACH FUGUE, HE BROKE INTO HIS SIGNATURE "*HONEYSUCKLE ROSE.*"

THOUGH IT WOULD BE OVER FIFTEEN YEARS BEFORE JACKIE ROBINSON TOUCHED OFFICIAL HORSEHIDE, SERIOUS DAMAGE WAS DONE TO THE COLOR LINE.

YOU SHOWED 'EM, THOMAS. THEY NEVER HEARD THE ORGAN PLAYED LIKE THAT!

YEAH? THEY NEVER SAW A NEGRO HIT A BASEBALL, EITHER.

trading cards. These contain portraits and biographies of artists like Bix Beiderbecke, Coleman Hawkins, Duke Ellington, Sidney Bechet, Big Bill Bronzy, Barbecue Bob, Blind Willie McTell, the Memphis Jug Band and Charley Patton.

Another Fantagraphics book that captures some essence of jazz in cartoon form, is *Cat On A Hot Thin Groove*. This reprints cartoons and covers that artist Gene Deitch drew for a publication called *Record Changer* between 1945 and 1951. Most of the one-panel gags revolve around The Cat, a bald, white, jazz enthusiast and his never-ending

search for rare records. The jokes hold up well today, and apply to all collectors of rare vinyl, whatever the music contained on the grooves. "Lemme tell you something about this record," says a rare record dealer to the Cat, "it was owned by an old lady who never played it faster than 20rpm." The book also contains some excellent portraits of jazz artists like King Oliver, Kid Ory and George Lewis. Deich also slipped social commentary into some of his work. One cover of *Record Changer* from July 1947, shows a white blues fan sitting on the bus with a new album, totally unaware that the artist concerned is

"...AND HE *PLAYED*.

"HE PLAYED LIKE AN ANGEL, SOARING OVER THE HEADS OF INFERIOR MUSICIANS, TRYING TO LIFT THEM WITH HIM INTO THE STRATOSPHERE OF TRUTH.

"BUT THEY BORE HIM DOWN. SHOWBOAT BUFFOONS LIKE *BUZZY TREADWELL*, WHO SOLD OUT HIS ART TO BE THE WHITE MAN'S FAVORITE *BOPPER*."

Batman Jazz, 1995
© DC Comics.

forced to sit behind him in the 'coloured' section of the bus. Another from September 1947 depicts a white audience enjoying the music of a black band, whilst a black couple outside the venue cannot get in. It is an excellent book, although, as *The Record Changer* did not embrace Bop, it gave us no cartoon portraits of artists like Thelonious Monk and legendary sax player Charlie Parker, although *Downbeat* magazine did contain some nice artistic illustrations of musicians.

Amazingly, Charlie Parker did get to appear in a comic book. In 1995! The curtain of the three-part 'Batman Jazz' story opens to reveal the Dark Knight rescuing an old saxophone-playing black man from assault by three young men. Once Batman takes care of the punching and kicking duties, he and the old man end up talking about jazz and the legend of Blue Byrd crops up.

"I've heard of him," says Batman, "he died in the '50s. Here in town. The father of Be-bop."

"Not "Be-Bop" corrects the old man, "Modern jazz."

Batman later drops by a run down jazz club – honest! – to see this old black man

called Willie Little play. Then, the story goes back in time to the '50s when Blue Byrd was at the top of his game and "played like an angel, soaring over the heads of inferior musicians trying to lift them with him into the stratosphere of truth." One of his partners on the bandstand is trumpet player Buzzy Treadwell who, with his beret, is basically Dizzy Gillespie in comic book form. Although the music they played in the '50s is brilliant, Byrd falls from grace due to drug use and dies of a Charlie Parker-type overdose. Of course, this being a superhero comic, Batman has to fight some villains, and these are the quaintly named Brothers Of The Bop.

'Batman Jazz' is basically a delightful examination of the Charlie Parker myth lovingly re-tooled with a happy ending. The black man Batman saved at the beginning of the story is, of course, Blue Byrd and thus – after a little bit of adventure and a reunion with Treadwell – Bird Lives!

Backtracking a little bit, Robert Crumb was instrumental in getting *Cat On A Hot Thin Groove* published and was also partly responsible for launching the career of another talent in the comic book field, who has introduced jazz in their work: Harvey Pekar.

"I started out writing jazz reviews in 1959 for a publication that was actually called the *Jazz Review*," recalls Pekar who wrote an appreciation of trumpeter Fats Navarro, "that magazine was edited by Nat Hentoff and Nat Williams. It only lasted about three years, but it was probably the best jazz publication that I ever wrote for. It was very good. Then I wrote for *Downbeat* and *Coda* and more recently I've written for the *Jazz Times* and *Jazziz*. I have written for a lot of different magazines over the years. I have been a jazz critic for longer than I have been a comic book writer."

Pekar turned his attention to comics after meeting Robert Crumb. Inspired by Crumb's self-confessional stories, Pekar began publication of his own comic called *American Splendor*. "It was an ironic or satirical title," he recalls, "When I was a kid I used to read all these DC comics, like *Star Spangled Comics* and *All American Comics* and stuff like that. I got the 'American' from that, and 'Splendor', that came from a movie called *Splendor In The Grass* with Natalie Wood. The title just seemed so ridiculous. I just happened to put those two words together, and obviously, most people would not consider my life to be very splendid at all, so it's an ironic kind of commentary."

Reviewing jazz albums was only one string on the Pekar bow, and financially a shoestring. *American Splendor* depicts Pekar's day-to-day life from his boring job as a filing clerk in Cleveland, selling records in hospital and the everyday events that happened to him. "I try to portray things about myself that a lot of the times are similar to other people who are subject to the same kind of frustrations on the job and stuff like that. At the same time, zany things happen to them at home. I like to be a kind of everyman figure that as many people as possible can relate to."

What also made *Splendor* interesting, was the revolving door of artists who Pekar used over the years to draw for him. This ranged from Crumb, Drew Friedman, Joe Sacco and even Alan Moore, "when I was putting them out myself, I had sixty pages a year to fill and you could not get one guy to do all that. A lot of these artists were doing other things and they had day jobs like I did. So I had to try and get a variety of guys to work on the comics, and then some of them would go and I would meet somebody else who was really good and I would want to work with him, so we would start working together. There was just that normal turnover."

With his love of jazz it was inevitable that music would creep into Pekar's strips. "That happened in the early 1990s," he recalls, "I was writing for the *Village Voice* and the editor knew my comic book work and liked it. He suggested that I do something in a comic book format about jazz. So I started doing stuff and it proved to be fairly popular." These miniature biographies were later collected into *American Splendor* comic books and included excellent strips on musicians as diverse John Zorn, Shelia Jordan, Lonnie Johnson, Slim Gaillard, Jabbo Smith, Sun Ra and even producer and arranger Teo Maceo. "I did a thing on his music," Pekar recalls "because I always considered him a really interesting musician."

Of course, since the film about his life, times and fun on the *Letterman Show*, things have been *Splendid* for Pekar. Things are not

so splendid for fans of classical music, as I found very few references in comics to the likes of Beethoven, Holst, Brahms and the like. But there are some. The short-lived *Top Spot* magazine that began publication in England in 1958 – 'man sized adventures in picture-strips' – ran a delightful two-page story about Waltz king, Johann Strauss, under the title of 'He Rocked And Rolled 'em In Old Vienna' depicting his career as some kind of embryonic Presley experience. In more recent times, Justin Green did an interesting 'Musical Legends' strip about 'The Day Jobs Of Philip Glass' – taxi driver and plumber – before he became a successful composer. There was also an interesting history of music in cartoon-form published in Belgium in 1978, called *Muziekgeschiedenis*. I don't read the language but the pages on Bach and Mozart look pretty good.

In closing we have to go to the opera. This musical form has been well served in comic book form through the singular efforts of artist P. Craig Russell. "I originally decided to do opera back in 1972 or 1973 when I was still in school in Cincinatti. When I was in my first year as an artist with Marvel comics I was completely besotted by (Wagner's) *Ring of the Nibelungen*, so in my first year in the business I decided that I wanted to do opera comics." This desire began to express itself in graphic form in stories like 'Parsifal', 'Pelleas' and 'Melisande' and even Mozart's *The Magic Flute*. "I was just looking for good stories to tell, and I was not interested the regular superhero stuff in any longer. I did not find the stuff that I was offered very interesting, and this was something that had some wonderful stories and that is why I was doing it. I did not care if the readers knew it

was from an opera or not. As a matter of fact, it counted against me a number of times! I had people come up to me on several occasions and say, 'I really liked such and such a comic and they were surprised because they did not like opera.' That floors me, because a story is a story and obviously what people don't like about opera is the singing, and there is no singing in a comic book. There is just a simple story."

Russell's masterwork in adapting opera to comics is the *Ring Of The Nibelungen*. This is one of Richard Wagner's classic operas and as it contains a magical ring, Gods, swordplay, heroic deeds and, uh, incest, was ideal fodder to be transformed into a comic book adaptation. Indeed, before Russell began sharpening his pencils, there had already been two adaptations. One by Numa Sadoul and France Renonce published in France and another version by Gil Kane and Roy Thomas published by DC comics in four parts in 1989/90.

However, Russell intended to produce a 400-page masterpiece that was to take up all of his time and energy. "It was the most nerve-wracking experience of my life," he recalls. "From start to finish it took about four-and-a half-years to do and this was right when the whole comics industry seemed to be collapsing in on itself. The challenge in doing something like that is to try to find a visual structure that replicates the musical structure in some way. You have these musical moments that have such an emotional punch to them, and the dramatic punch comes solely from the music. So when I am doing the visualisation, if it is not going to be dead on the page I had to come up with some sort of visual metaphor that hopefully succeeded in

He ROCKED and ROLLED 'em in Old Vienna

Here is the amazing story of the wonderful night when the music of Johann Strauss, who wrote "The beautiful Blue Danube," was first heard in Vienna, city of romance and song.

In 1840, Vienna waltzed to the music of Johann Strauss. This was not the Johann known to fame but his father, also a well-known conductor and composer...

It is not generally known today that Johann Strauss the elder had created a sensation in Europe with his orchestra and his music! Women adored him!

Two women worshipped him — his wife, mother of three sons...

HURRY, ANNA, I HAVE AN URGENT APPOINTMENT! YOU FUSS TOO MUCH.

BUT YOU CAN'T GO OUT WITH YOUR CRAVAT TIED LIKE THIS!

producing that same effect on the reader. So I was constantly challenged to try to come up with something more than just talking heads saying these lines from Wagner. That was the most challenging and fun part. "

Russell succeeded in this. Published in comic book form by Dark Horse between February 2000 and September 2001 the *Ring of the Nibelungen* was a triumph, especially when read in the form of the two collected graphic novels that were printed in 2002. As well as winning industry awards, the story of Votan, Siegfried, Siegmund and Valkyrie could be enjoyed by those who had no interest in opera. "Several of the people I have talked to at the Wagner Society have children or grandchildren who are crazy about it," Russell told me, "they are excited to be able to pass on their love of opera and be able to draw someone in through this more accessible medium." It also helped that the plot of Wagner's *Ring of Nibelungen* – written

and scored in 1875/6 – may have partly been the inspiration for a certain epic story written by Tolkien. "Enough words you filth!" screams Voton to Alberich who stole the Rhinegold from beneath the sea and forged it into a ring that not only gave him power to rule the world, but made him the Lord of the Nibelungs, "You've no…right…to…it!" Just like Gollum, Voton of course, wants the ring for himself which kicks off all kinds of trouble…

As well as Wagner's epic tale being given the epic treatment by Russell, opera stars can be used as figures of fun. Luciano Pavarotti made a surreal guest-appearance in the pages of a 2002 copy of Bob Burdon's *Flaming Carrot* comic which, come to think of it, even included a appearance by that famed samba-dancing jazz starlet The Girl From Ipanema – naked!

7

Destroy What Bores You On Sight

According to John Holmstrom, punk started with him.

It is difficult to argue with the man. After all, along with fellow conspirators Legs McNeil and Ged Dunn Jr. he began publishing *Punk Magazine* in January 1976. The first issue of this seminal publication featured an interview with an unsigned band called the Ramones. The star on the cover and featured inside the mostly hand-written pages was Lou Reed.

Punk Magazine is the perfect example of what happens when you lock music and comics together in the same cage. John

Holmstrom was a cartoonist who had been taught by – amongst others – the legendary Harvey Kurtzman at the School of Visual Arts in New York. Music fans unfamiliar with Kurtzman will surely have at some time thumbed through a copy of *Mad* magazine: well that long-running humour magazine was his creation back in 1952.

"He has been a mentor for so many cartoonists it is unbelievable," recalls Holmstrom, whose own inspirations are legion. "I was first influenced by Marvel Comics, Steve Ditko and Jack Kirby and early *Mad* comics, both the magazines and the paperbacks with Will Elder and Wally Wood. I would try to draw like those guys. Steve Ditko was my favourite. Then, when I got into High School I read all the underground books like R. Crumb, Gilbert Shelton and just kept going. I read every comic book I could get my hands on. When I got into art school Harvey Kurtzman introduced all of us to European comics."

As for *Punk Magazine*, seventeen issues published between 1976 and 1979 documented the emerging New York Scene. Although the Ramones, Patti Smith, Talking Heads and Television were strands of hair that were already growing there is no doubt that *Punk Magazine* was the comb, scissors and mirror that allowed more people than just those crammed into the sweaty venues like CBGB's to admire their style. According to Holmstrom, the magazine helped name the scene.

"I took that from *Creem* (magazine)", he recalls, "they were using the word a lot in 1974. Alice Cooper was 'Punk of the Year'. They used punk to separate the hard-driving rock and roll from stuff like Jobriath, Elton John or Rod Stewart. The Stooges were punk rock. The MC5 were punk rock. The New York Dolls were punk rock, but Roxy Music were not punk rock. We were hanging out trying to decide what to call the magazine. I had a couple of names but Ged and Legs did not like them. I said, 'What are we going to call the magazine that combines comics, fun stuff and music?' Legs said, 'Just call it *Punk*!' And it stuck."

The first issue of *Punk* nailed its colours to the mast in a handwritten editorial: "Kill yourself. Jump off a fuckin' cliff. Drive nails into your head. Become a robot and

join the staff at Disneyland. OD anything. Just don't listen to discoshit. I've seen that canned crap take real live people and turn them into dogs! And vice versa. The epitome of all that's wrong with western civilisation is disco. Educate yourself. Get into it. Read *Punk*." Lou Reed was as far away from disco as you could get, even if he had recorded an album called *Sally Can't Dance* and a suite of electronic music that was little more than guitar feedback. According to Holmstrom, the interview with Reed was a happy accident.

"We went up to CBGB's to interview the Ramones and Lou Reed happened to be there. So I interviewed Lou." Holmstrom not only drew a gorgeous cartoon image of Reed to illustrate the cover but broke the interview down into a comic strip format, "I always had the idea to do like a comic strip interview. Harvey Kurtzman had showed me similar interviews he had done for *Esquire* in comic strip interview form and I wanted to take it a step further and make it more comics."

In the interview we not only see a cartoon Holmstrom ask a cartoon Reed for an interview but alongside the handwritten transcription we are treated to a brief photo section of the conversation, as well as the interlude of the Ramones live set. Best of all, Holmstrom draws himself continuing the interview with Reed on the street after they leave the venue. Reed also tries to get Holmstrom to give him his tape recorder in exchange for a signed album! Although during the interview Reed was his usual self – "you're asking what everybody asks, y'know but you, since nobody reads your rag y'know, I really don't give a fuck what I say! Springsteen sucks!"

© John Holmstrom.

Lou Reed was so impressed with the cartoons that he met up with Holmstrom after publication to thank him, "Lou loved that issue," recalls Holmstrom, "He had forgotten that he had done it. He met up with me after it had come out because he wanted to meet me and thank me and stuff. He was knocked out by it. People always hear bad things about Lou but he was very nice and very encouraging."

The first issue of *Punk* contained sixteen pages and according to Holmstrom, 4,000 copies were printed and eventually sold. Although generally perceived as the first 'Punk Rock' fanzine, Holmstrom wanted *Punk* to become a proper magazine. The second issue of *Punk* hit the streets of New York in March 1976 and featured Patti Smith and Television. In subsequent issues *Punk* documented the emerging scene in New York and London

and transmitted the fun, energy and street culture of this new music and attitude.

"Everybody wanted to become our friend and before I knew it we were running the scene so it was totally weird," says Holmstrom. "I was like a huge music fan and would sit outside Madison Square Gardens for three days to get a front row seat for Alice Cooper. Then here I am with people begging me to put them in the magazine. Chris Stein is offering me naked pictures of Debbie Harry to publish in *Punk*. I was totally blown away. It was really weird, but it was great because most of the people I ended up hanging out with were really nice. I became great friends with Joey Ramone, Johnny Ramone and Debbie and Chris from Blondie and a lot of other people."

Of course, once it picked up momentum, the New York punk scene ran itself, but having a magazine that served as an outlet for interviews and photographs was vital.

Aside from editorial duties, Holmstrom drew some arresting portraits to grace the cover of the magazine. Typically, they reflected a love of music and comic books. Issue 3 featured Joey Ramone standing alone on a street corner, "that was my Will Eisner swipe. I kind of combined Will Eisner with Albrecht Dore." The cover of issue 4 featured an energetic portrait of Iggy Pop, "I based that on Marvel comics and the Incredible Hulk. It was the Incredible Iggy!" Comic history was even stitched into the magazine with number 3 from April 1976 featuring Robert Crumb and an interview with Harvey Kurtzman.

Although the meat of the magazine concentrated upon music, bands and photographs, there were also regular cartoons and strips. This ranged from an interview with Frank Zappa where Holmstrom drew how he imagined Zappa looked and felt at the other end of the line, "as that was also my first ever phone interview." There were also fun pages which allowed the reader to "fill in the dots and you'll find something to masturbate with!" Amazingly, although the editorial in the first issue had lambasted disco music, it took until issue 17 in March 1979 to devote a seven-page comic strip to parody that musical style. Holmstrom created a DJ who conceives the ultimate dance record that made people end up killing each other. 'Murder on the Dancefloor' indeed!

It would be wrong to suggest that cartoons and comics dominated *Punk*. Most interviews were in the traditional text and photo format (although handwritten) and it was this excellent coverage of the punk scene that attracted readers. Former lead singer with the New York Dolls, David Johansen, received similar treatment to Lou Reed with photos spouting speech balloons and hand-drawn cartoons. Famed music writer Lester Bangs also fought Dick Manitoba from the Dictators in a photo story complete with speech bubbles. *Punk's* crowning glory though, was the inside take of the Sex Pistols first and last American tour of 1978.

"The greatest story of all time," recalls Holmstrom who was on the tour bus with Johnny and co: "It was an adventure."

Punk moved into the realms of paper cinema with two issues – 6 and 15 – containing full-blown fictional photo stories featuring members of the New York punk movement as the cast. 'The Legend of Nick Detroit' in October 1976 saw original Television bass player, Voidoid leader and 'face' Richard

Hell filling the title role in this photo story with able support from Talking Heads' Tina Weymouth, David Johansen from the New York Dolls and Debbie Harry playing one of the Nazi Dykes! Things went from 35mm to the full 70mm in issue 15 where Holmstrom "produced and directed" the 'Mutant Monster Beach Party'. Again it was filmed in photographs and featured Debbie Harry from Blondie as The Beach Bunny and Joey Ramone as the surfer boy.

"Joey helped write scenes in 'Mutant Monster Beach Party'," recalls Holmstrom, "he wrote the scene where a UFO picks him up and takes him to the bikers. He also wrote some of the lyrics with Legs for the theme song where we just published the lyrics. He ended up using them later on in – I think – Danny says, 'You can't go surfing because it is twenty below.'"

Once again this example of paper cinema featured a host of guest stars appearing as themselves, including Andy Warhol, John Cale, rock writer Lester Bangs and various members of Blondie, the Patti Smith Group, Dictators and Voidoids. Great fun, although according to Holmstrom it totally bombed when it came to sales.

"It is ironic because 'Monster Mutant Beach Party' pretty much put us out of business. Both photo story issues were our worst sellers. We put them out there and nobody bought them. They are our most popular issues now, but at the time they were too radical even for our readers."

Financially, the history of *Punk* magazine was a struggle to make ends meet. At one stage it was selling more copies in England than it was in America, acting as seed corn for fanzines that ranged from Mark Perry's

© John Holmstrom.

Sniffin' Glue to Chris Donald's humorous *Viz* which ended up as a publishing sensation. Like any vehicle driven under the influence of drink, drugs, ego, cartoons and music, *Punk* magazine enjoyed some spectacular accidents along the route. One of the worst concerned issue 9 which never saw publication.

"That was a terrible, tragic case," rues Holmstrom, "We gave all of the artwork to a printer and we gave him all of the money and when we went to get the magazine they had disappeared. It was an empty warehouse. We lost all of the artwork and were never able to rescue it. We did not have Xerox machines back then so we did not even have a copy of it. We put Kiss on the cover of that issue as a big stab at commercial success. It never came out."

Money for the next issue was raised through two special benefit concerts at CB-GB's that featured bands like The Cramps, Suicide, Blondie and Richard Hell and the Voidoids.

The last issue of *Punk* hit the streets in May/June 1979 with a cover that featured the Clash drawn as cartoon characters in a suitable 'Last Gang in Town' pose, blasting their way out of a bank, city or indeed the confines of the punk movement itself.

According to Holmstrom, *Punk* magazine died due to a lack of financial backing and advertisements, "and then when Sid killed Nancy that was kind of tough. Punk became a four-letter word after that. It was associated with heroin and murder and the worst kind of description that you can think of. It was a very weird thing to have a front row seat for the entire punk rock revolution and watch it keep promising to take off, but nobody ever sold any records. We still did great work and it is great that people appreciate it years later."

When *Punk* magazine folded Holmstrom turned his attention to humour. He began publication of a tabloid called *Comical Funnies*. Although the first issue from 1980 featured the Ramones on the cover, they were soley there to introduce his character, Bosco, who acted like a version of *The Beano*'s Dennis the Menace that had grown up, shaved his head and discovered beer. Featuring Holmstrom, early work from Peter Bagge and Drew Friedman, *Comical Funnies* was an adult-orientated magazine that holds up well today. Holmstrom next published another humour publication called *Stop* that was notable for featuring cartoons drawn by Joey Ramone in issue eight.

The legacy of *Punk* magazine remains its coverage of punk and New Wave bands like the Ramones, the Sex Pistols, Television, Blondie, Suicide and the Clash. The door of the editorial office was however, wide enough to admit acts like Brian Eno, AC/DC the Bay City Rollers and even Thor.

I know, if you are a fan of Marvel comics the name summons up images of the God of Thunder who, with his trusty hammer, flies around battling all and sundry speaking cod Shakespeare like the eccentric former English boxer Chris Eubank. In fact, the image of the lead singer of this Canadian metal band was little short of a real flesh and blood superhero. A pathological dedication to pumping iron gave the young Jon Mikl a physique which saw him win the Mr Canada bodybuilding contest in the late Seventies. When he moved to New York, his long bleach-blonde hair would have drawn a sustained round of applause from a longboat of passing Viking warriors.

Whilst Gene Simmons from Kiss spat fire and gurned blood live on stage, Thor had a more physical way of winning attention. As well as singing, he thought nothing of lifting his lead guitarist above his head with one hand, bending steel bars and allowing members of the audience to employ a sledgehammer to break concrete slabs on his chest. What this did to his singing voice is open to question but his debut album from 1977 – *Keep The Dogs Away* – was pretty solid rocking thunder. Typically, it featured a track called 'Superhero' which contained lyrics like "we're living in the world of the superhero, everybody catch the show" and "Superman he went insane, he couldn't take this crazy game, and now he's in the gutter with a bullet in his brain." Another track called 'Thunder' also had something to do – "Thunder! Thunder! Thunder!" – with the Norse God of the same name. Although a million miles from punk rock – it was a few miles per hour below the required speed limit – John Holmstrom was impressed when the Thor album was released in America in 1978, "we liked the first record so much. It was sent to *Punk* and we put it on one day and we loved it. We went to see this guy live and he would have people break a brick on his chest with a sledgehammer, blow up hot water bottles into balloons and bend iron bars with his teeth. All these strong man stunts!" Bare-chested at all times with a studded neck collar, Thor looked like Mick Ronson on steroids. So, it was only right that he would end up in a comic book.

Of course it was not a major label deal. Back in 1979, Marvel and DC comics were the Warner Brothers and EMI of the American publishing industry, and as such were not going to incorporate punk into their pages, let alone a screaming Canadian psychopath – unless he was called Wolverine. Peter Parker was never sent down to CBGB's in 1976, 1977, or 1978 by the *Daily Bugle* to photograph this emerging street culture. Even though Daredevil prowled the streets of Hell's Kitchen he never encountered any punk rockers, apart from the time he handed out Hostess Fruit Pies (see opposite).

The same applied to DC's Superman, Green Lantern and company. Robin never baffled Batman by cranking up *Never Mind The Bollocks* in the music room of Wayne Manor, or the car stereo of the Batmobile. To be fair, Captain America's alter ego Steve Rogers was once asked at a party whether he thought that Elvis Costello was the new Bruce Springsteen, but did not care to give an opinion. Anyway, Thor the singer appeared in an independent comic published by an artist called Ken Landgraf, who, as

synergy would have it, was an old classmate of John Holmstrom at the School of Visual Arts in New York.

As an artist Landgraf, had drawn comics like *Hawkman* for DC, as well as an early Wolverine story for Marvel. Landgraf was however, interested in publishing his own comic and "wanted artistic independence. I loved the idea of drawing anything I felt and publishing it myself." To this end he decided to self-publish a comic based on music and to make sure that there could be no mistaking its content he called it *Rock Comics*. A fan of important comic book artists like Batman artist Neal Adams and Jim Steranko, whose work on *Nick Fury Agent of Shield* was literally Dali-does-comics, Landgraf was keen to push the envelope when it came to format. "I used the large size because of Steranko's push towards the tabloid size. Also Marvel were producing tabloid comics. I was hoping that the large size would be a commercial hit, I thought it was cool to print the work the size it was drawn." Therefore when the first issue of *Rock Comics* was published in July/August 1979, it was the same size as a newspaper.

The cover image was striking and featured the star of the comic, Axe McChord, with a guitar raised above his head preparing to crash it down upon the head of a convenient villain. McChord was a composite heavy rock star created by Landgraf.

"I saw Ted Nugent and Johnny Winter on TV. I liked the idea of a dynamic lead guitar player, so I came up with Axe McChord."

As his name suggests, Axe is an ace with the guitar and the comic makes no bones about it, "like his innovating forerunners, master guitarists Jimi Hendrix, Eric Clapton, Ted Nugent and Jimmy Page, Axe has bypassed

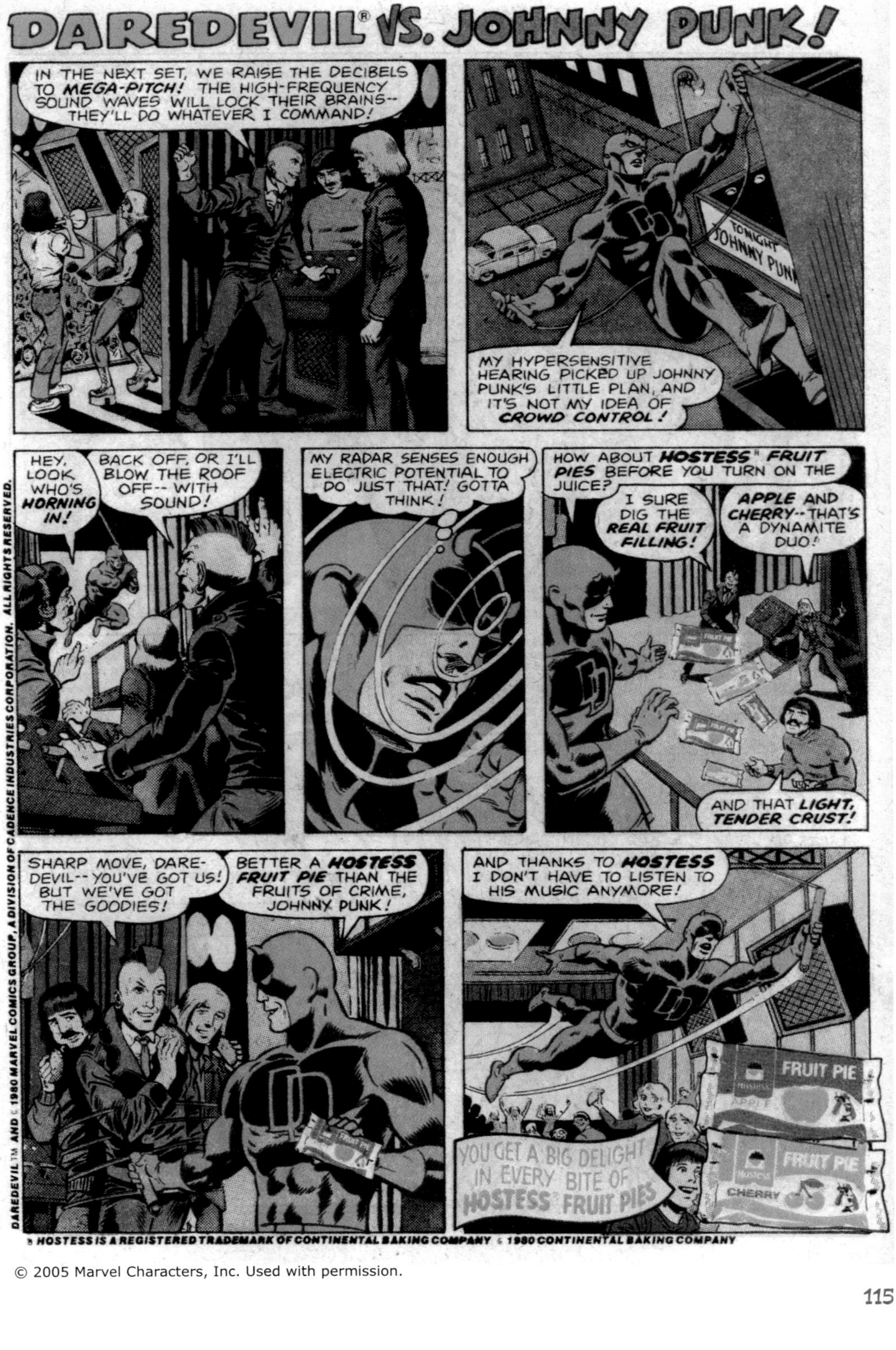

© 2005 Marvel Characters, Inc. Used with permission.

© Ken Landgraf.

even their musical achievements. His intense blazing guitar style incorporates the advanced technology of the future. Using high-powered chording techniques pioneered by the Yardbirds, this visionary of the Eighties has moulded modern technology with great musical genius. The audience senses this is more than just music – they dig the man behind the machine!!"

After this fulsome introduction good enough to grace a Las Vegas heavyweight title fight, the story opens with McChord's band playing a concert. Their heavy metal version of a Chick Berry (sic) song, recorded by the Meatles, 'Turn over Beethoven' (very sic), is played at such loud volume that the

sound wafts out onto the street and down the road to a convenient cemetery, where "the manhandled notes and chords call out to their father, the master of music himself... Ludwig Von Beethoven!" At this stage Landgraf is kind enough insert a footnote informing his readership that "sure we know Beethoven is buried someplace in Europe... but this is only Comix folks!"

Beethoven is furious that his name is being associated with such music and – suitably resurrected – slips on a costume and takes on a new identity as Captain Feedback! He then vows to punish Axe for mangling his music, "for he who lives by the chord must die by the chord!" Swiftly walking onto the stage he does battle with McChord. When Axe fights back with the cosmic powers of his guitar (called Valkyrie), Beethoven initiates backup from "Tchaikovsky, Bach and all the other great composers whom I have called from the grave!" Great fun.

The entire comic is a blast with Landgraf, Neal Adams and Armando Gil delivering superb art.

"Since I had been an organist in garage bands in the Sixties, I liked the idea of working with other artists to achieve artistic goals," recalls Landgraf. 'The King of Punk' story looked at the New York punk scene with a band playing CBGB's thinly disguised as Heebeejeebies. The band – the Fleabags – resemble the Ramones, and enjoy playing songs like "Puke On Da Floor" whose lyrics are choice; "When mah gurlfren' come home an' she puked on da floor/I got a spoon an' asked fer more!!"

The lead singer becomes the king of punk after shooting dead a girl who told the band that they were awful, and got up on stage to prove that she could do better herself. When she proved that she could sing like a bird – or a female Barry Manilow – the lead singer reaches for the gun.

As for Thor, he makes his appearance in a glorious four-page biography drawn by the legendary Neal Adams.

"Thor was around the fringe of stuff," recalls Adams, "He was one of the guys who really liked superhero comics and was a really big fan of mine, so I think he probably thought of any excuse that he could to get me to do something for him. I thought that was terrific."

In fact this strip was supposed to appear as an inset inside the first Thor album *Keep The Dogs Away* but "there was a fallout when the (record) company did not pay Neal for the art, so Neal offered the strip to me to publish," recalls Landgraf. As we discover in the story, not only did Thor have a fascination for comics as a child, but went to school dressed as a superhero. Which was all true.

"I was actually fascinated with superheroes at a very young age, like five years old," recalls the Rock Warrior, "I took it so far. I was much more into Superman than anyone else where I went to school in Vancouver. I would draw Superman insignia on my schoolbooks and on the chalkboard. I would have notes sent home to my parents that I was too fascinated with superheroes. It went even further when I went into school with a Superman costume underneath my clothes and then dressed as Superman in recess. One time, as the other kids watched, I actually jumped out of a first story window and got a concussion at school with my Superman costume on. So I would pretty much say I was a fanatic!"

As he grew older he also pumped iron to develop a bodybuilding physique. "Thor is the first rock and roller who could beat Conan the Conqueror in a fair fight, " trumpets the text of the comic strip. Thor is equally forthright, "Rock is thunderous, muscular and explosive strength is its natural compliment." As he is waving his fist in your face on the page you are hardly going to argue with him. The bending of bars live on stage was totally true:

"Thor did bend the bars," recalls Landgraf who attended a Thor concert, "I tried to bend the bar by stepping on it myself. It didn't bend!"

Sadly *Rock Comics* lasted for one issue. It was circulated by one of the first independent comic distributors in the New York area, Phil Suelling, and sold around 10,000 copies – which was more than *Punk* magazine! Despite being eye-popping, the tabloid size was a problem.

"Phil Suelling suggested that I change the format to magazine size and I did," recalls Landgraf, "he thought that I could reach more viewers that way, since it would fit on news-stand shelves better. News stand dealers did not like the tabloid size as they had to fold the book in half."

The adventures of Ace McChord were transferred to another Landgraphics publication called *Star Fighters*, "and this featured the last appearance of Axe." *Star Fighters* was a kind of American *2000AD* with three or four science fiction stories running each issue. After finishing off Beethoven, Axe tries to go on vacation with his band that includes his wife, the drummer Penny Laine – who probably knew a barber who liked to take

"...I'LL FIGHT, TO THE CRACK OF DOOM, THEIR CRATER CAVES WILL BE THEIR TOMB

© Ken Landgraf.

photographs – but ended up tangling with aliens.

Although Landgraf's publishing venture failed to survive, he was asked to illustrate a magazine sized comic called *Vikon* in 1982, which transformed Thor into a superhero in his own right. According to Landgraf there was also a practical purpose. "It was to be a Broadway play featuring Thor." A harder rock version of the *Rocky Horror Show* which, incidentally, was turned into an excellent three-part comic book in 1990.

According to Thor, "This was a whole different period where we were developing a huge musical with Charlton Heston's chariot, the actual one that he used in *Ben Hur* (on stage). We had midgets, giants and we actually rehearsed for a long time in New Jersey putting together this huge show, and we were playing around with different names, we came up with *Vikon*."

Reading the comic today – which features the chariot – it is a cracking story and even features lyrics taken from proposed Vikon songs: "Shoots the crystal's golden spark, Beware its magnum force – Lightning strikes, lightning strikes again, lightning strikes, lightning strikes again" sings Thor. Although the Broadway show did not happen, Thor went on to appear in several movies and record more albums. He continues to trade today, has won a new generation of fans and at fifty years of age continues to bend steel bars with his hands and teeth.

There have also been two more comics lushly illustrated by artist Mike Hoffmann depicting Thor in Frank Frazetta-style as the legendary God of Thunder complete with hammer. Have Marvel have ever threatened to sue the Norse God of Canada? "Never!" he blasts down the phone, "I am incorporated as 'Thor The Rock Warrior' and theirs is 'The Mighty Thor'. I have been doing it for so many years and Thor is a legal part of my name. I have my own trademark and have even met Stan Lee. I went into Stan's office years ago and blew up a ten year-guaranteed hot water bottle in his office. When it exploded knocked it down a shelf of comic books and stuff."

New York may have been the cradle of punk, but the rattles of this healthy and rude offspring were also thrown around in Los Angeles and San Francisco, but it was

England where the child thrived. In attitude, music, look, intention and all-round enemies of the people, the Sex Pistols were the greatest band to emerge out of punk. That they inspired the Clash, the Damned, the Buzzcocks, Joy Division, Adam Ant, Generation X and as time wore on, a whole host of other bands like Megadeth and Guns 'N Roses is well documented.

Although the English music press was initially sceptical about this new breed of upstarts, they swiftly began to cover the punk and New Wave scene along with existing trade routes where Bob Dylan, Wings, Pink Floyd and other bands plied their wares in the music business. Unlike America, England enjoyed weekly music papers like the *New Musical Express*, *Sounds*, *Melody Maker* and even *Record Mirror* which were in the perfect position to cover the shifts and turns of the English music scene which, from 1976 to 1981, threw up new bands and movements with seismic regularity.

Brilliant journalism and photography aside, there was also a comic element inside these publications. For years Tony Benyon's *Lone Groover* prowled through the pages of the *New Musical Express* and Ray Lowry's sharply compelling strips also made telling points. But with punk, a new type of cartoonist emerged. Brendan McCarthy drew the punk rock-inspired and Peter Milligan scripted *Electric Hoax*, a one page strip for *Sounds* in 1978, which was replaced by the work of an ex-Northampton gas fitter called Alan Moore, writing and drawing under the name of Curt Vile. Although the quality of McCarthy and Moore's work was undeniable, the artist who aptly reflected the light back at the emerging buzzsaw of punk,

New Wave, Ska, Mod II, The New Wave Of Heavy Metal and other musical ports was aptly named Savage Pencil.

"That name came way way, way before that, because I was drawing cartoons," recalls esoteric music journalist and illustrator Edwin Pouncey who used, and still uses, Savage Pencil as his stage name. "I used to read Marvel comics – the American ones – EC horror comics and things like that. Then underground comics came up like *Apex Novelties*, *Last Gasp* and stuff like that. I really wanted a logo of my own, so that I could say that this was a Savage Pencil comic. It really didn't apply to me, it referred to my imaginary publishing company, which from the very outset was called Savage Pencil, a name that went back to the late-Sixties and early-Seventies before punk happened."

When punk exploded, through a happy accident, Pouncey was to get an opportunity to have some fun.

"He was working as a postman when I first met him," recalls Alan Lewis who edited *Sounds* at that time. Vivien Goldman, who was a reviews editor at the magazine, introduced Pouncey to Lewis. Pouncey was a temporary postman whilst he was studying at the Royal College of Art, and when he met Goldman mentioned that he drew cartoons; she told him that *Sounds* was looking for a cartoonist. Before his meeting with Lewis, Pouncey quickly knocked up some samples of artwork he hoped the editor might like.

"I had drawn what I thought would be humorous one-panel gags for *Sounds*, which dealt with punks and animals and things like that. I had decided that I was going to draw people like animals – give it a Warner

Brothers kind of feel, that kind of amorphic animal idea."

Alan Lewis was, and remains, a decisive editor who acts fast.

"I went to see him," recalls Pouncey, "nice guy, sort of looked through the stuff and says, 'this is great, really funny, we can use this stuff.' I had this really beautiful sketchbook and he just started to tear pages out of it. 'We'll have that one and that one...' I was thinking, 'Don't you have a photocopying machine?' So he tore them all out and gave them to this bloke and said, 'Do something with this!' He then turned to me and said, 'What shall we call it?' I said, 'Rock'n'Roll Zoo?' He said, 'Yeah! Brilliant! Rock'n'Roll Zoo! We'll call it Rock'n'Roll Zoo! Let's do a logo, can you do it over there?' I said, 'OK.' It was brilliant. It was real DIY mentality; even the editor had a DIY punk mentality where he just ripped things out."

Pouncey was still reeling from having to knock up the logo so quickly, when Lewis told him how much he was going to be paid.

"He said, 'we want a half page spread every week. As this is going to be a page I'll give you £100 for this one and £50 for each one that comes out'."

Not bad for 1977, although more important to Pouncey was the fact that this, "was the opportunity I had dreamed of. Drawing cartoons and being paid for it, it was brilliant! I just went off and kept cranking it out for £50 a week."

The first broadside of Rock'n'Roll Zoo was cranked out in Sounds on 12th February, 1977, featuring "The Fan, The Cult Hero, The Hip DJ, The Critic, The Rasta, The Punk..." all drawings that had been ripped

and torn out of Pouncey's sketchbook. Over subsequent weeks Pouncey featured a host of animal-based characters who perfectly reflected the punk and new wave movement.

"My reasoning was that I thought animals looked more interesting, and I could get more characters out of animals than human heads. For example, I had one of Nick Moult who had signed up the Sex Pistols at the time. I had him as Mickey Mouse because he was some kind of corporate bloke who had signed the band to make money for EMI. In the strip he was saying, 'Well, blah blah blah', and the other character glaring at him with evil intent in its eyes was a punk anteater. The joke being that the anteater had this great big ring in his nose and a big chain that probably went up to its ear – punks used to have chains in their nose and their ears – and this one was three yards long because it was an anteater. I thought that if you gave them animal personalities you would have more opportunity for jokes and funny things like that."

Apart from the characters, what gave Rock'n'Roll Zoo its flavour was Pouncey's witty and cynical take on everything. Rather than simply snipe at established musical dinosaurs and disco, he also attacked the punk and emerging new wave movement itself. His strip the week that the Sex Pistols split at the end of their first and last American tour in early 1978 was choice; with Malcolm McLaren, Sid Vicious and John Rotten all giving their take on events. As for Paul Cook and Steve Jones, despite a microphone being thrust into their faces, neither could think of anything to say. An imaginary fantasy about the effects of Sandy Pearlman's influence on Joe Strummer and Mick Jones when he

© Savage Pencil / Edwin Pouncey.

© Savage Pencil / Edwin Pouncey / Shock Publications (1992)

produced the Clash's second album *Give 'Em Enough Rope* was – and remains – hilarious.

What made Pouncey's work compelling was his style. His portrayals of Joe Strummer and Mick Jones looked nothing like them at all. In fact, the late Joe Strummer looks like a singing carp, but the energy, power and intent of the lines was vital. To the untutored eye it looked as if Pouncey could not draw at all, or who only went to the drawing board after downing ten pints of lager and several packets of cocaine-soaked crisps. In fact, it was literally a new wave style which became known as the 'ratty line'. "It just happened," recalls Pouncey, "I did not draw specifically that way, that was just how I was drawing at that time with a ratty line."

As you can imagine, Pouncey loved his work.

"It was a musically rich period wasn't it?" he recalls, "There were so many characters out there. I didn't know where to turn, as there were so many coming at you."

They ranged from Bob Dylan's conversion to Christianity, 'A Day In The Life Of Neil Young', a Royal Jubilee Special, street culture, record company politics and Pouncey's own search for weird, wonderful and obscure music – "Devo bootlegs are th' latest trend, n' good quality recordings are saleable items."

Being challenging work, naturally readers would respond in the letters pages either commending or slating his work.

"Most of it was really, really weirdly positive," he recalls, "People reacted to it. All the kids who had been reading comics all their lives could appreciate the punk aesthetic of it. Really appreciate it. I used to get quite a reaction, people were moved and outraged – just as I hoped."

It was only logical that the poacher had already turned gamekeeper. Pouncey formed his own band whilst at art college. The suitably named Art Attacks played live in 1977 and released catchy singles like 'I Am A Dalek' and 'Punk Rock Stars'.

"It used to really annoy me that people used to say that it was my band," recalls Pouncey, "because it was not my band, it was everybody who was in it. I was just the vocalist. At that time it was a big deal – the rest of the band did not mind, but I did."

The Art Attacks brief, two-year career included highlights like supporting Generation X and generally having a good time, although it was the art attacks on the printed pages of *Sounds* that spread butter onto Pouncey's bread. *Rock'n'Roll Zoo* continued until the mid-Eighties, whilst in parallel Pouncey self-published his own comics like *Nyak Nyak* and *Corpsemeat*. He was also more than happy to design record covers for bands whose music he liked, and this – along with music journalism – continues today.

"I still love the stuff. Why have I stuck at it for so long? I could have gone off and become a multi-millionaire comic book artist if I had pushed myself more but I would not say that it has held me back. I feel that I am rich because I have had the opportunity to meet all these people. I've done what I wanted to do. I have not given any quarter in what I've wanted to do. I've worked with bands that I have wanted to work with. They approach me and if I like it I get on with it.

At the moment I'm working with a band on a T-shirt and poster. For me, it is one of my favourite drawings so far. It is a goat's head but done in a trance state so it does not look like a goats head, it looks like a

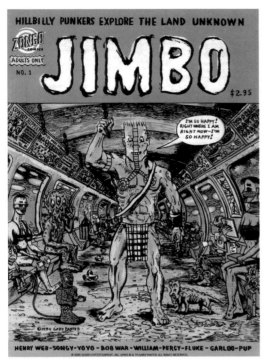

HILLBILLY PUNKERS EXPLORE THE LAND UNKNOWN

ZONED
COMICS
ADULTS ONLY
NO. 1

JIMBO

$2.95

I'M SO HAPPY!
RIGHT WHERE I AM
RIGHT NOW—I'M
SO HAPPY!

HENRY WEB·SONGY·YOYO·BOB WAR·WILLIAM·PERCY·FLUKE·GARLOO·PUP

million monsters rolled into one. They are all abstract. I'm really proud of it and to think that some kid is going to be wearing that, some kid who likes this band that I really like wearing it or having it as a poster on their wall – that is great."

When it came to the ratty line Pouncey was not alone. Totally independent of Pouncey, an American artist called Gary Panter developed a similarly vibrant style. Panter's work initially began to appear in Los Angeles *Slash* fanzine, a West Coast equivalent to *Punk* magazine.

"I saw *Slash* at the old Gower Gulch newsstand. I asked around and eventually went to visit (editors) Steve Samiof and Claude Bessy at the *Slash* office," he recalls, "showed them my comic and they gave me space in their mag."

Panter's 'Jimbo' character began to appear in late 1977, "before that I was drawing Jimbo with a pompadour, but once I started drawing for Slash, I cut his hair a little." The punkish Jimbo, dressed in a loincloth, remains one of Panter's great creations and his adventures were ideal for the *Slash* audience, much to Panter's surprise.

"People liked my stuff – even punks liked it – which surprised me because I thought my stuff was probably too panty-waisted for them!"

Panter hung out on the L.A. music scene seeing bands like the Germs, the Zeros, Fears, X, Black Flag, the Weirdos and the Screamers, "because they were playing in town all the time. It was noisy and people smoked and the clubs smelled of rancid wine, beer and vomit."

It was inevitable that Panter's work would find an outlet through music, designing sleeve art for different bands including underground art rockers the Residents. As Edwin Pouncey was also a rabid fan of the beautifully strange music of these anonymous San Francisco cult artists and had reviewed their *Nibbles* album in comic strip form, it was not long before they met. The confluence of these two ink rivers was facilitated by Panter.

"I saw Edwin's work in *Sounds*," he recalls, "and wrote him a fan letter, because I could see that we were both onto some similar terrain. We've been friends ever since. When I first met him, he came to see me in LA. He had long hair, which he kept inside his great peacoat. It was a hundred degrees out! I thought he was very modest to be wearing it in hot weather."

Ignoring the peacoat incident, Pouncey agrees that they were artistically blood brothers.

"We got together and it became apparent that we had both got a similar technique but we weren't copying it off each other. I suppose in a way he was more influenced by me than I was influenced by him, because I didn't even know him, but it somehow clicked in that ratty line thing. We both got it from Cal Schenkel who did the Mothers of Invention covers like *Reuben and the Jets*. He also did *Billy The Mount* and things like that. You know the booklet from *Uncle Meat*? Jello and all the animated snippets from *200 Motels*? That is where we got the ratty line from, Cal Schenkel. We wanted to be Cal Schenkel, he is brilliant. I got the animal things from (Zappa album) *Reuben and the Jets* where he drew all of the Mothers as cartoon dogs, they were like Disney characters with stupid rubber ball noses."

In fact, when he first moved to Los Angeles, Panter knocked on Schenkel's door.

"Yes I am a big Cal Schenkel fan, so I looked him up and he was a very nice guy."

In a satisfying act of synergy, Panter also went to design covers for Frank Zappa albums like *Studio Tan* and *Sleep Dirt*. Like Pouncey, Panter also submitted to the gravitational pull of that black hole called the recording studio and recorded a track called "Precambrian Bath" which was given away as a flexi disc with a suitably musical themed comic book called *Invasion Of The Elvis Zombies*.

"Jay Condon and I did the basic 'Precambrian Bath' tracks together on a two-track tape recorder in college in Texas. In LA, Jay and I stayed up for a few days arriving at the basic cut-up tape composition and then Jay took it into a studio and worked on it more. Jay and I met in tape composition class in 1971. It was lots of fun and lots of work. Regarding my own music, I have not often had access to recording studios and whenever I did I tended to do songs; which is never what I intended as I listen to noises a lot more than songs. I am surprised about that."

Above and opposite: © Gary Panter. *Jimbo In Purgatory* published by Fantagraphics Books.

This is true, as the 1984 album *Pray for Smurph* confirms.

Today after a career that has embraced design work for television – *Pee Wee's Playhouse* – and cartoons, Panter is a successful artist. Jimbo has recently returned in the delightful and massive *Jimbo in Purgatory* book published by Fantagraphics, which is well worth seeking out, especially as it contains guest appearances from Boy George, Frank Zappa, Keith Moon, Jim Morrison, John Lennon, Yoko Ono, Alice Cooper...

It would be wrong to state that music comics, punk and the New Wave were joined at the hip. Although Sid Vicious told *Punk* magazine early in 1978 when he was recovering in hospital from a drug overdose, "what I want is like a very, very large pile of Marvel comics," many musicians had no interest in comic books at all. Savage Pencil and Curt Vile cartoons only filled one page of a very thick and readable copy of *Sounds*, and for every John Holmstrom or Gary Panter single or album cover there were – "Gabba! Gabba! Hey!" thousands of others with typical band

photos glaring, pouting or mincing at the potential buyer. That, or a tender part of female anatomy being displayed. Even the famed Sex Pistols' "Holidays In The Sun" cartoon cover was taken from a travel brochure rather than a comic.

Saying that, as the Sex Pistols career unravelled under the harsh media spotlight, the band was literally transformed into cartoon characters, not only in the pages of the English music press. Sid Vicious became a caricature of himself and was animated as a cartoon for the *Great Rock 'N' Roll Swindle* film. Since his death, he has made many guest appearances in comics and been immortalised – at last count – in four action figure toys. It's Something Else to think that young children can pit Sid against Spider-Man, Batman or Wolverine toys in the battlefield sanctuary of their bedrooms. To paraphrase the Vivienne Westwood T-Shirt, 'She's dead, I'm Alive, I'm Yours'. Indeed.

In England at least, punk made underground comics appear dated overnight. Adventures of bearded hippies seemed out

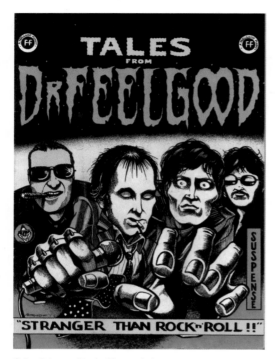

© Joe Petagno. Used with permission.

music content. Although the French have always adored rock'n'roll, punk made a big impression and *Hurlant* gave the movement excellent coverage. The cover of *Metal Hurlant* 22 not only depicted a glam/punk/metal guitarist adorned in swastikas having sex with a demonic woman as he played, but inside it offered "Star War, Sperm Opera and Sex Pistols."

Metal Hurlant also produced themed issues, such as a 150 page *Rock Special* from 1979, which was superb and covered all musical bases. Best of all was a five page 'Dossier le Cid…' which, with almost photographic realism, documented the life and times of Sid Vicious. The success of *Metal Hurlant* led to American reproduction in the form of the magazine *Heavy Metal* that also produced a stand-alone music issue in October 1980, although there was no punk or new wave in evidence apart from an interview with Edwin Pouncey about his Savage Pencil work.

Comics were employed as a marketing tool to help promote bands. Indeed, the Stranglers got their first management contract through Hugh Cornwell sending the company a comic strip.

"I used to portray them in their offices with their feet up not doing any work falling asleep, throwing paper clips at each other, he recalls, "Basically being very lazy and not doing anything. Then in the comic strip the Stranglers send them a package and they leave it in the hallway as they are so lazy and it starts growing. I started sending this strip every week and they kept ringing up saying, 'we have not had our strip instalment this week when are we going to get it?' It was partly because of that that they took an interest in us. It set us apart."

of synch with the times. Saying that, Brain Storm Comix adapted themselves to this new movement by adopting a mock Jamie Reid Sex Pistols logo that read "Comix In The UK." Their *Amazing Rock and Roll Adventures* (1977) featured the first of Bryan Talbot's marvellous Ace Wimslow Freelance Rock Reporter stories which, as well as containing a punk flavour, sees him investigating a band called Omega, whose music wins converts through mind control. Punk attitude and excellent work was also evident in the French comics publication *Metal Hurlant* which began publication in 1976. Although full of vivid, beautiful, challenging no-holds-barred work from the likes of Moebius, Dionnet, Druillet and others who explored the world of science fiction and beyond, there was also some glorious

Of course, *Love and Rockets* was an illustrated fanzine with minimal distribution and sales. This was to change when 'Los Bros' sent a couple of copies to Gary Groth of the *Comics Journal* for review. To this day, the *Comics Journal* prides itself not only upon a strident advocacy of comics as a vital medium of communication, but seeks to review, advocate, interview and promote artists and writers from the mainstream, midstream and backwaters of the form. They can be as vicious in their criticism as a music journalist reviewing a Posh Spice solo record, or a Barry Manilow Christmas album. Los Bros sent copies of *Love and Rockets* to the *Journal* for this very reason, "I thought, 'God, these are the meanest sons-of-bitches in the world (laughter),' says Gilbert, 'If we can take their abuse, we could take anything.' See, that was my punk attitude working."

Rather than pour scorn on *Love and Rockets*, Fantagraphics was impressed enough to offer the brothers a deal to publish subsequent issues of *Love and Rockets*.

"Gary Groth, the publisher was like, 'Yeah, we like what you are doing and go for it!'" recalls Jaime, "We went, 'OK. What have we got to lose?' and took it from there."

Therefore, in 1982 the *Journal's* publishing arm, Fantagraphics, began publishing *Love and Rockets* comics.

The ongoing stories were outstanding. The initial science fiction element was swiftly dropped, and stories concentrated upon compelling relationships which demonstrated an amazing empathy for women. As time progressed Gilbert began to concentrate upon stories set in the fictional republic of Palomar. Jaime, immersed himself in the adventures of Hopey and Maggie and their friends, who operated on the fringes of the Los Angeles punk scene. Hernandez drew upon his own experiences for these stories, with Hopey and Maggie reflecting the music scene from the perspective of the fans themselves. Trying to get into concerts, bumming cash for the ride home, the ups and down of their own band, as well as being perceived as legendary punk girls by some of the guys who tried to date them. Alongside their musical exploits was the unfurling carpet of their lives, loves and relationships.

"Obviously, with Maggie a lot of her is me," recalls Jaime, "and she is a mixture of everyone I have ever met in my life, because her character is so in your face. So she is not based on one person. Hopey comes more from a look that was going around LA in '78 when a lot of punk girls sported the hair and attitude and that was what got me excited to do these characters in the first place. These little spunky girls that were smaller than everyone, but they were actually running the show!"

Jaime also captured the fun, energy and tangle of limbs that were trademarks of early punk gigs.

"That was the stuff I liked about the whole punk scene. That was the first time I was ever part of any – I guess for lack of a better word – kind of revolution that was going on culturally. I just thought that this stuff is worth telling in comics. There were a lot of stories there, and it kind of wrote itself because that was what I was living. We realised that our lives were more exciting than what we were reading in comics. It just kind of fell into place, it was not a big game plan, we didn't notice it at the time. It just turned out that

© Jaime Hernandez. *Love and Rockets* is published by Fantagraphics.

way and the more response I got, the more I wanted to do it."

What made *Love and Rockets* vital was the glorious artwork and that fact that this was an America seen and lived from the perspective of Mexican-Americans. Glorious work and recommended to all. Actually, the Maggie and Hopey stories have now been collected into one beautiful volume called *Locas* published by Fantagraphics which is a perfect way to enjoy their adventures.

Love and Rockets quickly built up a devoted readership, although like *Punk* magazine, was at one stage apparently selling better in England than America. One copy – perhaps

purchased in Northampton – strengthened further the links between music and comics.

Between 1979 and 1983 Northampton-based band Bauhaus had been roasted by music critics, but adored by their loyal fans. After the release of their debut single "Bela Lugosi's Dead" they literally invented Goth Rock and their Bowie-inspired glam stylings, dark pop sound and the cheekbones of their gorgeous lead singer, Peter Murphy, made them the hottest and most theatrical band on the English live circuit. When the band split in 1983 – ego, artistic differences, ego, ego and ego – it was widely assumed that Murphy would step into the magic shoes of a successful solo career and the remaining musicians melt away like ice cubes on a fired-up radiator. But Daniel Ash (guitar/vocals), Kevin Haskins (drums) and David J (bass/vocals) decided – after various solo twiddles – to continue as one unit and they were looking for a suitable name…

"I was into that comic at the time," recalls David J, "and it (*Love and Rockets*) was literally sitting on a table when we were all together playing and trying to get our new band off the ground. We were trying to think of a name. There it was, just staring at us: Love and Rockets."

So, without further ado J, Ash and Haskins joined the ranks of bands like The Teardrop Explodes, and later on, Massive Attack who took their names from the pages of comic books. Love and Rockets began touring England and releasing records under the name.

"Then I got a phone call from Jaime Hernandez" recalls J, "who had found out about it. He wanted to know who this gang of upstarts were appropriating his name. So I told him. He said, 'Well, the thing is I have got a band and what if I want to use the name in the future, what if I want to use that name and you have got it?' I said, 'Well, what can I say? If you want to use the name it is obviously your choice. Taking the name was cheeky, but I love the comic and it is a nod in your direction and it has been done out of respect. Also out of respect, if you don't want us to use it I'll drop it.' He said, 'Well, send me something.' I can't remember what I sent him, it might have been our first single "Ball Of Confusion" as we had just done that. He said he liked the music and something like 'go ahead with our blessing'."

When asked for his take on events Jaime recalls something of a different view.

"We didn't like it because it was ours. I have nothing personal against anybody; we just felt violated. Someone says, 'We want to use your name. How cute of us.' We were like, 'No we kind of want the name for ourselves.' They are like, 'We are going to do it anyway'."

Of course, if the musical Love and Rockets had remained a small cult phenomenon – like the comic – things would have not been so bad, but through constant touring, great songs and – lest we forget in the age of MTV – quirky videos – Love and Rockets became a huge commercial success in America. Initially this was confined to the independent scene, but their high water point was in 1989 when the single "So Alive" went to number three in the charts and their fourth album – *Love and Rockets* – got to number 14. What the Los Bros thought about this was reflected in *Love and Rockets* 35 when one character says to another – who happens to be a guitarist –

"I… really hate that English band Love and Rockets…"

"That's good to hear," replies the string strummer, who, later receives a pre-concert blow-job.

"A faithful snipe there!" laughs J when asked about the reference although he did later communicate with Hernandez after moving to America.

"One of the members – I can't remember which one," recalls Jaime, "moved to California and they coincidentally shopped at the comic store I shopped at when I lived back at home. The guy at the store told me – because I go back there once in a while every chance I get – 'Hey, one of the guys from Love and Rockets came in!' I was like 'Oh, yeah.' Grunt! You know! He says, 'Hey they left you a note.' And the note went, 'Thanks for the name.' (laughs). I was like 'Oh, You motherfucker!'" (Laughs uproariously).

The Hernandez Brothers did get the last laugh as Love and Rockets have now disbanded, and the comic, despite initially retiring after 50 issues, is now in its second ministry and artistically still going strong.

After 1977, punk characters became a stock-in-trade of newspaper comic strip artists and weekly publications, ranging from the weekly science fiction magazine *2000AD*, to the pages of the *Beano* and *Dandy*. *2000AD*, launched on February 26, 1977, was in some respects punk in attitude.

Inspired by the violent, gritty and almost banned comic *Action!*, 2000AD was a clear break away from old trends and aimed to give comic books readers something new. Unlike war comics such as *Victor* and *Warlord*, it did not aim to keep re-fighting the Second World War thirty years after it had ended, but served up excellent, witty, lush, gorgeous science fiction and adventure stories spearheaded by 'Judge Dredd'.

As issues – or ahem, Progs as they were known – rocked out across England week-by-week, punk hairstyles began to creep into the pages. Indeed, in Prog 110 published in early 1979 the Judge Dredd story 'Punks Rule' drawn by Brian Bolland, detailed how a gang called the 'Cosmic Punks' – led by Gestapo Bob Harris – take the law into their own hands and have to be put in their place by Dredd. In a recent interview in the excellent overview of English comic book artists, *True Brit* (TwoMorrows), Bolland stated that the look of Judge Anderson was based on a certain punk legend.

"I think at the time, Debbie Harry was on the go," he told George Khoury, "and I think it was probably Debbie Harry to some extent, a young Debbie Harry."

No wonder Judge Death wanted to rip her to shreds!

To be honest, the history of *2000AD* is littered with musical references and puns ranging from song titles approximated as story names – 'Final Solution', 'Sunday Night Fever', 'Beggars Banquet', 'Riders On The Storm', 'Reasons To Be Fearful' – to a cattle train of musical references in stories that continues to this day. One of the best *2000AD* crossovers were two Muzak Killer stories penned by Garth Ennis in Progs 746-748 and 837-839. Marty Zpok is a devoted fan of 'antique' music like The The, The Pogues, The Fall, The Happy Mondays, Big Black and the Smiths to name a few. He hates 22nd Century pop, especially the 'Muzak stars who act as chart and video fodder'. So, he decides to start killing them.

"I got the idea of killing Muzak stars while listening to a record backwards," he relates with glee.

Zpok sets about his business whilst listening to REM, the Doors and the Clash on headphones, although is finally shot and put in prison by Judge Dredd. In the second story Ennis has Zpok being sprung from prison by devoted fans who dress up to resemble famous ancient pop stars like Robert Smith, Kurt Cobain and Fergal Sharkey. The killing begins again, with a music journalist who bears an uncanny resemblance to Morrissey feeling the caress of a chainsaw, before Zpok hijacks a late-night music show called *Word Up* hosted by a carbon copy of Terry Christian. Zpok begins to kills Muzak star guests

– he shoots a Sinéad O'Connor look-alike in the head – and even watches as a member of Crazy Sken Moaners tries to burn 'For Real' onto his own forehead in emulation – no doubt – of Richie from the Manic Street Preachers. Of course, if you tolerate this,

Can Rock & Roll Save the World?

then your ass will be next and Zpok ends up being shot in the head by Dredd as he sings "My Way" (Sid or Sinatra?). The sting in the tail of the story is that Zpok lives on, but so much of his brain was removed by the bullet, that he now loves Muzak especially Kylie Minogue!

Although Seventies punk rock is now over a quarter of a century old, it still serves as inspiration for comic books. In 2003, a four-part series called *Tupelo* was published by America's Slave Labor Press. Written by Matt De Gennaro and illustrated by Phil Elliott, what made the series delicious was that it featured a man with powers – Captain Tupelo – a junkie, and former member of legendary punk band the Famous Monsters.

"The Famous Monsters were a band that you had never heard of, but I was trying to make the band like an actual real thing, a real band from the Seventies that were never really big," De Gennaro told me, "like the Sex Pistols without a record, but having all of these bootleg tapes all over Greenwich Village."

As for the drugs angle, what exactly Captain Tupelo injects into his veins is unknown, but it gives him strange powers that seem to involve his hands being able to discharge molten lava for short periods of time. Rather than fight super-villains, Captain Tupelo fights against "bullshit" although most of the time because of his addiction he is in a trance state. The contemporary plot contains many flashbacks to the Famous Monsters short-lived 1977 heyday, as the best punk band on the block.

To give a feeling of realism, the comics contain bogus biographies of the band, fake flyers for gigs at Max's Kansas City and hand-written lyrics. When the four issues of *Tupelo* were collected into a trade paperback, a five-track CD with songs by the Famous Monsters was included.

"That was a lot of fun," recalls De Gennaro, "I was in a band about ten years ago and had all of these songs. I thought we were going to be the Rolling Stones, but most of the time we sounded like the Rolling Stones castrated! Anyway for the CD we used a couple of songs that I had from ten years ago, and I wrote a couple of songs. Then, over a weekend I grabbed a couple of my friends – in fact I hijacked them – and threw them into my basement and told them we were going to play and record some punk songs. It was great fun, drinking and messing around and we got a pretty good sound that carried the punk emotion well."

De Gennaro also included a tribute to the Ramones in *Tupelo* with the late Joey making a guest appearance in a dream sequence.

"I love the Ramones. The Ramones are great. I thought it would be great to have Joey Ramone hang out with Captain Tupelo."

Best of all, the Captain's loyal side-kick who keeps him out of trouble in the real world, as well as injecting him with the mystery drug – "ouchie!" – is his former bass player, the 11 O' Clock Man. Of course, this character was based on a certain rock legend.

"I'm waiting to get sued by Lou Reed," laughs De Gennaro.

A comic book character based on Lou Reed? Which is, of course, where we came in....

8

Alan Moore Knows the Score

The living room of the small terraced house in Northampton, is what male students would call comfortable – and their mothers would define by an imaginative use of expletives. The walls are painted blue and adorned with mystical signs. Shelves heave with books, the subject matter embracing murder, magic, science fiction and literature. The carpet has seen better days, or some great nights, and there are Federal Express boxes strewn around or piled up like empty pizza containers. Colourful American comics are stacked in various places, including the kitchen, that is best described as 'industrially functional'. Overall you get the distinct impression that these downstairs rooms are inhabited not by a person, but by a mind. Welcome to the habitat of Alan Moore.

In person Alan Moore looks like, well Alan Moore. Tall, dressed in black, with long hair and a vast beard shaped like the Florida Peninsula in need of pruning. When he opens the front door he is on the cusp of a half-century of years and is friendly, warm and inviting. Those unaware of Moore's profession might mistake him for something other than one of the most brilliant writers in the comic book field. The long hair, beard and impos-ing build suggest a retired professional wres-tler, night-club bouncer or a character actor in a low-rent horror film set in the Southern states of America. Then again, flip the coin and the searing intellect burning from his eyes suggests he would equally be at home in a loose-fitting toga and a life as a Roman senator or a Greek philosopher. But pour him into black jeans, T-shirt and drench both hands in a number of solid silver rings and what you get is Alan Moore.

Moore's long and successful career as a comic book writer, author and all-round Northampton landmark has strayed into music on several occasions. The title of this chapter is culled from a song "Can U Dig It" by the group Pop Will Eat Itself, where they name-checked him and his *V for Vendetta* story and graphic novel. Moore has even en-joyed sensations similar to those experienced by Elvis, the Beatles, the Bay City Rollers and Duran Duran. When his *Watchmen* series was lighting a forest fire in the com-ics industry in 1985, the blaze could be seen around the world. *Watchmen* brought super-heroes kicking and screaming into the real world, trying to cope with the physical limi-tations of middle age, political manipulation and psychological trauma. Along with Frank Miller's *Dark Knight* take on the Batman myth, *Watchmen* simply redefined superhero comics. Compiled as a stand-alone graphic novel *Watchmen* made Moore a comic book celebrity to the extent that he was mobbed at comic conventions.

Like the Beatles in *A Hard Day's Night* and Duran Duran when they were the poster boys of the New Romantic movement, he had to flee into a convenient fire-escape to get away from a horde of admiring comic book fans who simply wanted to touch him. He was even pestered for autographs when going to the toilet. Whether he was asked to shake and sign simultaneously is unknown.

Of course it was – indirectly – music that led to Moore being mobbed and celebrated. It would be delightful to report that he inflamed comic book convention crowds by dressing in a tight-fitting silver costume and screaming out an incendiary version of Gary Glitter's 'Do You Wanna Touch'. But this was not the case. The truth is that some of Moore's first paying work in the form he came to dominate as a writer, was for the English music press in the Seventies.

At the age of twenty-five Moore was work-ing "in a fairly depressing job for a gas board subcontractor. I was starting to reach the point where I thought I'd always wanted to be an artist or a writer or something like that to make my living, some creative medium or other. I thought if I don't do it now, I prob-ably never will do it."

With his wife conveniently announcing that she was pregnant with their first daugh-ter, Moore gave up his job and went on social security. He admits now that it took him some time to get over "basic inertia". He would start projects without finishing them, for fear of having to submit them to publish-ers and getting rejected.

"Once I realised that I was doing that and how pathetic and screwed up it was, I decid-ed to do a couple of episodes of an ongoing comic strip for *Sounds*."

Sounds was at this time one of the thriving weekly music magazines along with *Melody Maker* and the *New Musical Express* that re-flected the prism of the English music scene.

The editor liked his work and via telegram – Moore didn't have a telephone – offered him £35 per week for a weekly strip. Shortly after this, Moore also landed "a five panel weekly gag strip in a local newspaper, that was an extra ten pounds a week." Although the combined sum was little more than the dole money he was receiving, Moore was able to "sign off, make an honest man of myself and scrape a first precarious living just doing that."

Moore's first weekly strip appeared in *Sounds* on 31st March 1979 and ran in various forms for four years. At this time the English music scene was still going through seismic landscape changes inspired by punk. Moore's strips reflected music, science fiction and reading material like H.P. Lovecraft in ongoing strips like 'Roscoe Moscow: Who Killed Rock'n'Roll' and 'The Stars My Degradation' and fitted in perfectly with the anti-authoritarian view of the music press. Alan Lewis, who was editor at *Sounds* at the time, recalls that Moore used to come in to personally deliver his work, "this huge bear of a man in an astrakhan coat."

Once this business was out of the way, Moore would repair down the pub. Moore was earning his living as a weekly strip artist in the tradition of English comic that required fresh material every week. Moore conceived, drew, illustrated and lettered everything himself. Although he greatly enjoyed the work, and he relished slipping rock stars like David Bowie, Iggy Pop, Kraftwerk and Lemmy into the strip, it was time consuming.

"I started to realise that I could not actually draw well enough to make a living out of it. I could do stuff that looked OK if I spent ages on it, but if you are a commercial artist you can't afford to do that."

Moore has taken steps to ensure that this work in *Sounds* will not be reprinted. This is a shame, as it is a *tour de force*, with some biting satire and great art. *Sounds* devoted a whole page to cartoons with Edwin Pouncey – Savage Pencil – providing the other strip with his animal-inspired *Rock'n'Roll Zoo* which Moore was a great fan of. This is best illustrated in a letter penned by Moore as a response to a criticism of 'Roscoe Moscow' in May 1980. "I'm not claiming that 'Roscoe Moscow' is a good comic strip or even a mildly funny one. For my money Savage Pencil has got the edge any day of the week."

Typically, on one occasion in 1981 Pouncey and Moore decided to have a little fun.

"I remember one famous occasion," recalls Pouncey, "we decided that it would be funny if we swapped strips, so I did his strip and he did mine. And he killed off all my characters! So I could not use them anymore – which was quite funny really."

Despite murdering all of Pouncey's characters, Moore did allow this strip to be reprinted in the Savage Pencil compendium *Rock'n'Roll Necronomicon*.

Moore had dabbled in music as a teenager in the Northampton branch of the Arts Labs that had swept the county in the Sixties and Seventies. However, it was not until 1983 that his voice was stamped onto a piece of 7" vinyl. Deliciously, the catalyst for this experience was Goth rock. Although now classified as a musical genre in its own right, back 1979 it was Northampton-based band Bauhaus who hammered out (and hammered up) the image and musical template. Peter Murphy (vocals), Daniel Ash, (guitar), David J (bass) and Kevin Haskins (drums) nailed their colours to the mast with an astounding debut 12" single suitably called 'Bela Lugosi's Dead'. Influenced in equal parts by Glam Rock, Punk Rock, Brian Eno, the Banshees and an overwhelming desire to look good, they pulled off the impressive feat of building up a huge following whilst alienating most of the English music press. Live, the cheekbones and Iggy-as-Messiah performances of lead singer Peter Murphy attracted most attention, although as a visual foil, Daniel Ash was not far behind in the fashion stakes. When Murphy toyed with the possibility of simulated buggery of Ash on *Top Of The Pops* it brought to mind the antics of Bowie and Mick Ronson. Quite apt, considering that the hit they were promoting was a cover version of "Ziggy Stardust". Bass player David J wisely decided not to compete for attention with these two blow-torch performers and thus took out a lifetime subscription to the Bill Wyman school of statuesque bass playing.

J had an enquiring mind and filled it full of films, art and literature. Comic books were also an interest. Although like most English children he started off with weekly titles like the *Beano, Dandy* and *Topper* as he grew up he was attracted to more testing fare.

"I had my mind blown around 1968 when I went to the market – they used to have a market in the middle of Northampton – with second-hand books and comics. American comics, I really got into them. There was something magical about those comics. I used to sniff them. They had a particular aroma. Things like *Doctor Strange* and *Iron Man*."

Typically there was also a box of taboo comics that the owner would not let the young innocent boy peruse. These were underground comics featuring Robert Crumb, S Clay Wilson and Robert Williams, and on subsequent weekly visits J pestered the man to buy one.

"I took home a copy of *Zap*. I hid it under my bed and would bring it out and read it. It just amazed me."

With Northampton being a small place, it was inevitable that the paths of Moore and J would cross. This first happened in 1977 when Moore had put an advert in the local paper seeking not musicians but "co-conspirators".

"So I called this number up and met up with Alex Green," recalls J and we had a long and very interesting talk and he told me all about Alan, this mad poet they were rehearsing with in a cellar. Next night he took me down there and Alan did a recitation for all these weirdoes with saxophone, toy keyboards and a guy with a twenty five-dollar guitar. I got to know Alan a bit and he was just starting to do some strips in the local paper."

They kept in touch, indeed Moore wrote the surreal sleeve notes inside Bauhaus' second album *Mask* and even recited these words in a recording studio so that they could be played as the introduction before concerts on the subsequent tour. Even though Bauhaus took up most of his time, J still found time for external collaborations. He worked with one of the original Bauhaus artists, Rene Halkett, and an accident led to forming a ramshackle outfit with Moore called the Sinister Ducks.

"We put them together on the spot," recalls Moore. "There was a string of gigs at a local Victorian Pavilion that a very eccentric and brilliant musician Dr Liquorice had decided to put on at Saturday lunchtime. There would be punk bands, local bands and vintage cartoons that he would show. It had a playschool air about it that was quite interesting. Anyway, one of these particular days the main band had not shown up, so he asked me and David and a couple of other musicians if we could put something together in ten minutes and do a set. We quite liked the challenge, so I did a piece of reading with music in the background."

The Sinister Ducks did a few concerts and it was obvious to J that they should record a single.

"It was easy. We went to Beck Studios where we did all of our Bauhaus stuff, and Alan wrote the words. The 'B' Side – "Old Gangsters Never Die" – was part of a play that he had written that dated back to the Arts Lab before I had met him. He resurrected it and made it into a pop song and me and Alan put some music to it."

The Sinister Ducks single was released in 1983 and received some intriguing reviews. Due to Moore's appearance, the single is quite collectable today not only for the music – uh the lyrics go "quack, quack!" – but the delightful fine art packaging.

"It was two way traffic – comics and music," recalls Moore. "It has got a Kevin O'Neill cover on it. There is a rare comic strip version of Old Gangsters Never Die done by Lloyd Thatcher. There is a Savage Pencil graphic on the back, which Sav was telling me was the first time that he had drawn his subsequently popular Dirty Duck character. He got the idea from the Sinister Ducks."

The Sinister Ducks even performed on water at Bauhaus drummer Kevin Haskins' birthday party on a canal barge.

Another collaboration transferred J's musical talents into comic book form. Moore had started to write stories for English comic books and his work had appeared in *Dr Who Weekly* and *2000AD*. Music was neatly incorporated into what is considered as one of Moore's first pieces of seminal work. Founded by Marvel UK editor Dez Skinn, the comic *Warrior* began publication in March 1982 following in the footsteps of *Action* and *2000AD*, looking to offer stories with a science fiction, fantasy and superhero bent. Moore had reinvented an old English superhero Marvelman and given him a delicious contemporary twist. *Warrior* also began to print a new story called 'V For Vendetta' written by Moore and illustrated by artist David Lloyd, which detailed the exploits of a mysterious anarchist in an English Police State.

"In the first episode of book two of 'V'," recalls Moore, "I decided would it be possible to do a comic strip and record a piece of music and we would have the music actually printed in the comic."

When it came to writing the music for the song "This Vicious Cabaret", Moore turned to J.

"Alan asked me if I could write some music to his lyrics. He described what he wanted. He wanted something like an old cabaret number. So he sent me these lyrics. That was great. It was quite interesting as I got them through the post – I was waiting for them – and sat down at the piano and just played that through. I called him up and said, "I've done it." He said, "What are you talking

about, I've just sent the words over! I'll come around." He came around and I played it to him. Then we transcribed it so you have the music written out in the comic, so if you want to play it you can." Inspired by *V For Vendetta*, J also released an EP in 1984 featuring 'This Vicious Cabaret', as well as some other tracks inspired by the comic "imagining if *V For Vendetta* was a little movie what the incidental music would be."

When Moore's career began to take off in America via *Swamp Thing* and other work for DC Comics, his musical endeavours took a backseat to the creative well-spring that generated the famed *Watchmen* series. Saying that, he did write a film script for Malcolm McLaren and music also, at times, coaxed his creative mood. When he was drawing for *Sounds* he would listen to music when inking his strips, although when it came to

creating his legendary detailed comic book scripts – "Right Kevin, here we go. Starch your collar and tighten your corset. We have a six-panel page to open with," – songs and singers could get in the way of the creative process.

"So I started listening to purely instrumentals until I found that the rhythms were actually getting in the way of the sometimes complex prose rhythms I was trying to set up in my writing. Then I thought ambient music would do it! So I started to listen to lots of Harold Budd, Brian Eno and things like that. That was best, but the atmosphere of the ambient music got in the way, it wasn't always the atmosphere of the scene that I wanted to be writing."

He does recalls one episode of *Swamp Thing* where there were detailed descriptions of the sounds of the Bayou, "because I was listening to some very drippy ambient music. In one episode of *Marvelman* there are images that only came up because I was listening to 'Lovely Thunder' by Howard Budd on continuous loop."

Although he eventually wrote in silence, music did, on occasion, play some part in Moore's work, even if it was indirectly.

"When I was doing *Big Numbers*, sadly an aborted project, there were a lot of things that that was about. Practical maths, community shopping and stuff like that. We brought that out in a square format that had not been used for comics before, partly because that gave us more possibilities with page composition, also partly because it looked more like an album than a comic. It looked more like a ten-incher or something."

Big Numbers was self-published by Moore's own Mad Love imprint and only lasted for two issues, both printed in 1990. According to Moore, *Big Numbers* was partially inspired by music.

"The thinking behind *Big Numbers* was to try to do comics that left you with the same feeling as good contemporary pop music. One of the big influences – which would have probably been more apparent and obvious if the strip had survived beyond two issues – was the Smiths. There was something in that forlorn, yet humorous vision of a grey, poignant England that was in Morrissey's early Smiths songs that I wanted to portray. I didn't have a girlfriend in a coma, but I did have a boyfriend in a coma.

One of the characters was the boyfriend of the main character's sister who would have been in a coma all the way through the (proposed) twelve issues. I've got some lovely little scenes of people talking to this comatose person as people do. I've also got a shoplifter – an elderly female shoplifter – as one of the main characters, which was probably suggested by 'Shoplifters Of The World Unite'. There was a dream sequence in the first issue which I based upon a dream my girlfriend of the time told me she had, but there is also a strange instrumental track on one of those Smiths albums that has almost got the sound of a crowd in the distance, an unruly crowd, a football crowd or something, and these quite sad Johnny Marr chords. It is just a little piece on its own and lasts for a couple of minutes and there are no lyrics to it. That was what I was trying to get over with that particular dream sequence. That was what was in my head."

In the same way as other comic book professionals like Peter Bagge, Mike Allred, Edwin Pouncey, Grant Morrison, Joe Quesada and Robert Crumb, Moore also trod the boards as the member of a band.

"In the early 1990s. I was in a local band we put together called the Emperor's Ice Cream, which was pretty good while it lasted. We had a girlie backing group called the Lyon's Maids, which included Melinda Gebbie. We did very theatrical gigs. I've got a huge white zoot suit that Melinda made for me, where the waist of the trousers is up here (indicates legendary chest) somewhere and the arse is down there (indicates legendary arse) and is massive. We had lights; we used lightshows and had backdrops, theatrical touches. It was a good show and we wrote some good songs."

Sad to say, the Emperor's Ice Cream never released any singles or albums, although one imagines that there are live tapes locked away somewhere. The band eventually split up due to internal frictions and the fact that "I was starting to feel that while we had done some very good little pop songs the world does not need that many more good little pop songs. It has got some great pop songs already and I did not feel that we were contributing. I used to have delusions of adequacy as a singer as well. But I was starting to feel that I was not going to be best remembered as a svelte and androgynous David Bowie figure."

Although retired from the pop arena, this did not mean that Moore was through with performance.

"I enjoyed working with musicians and I continued with Tim Perkins. He is Northampton born and inbred, same as me. David J drifted back into our orbit around the time that I started to get into magic."

Indeed, when Moore turned 40, he decided to become a magician and began to investigate ritual. This led to collaboration with Perkins and J, which culminated in performances that incorporated spoken word, theatre, magic and music.

"Paul Smith at Blast First (records) was organising a three day event in Bridewell Lane, just off Fleet Street, called *Subversion in the Street of Shame*. We were on the last night and that went really well."

The performance in July 1994 was well-received and led to similar events, with Moore painting his face and arms with symbols – although he still did not resemble David Bowie!

Joking aside, the performances were compelling with, for example, *The Birth Caul* exploring feelings of childhood provoked by the death of his mother. It was agreed by all three parties to go into the recording studio and document it on CD.

"It was amazing, very spontaneous," recalls J, "we were bouncing off each other. He (Moore) would have an initial idea and start writing in the studio, writing the words. I would listen to it and try to get a feel for the essence of what he was on about. For example, *The Birth Caul*, a lot of it is to do with childhood. He would say, "What is the sound that is representative of childhood? What immediately comes to mind? I said what immediately comes to my mind is that when I was a kid I used to have a bike and used to stick bubble gum cards in the spokes. Peg them to the spokes and then ride around making that flapping noise, like a machine. 'God!' he said, 'that's it, let's get a bike and record it.' So we got this bike, put paper cards in the spokes, miked it up and fed it through echo units and pitch shifters and let the wheels go round. That was the underlying theme that you hear – a kind of glue that binds the record. Something like that is how we worked."

This recording, and those of other Moore performances, like *The Highbury Workings* are fascinating and well worth seeking out. The link between music and comics was extended when artist Eddie Campbell asked Moore if he could adapt *The Birth Caul* CD as a comic.

"He asked me how I felt about it, and I thought that if anybody could do a good job on it then Eddie could," recalls Moore. "I would be interested to see how a comic strip turns out when I have not written my usual obsessive, control-freak script, but Eddie has taken a copy of the CD and he is transcribing and breaking it down as he wishes. I thought that it turned out marvellous."

This is true, and Campbell also interpreted

Simmons had arrived in America as a young Israeli immigrant and lived the American dream with a vengeance. Kiss formed in 1972 and comprised of Simmons, Paul Stanley (rhythm guitar/vocals), Peter Criss (drums/vocals) and Ace Frehley (lead guitar/vocals). The first act to sign to Neil Bogart's Casablanca label, their live shows and tough rocking music soon won a devoted following. Album sales though, took a while to go through the roof as the all powerful FM/AM radio DJs refused to play music from long-players like *Kiss* (1974), *Hotter Than Hell* (1974) and *Dressed To Kill* (1975). When Kiss album sales did shoot upwards, the roof was that of a penthouse and their fourth album *Alive!* was the first ever long playing piece of vinyl to go platinum. By 1977 they were the biggest band in America – by several country miles.

To say that Kiss enjoyed their success is an understatement. When it came to the first part of the sex, drugs and rock and roll equation, Simmons coyly admits in his stonking autobiography *Kiss and Make-Up* that he was "indiscriminate" when it came to his sexual partners. When not increasing the profits of contraceptive manufacturers or during post-coital resolution phases, Simmons also enjoyed reading comic books. Actually, devoured them would be a better term, because Simmons was obsessed by superheroes.

"When I came to America as a little boy, I was nine years of age," he barked at me down a transatlantic telephone line, "and I could not speak a word of English. Everything about America, more than any other country on the face of the planet, I have learned over the years is about big, is about modern is about the future instead of the past. All of the other countries in the world – including England – talk about the greatness of the past, and while they are doing that, America is walking on other planets. That notion by itself completely overwhelmed me and continues to this day. So when I discovered television and people flying through the air like Superman, I could not believe my eyes, because it broke every rule and only in America of course would superheroes be invented."

One of the first superhero books that the young Simmons picked up was *Superman* and even though he could hardly read English.

"I could not put it down." Simmons had a lot in common with the man of steel: "I also felt like a stranger in a strange land, and even though Superman was a real alien from another planet and I was a figurative alien from another country, I saw that I could rise above the handicap of not being able to speak English."

Like many immigrants who came to America, rise above the handicap he did. Simmons addiction to comics was intense, and played a large part in helping him to swiftly learn to read English. Of course, although he enjoyed *Superman*, *Batman* and other DC titles he quickly gravitated to Marvel.

"I voraciously read everything from *Tales To Astonish* to *Tales of Suspense* which were sort of Marvel monster comic books. Every issue had a huge new monster like Fin Fang Foom, which was a dragon that could talk. If it said 'Marvel' I knew it was going to be exciting."

Of course, Simmons was fortunate enough to read some of the most exciting superhero comics ever printed, such as Marvel's Silver Age masthead titles like the *Fantastic Four*, *Spider-Man*, *Thor*, *Iron Man*, *Doctor Strange* and *The Avengers* to name a few. Simmons was so addicted to the Marvel name, that as well as the superhero titles he would even occasionally buy western titles like *Millie The Model*, although one wonders if Simmons' interest in the attractive Millie was purely platonic...

It would be wonderful to say that the entire look of Kiss, with their over-the-top costumes, make-up and the great pains taken to conceal their real faces – secret identities – was inspired by Simmons' comic book heroes. Sadly this was not the case.

"It is a little too simple and a little too black and white to say that Kiss were superheroes," says Simmons, "because not everyone in the band, in fact I am the only one in the band who loves comic books and so saw the connection."

In truth, the look of Kiss was more inspired by the entire Glam hoopla that sprung up in the early Seventies. Of course, as they tottered on their custom-made towering platforms, sweated in their studded codpieces and rocked and rolled their way around America, Simmons did begin to play up the Kiss-as-superheroes angle. The most striking example was in photo shoot for the cover of their fifth album *Destroyer* (1976).

"The artist and everyone else in the band was saying that you have to have a destroyed city in the background," cackles Simmons, "I'm going, 'To hell with the city or whatever you want to do with the background! Let's just look like superheroes, get rid of the guitars, don't pose with guitars. We're bigger than our guitars!'"

By that time Kiss were bigger than any other band in America. Their stunning live shows employed so many pyrotechnics that

it was like a bonfire night every night. Simmons would actually breathe fire, fake blood would gurn out of his mouth and he would weave his long, pointed tongue around like an agitated steak knife. Peter Criss would also climb out from behind his drum kit to sing the tender ballad 'Beth', the first massive Kiss hit single. Then it was back to a high energy, hard-rocking show that visually and sonically would give their fans more bang for their buck that a high price hooker. With its Kiss-as-superheroes cover, *Destroyer* confirmed Kiss's domination of America and the Far East. Simmons also took the comics link further on the cover of their next album, *Love Gun*.

"The *Love Gun* cover, portraying us standing with pillars, is my homage to Frank Frazetta, the great artist who did all those great *Conan* (the Barbarian) covers. And of course the rest of the band said, 'Why the hell do we want to stand next to pillars?' And I said, 'Cause we're larger than life. We'll get the girls grovelling at our feet. That is what *Conan* covers are like, and we are like that." That was the sort of language that the other boys in the band could understand and they posed accordingly. The Kiss merchandising machine also began to get in gear with the now famed KISS logo being slapped on items that ranged from T-shirts to lunch boxes. Was there a Kiss condom? There were two, with a Simmons Special and a 'Studded Paul' Stanley version.

Kiss made their first comic book appearance in a Marvel title called *Howard the Duck* in June 1977. Like Kiss, during the early Seventies, Marvel appeared ready to steamroller the world. Along with the blue chip titles like *Spider-Man, The Fantastic Four, Thor, The X-*

Men, The Avengers, Daredevil and *Iron-Man* they also launched several experimental titles. *Ghost Rider, Man-Thing, Tomb of Dracula* and most amazing of all, *Howard the Duck*. The premise of this character seemed so deliciously unsound that it makes you wonder if Howard's creator, Steve Gerber, was an acid casualty, mentally unhinged or criminally insane. Howard was, as his name suggests, a cigar chewing, foul-mouthed duck who fell to Earth from another dimension. Unlike David Bowie, who performed a similar feat in Nick Roeg's *The Man Who Fell To Earth*, Howard did not become a rock star but had to come to terms with being "trapped in a world he never made."

Gerber actually blames salsa music for the origin of Howard, who first appeared in a *Man-Thing* comic.

"I had been writing a story called 'Adventure Into Fear' for the Man-Thing character. It had to do with realities colliding. The basic premise of the piece was that every reality existed on some plane of existence somewhere in a multi-faceted universe. I needed a gag to top a barbarian jumping out of a jar of peanut butter that happened earlier. At that time I was living in a Brownstone (apartment) in Brooklyn and my office was a room on the ground floor that faced out onto a row of backyards. Someone in that row of back yards had apparently bought a new stereo system and I can only assume that it was a really expensive stereo because the guy could only afford one record, which he kept playing over, and over, and over again. It was this salsa record; that Latin beat over, and over, and over again, and the same words. I don't speak Spanish so I don't have any idea what the words were. I suppose it literally put me

into some kind of trance (laughs). The music was there, the typewriter was there – this was the days before computers – and the next thing I knew I was writing something about a duck walking out from behind a shrub in the middle of the Man-Thing's swamp."

Howard; witty, foul (and fowl), verbose and courageous, swiftly got his own comic.

"When I proposed the book to Stan Lee," Gerber recalls, "I just basically walked into his office one day and said, 'Can we do a Howard the Duck book?' He stood up and said, 'Yes!' That was the whole pitch process."

With the blessing of 'Stan The Man', Gerber began a 27-issue run that was breathtaking in plot, wit and execution. *Howard the Duck* was – to my mind – a watershed comic, because Gerber's writing had a vibrant, witty intellectual touch that treated the readers as informed adults rather than children. Gerber had grown up with the Marvel universe and Sixties pop culture, giving his brilliant writing and seat-of-the-pants plotting a delicious, compelling and contemporary flow. As a body of work it has stood the test of time and all readers are advised to read Gerber's first *Howard* ministry, conveniently available as a dirt cheap (but black and white) *Marvel Essentials* collection.

As for the plots, Howard spent time trying to find a job, masters Quack-Fu and fought villains like the deliciously named Dr. Bong, a former rock critic who turned to evil ways after his left hand was chopped off live on stage when appearing with Mildred Horowitz and his band; "the most popular, most outrageous rock group of the early 1970s". There was also a barely concealed sexual frisson between Howard and his female friend

– part-time Go-Go dancer – Beverley Switzler. Unlike a waddling character owned by a certain corporation, this duck looked like he might want to fuck. Howard's troubles on earth were given realism by one of Marvel's great artists: Gene Colan. Colan was on board as the lead guitarist – penciller – for twenty of the Gerber-scripted issues.

"When I start a story I try to make believe – it's all make believe – a fantasy trip that I take," Colan told me. "I try to make believe that I am watching it on the screen as if I have gone into a movie theatre and I am watching a Hollywood production. Starting with that I try to imitate what I imagine that I would see up there."

Kiss got involved in *Howard the Duck* because Gerber was a Kiss fan.

"We were thrown in almost as an afterthought," recalls Simmons. "Howard's friend was being possessed, and of course through her dreams here comes KISS. But again, we were more like Demons instead of a rock band, as there were no guitars or anything."

Kiss appeared in the last full page of *Howard the Duck* 12 in June 1977.

"They supplied me with photographs of the Kiss group," recalls Colan, "Gene Simmons is the lead singer and I've met him a few times since. Very nice fellow."

As Simmons stated, Kiss appeared from Beverley and Howard's friend Winda's head after having a nightmare. In the first two pages of the following issue Howard is so stunned by their appearance that he watches in what Gerber describes as "drug induced apathy as the Catman, the Demon, the Starchild and the Space-ace move in for the word."

The Catman (Peter Criss) whispers into Howard's ear, "When you meet reality head-on – kiss it, smack it in the face! That's the word! Pass it on!" On the next page Kiss vanish back into Winda's head although not before this strange meeting of real-life musicians, fowl and comics has been captured on photographic film by hospital intern.

According to Simmons, Kiss appearing in *Howard the Duck* gave a great boost in sales for the flagging title.

"When Marvel saw the reaction to the Kiss appearance there, they were astonished. They did not understand that Kiss could also be superheroes and it was not long after that I sat down with Stan Lee and off we went into the comic book world."

According to Gerber, Marvel took some time to commit to the Kiss comic project and perhaps the appearance of Kiss in *Howard the Duck* was intended to test the waters.

"Marvel had no idea who Kiss was or what is that loud guitar stuff? (laughs). Someone mentioned it to me – it might have been Stan (Lee) I'm not sure – I thought that it sounded like a great idea and had a couple of meetings with the guys in the band and their managers."

To complete their market research Gerber and Lee also attended a Kiss concert in Philadelphia,

"I got to watch Stan at a rock concert," chuckles Gerber, "I think he was interested and strangely baffled by it. All the pyrotechnics, as these guys put on quite a show. To tell you the truth I had never seen anything like that either. I had been to a couple of Beatles concerts and Stones concerts but in those days they did not do the fireworks, the

explosions and special effects and stuff."

A deal was hammered out between Kiss and Marvel comics. With Gerber undertaking writing duties Marvel would produce a 68-page comic that transformed Kiss into superheroes. As much as he was a Marvel Comics fan, Simmons wore a hard hat to business meetings.

"I insisted on charging a dollar fifty for the comic book in the days when the comic books were twenty-five cents. I insisted in making the format magazine-sized because comic books didn't have any respect and they still don't, and you have to go to the comic book section where the kids are. What I always thought was that they should be right next to the magazine section. In those days comics didn't come magazine-sized."

The Kiss comic also broke new ground around Marvel's stringent work-for-hire practices, where writers and artists were paid a flat fee. For the first Kiss comic as per the music business, Marvel gave royalties to the artists and writers, "Basically, because I insisted upon it," recalls Gerber.

Gerber later took Marvel to court over ownership of *Howard the Duck*, whose success spun off at one stage into a daily newspaper strip written by Gerber and illustrated by Colan, together with a full-length George Lucas feature film which made Jude Law's *Alfie* look like Shakespeare.

As with everything related to Kiss, there had to be a special marketing twist and Simmons and the boys came up with something brilliant: the idea of adding their own blood to the printing ink so that the front of the magazine could scream, "Printed in real KISS blood." True to their word, the band were photographed donating blood, and

flew up to the printing plant with Stan Lee to add their personal claret to the red ink.

"Oh I couldn't believe it!" Simmons recalls twenty-eight years later still with a thrill in his voice, "I remember we were on a DC3, a prop plane, going up to Buffalo. The band was in full make-up and Stan Lee was with us. This was my hero from my childhood, the man who co-created *The Fantastic Four*, *Spider-Man* and just about every other marvel character, who along with the artists Steve Ditko and Jack Kirby created the books with him. I knew more about him that he thought anybody ever knew."

Lee also enjoyed the experience and even makes reference to it in his rather skeletal autobiography *Excelsior!*. He was shocked at the extraordinary popularity of Kiss, and when driven from the airport to the printing plant under police escort, "there were cops at the street corners holding up traffic while we passed by like some sort of presidential motorcade."

As well as Gerber's excellence, Marvel employed some of their finest artists on the *Kiss* comic. Alan Weiss, John Buscema, Rich Buckler and Sal Buscema did sterling work with their pencils, whilst inker Allen Milgrom and colourist Marie Severin went to town. As for the plot, no holds were barred and Kiss got to take on Doctor Doom, the biggest super-villain in the Marvel Universe, in a three chapter saga that also featured guest appearances by Spider-Man, The Avengers, Doctor Strange and Simmons' beloved Fantastic Four. Gerber also had some fun,

"Th-they're hideous Reed... such evil in their faces," says Invisible Girl Sue Storm looking at a picture of Kiss printed in a newspaper.

"We mustn't judge by appearances, Sue," says Mister Fantastic who probably listened to Beethoven, "That's tellin' her stretch!" says The Thing who, as always, looked like a man made out of bricks, "besides, I think they're kinda cuddly-lookin!!" In addition to the main story, the magazine was filled with a band biography, photographs and a spoof advert for Air Latveria which was, of course Doctor Doom's fictional kingdom.

When the *KISS Marvel Comics Super Special* was published in November 1977, it sold a million copies. Simmons remains proud of this achievement, especially as "regular comic books sold a hundred to two hundred thousand, at twenty five to thirty cents." To be fair Marvel's *Kiss Super Special* was an excellent publication. Kiss already wore costumes on stage and it was easy to turn them into perfect superheroes with special powers to boot.

With such phenomenal sales, Marvel were keen to go back to the well.

"They did not know what hit them," cackles Simmons, "they discovered a brand new world that existed out there and distributors took it and it exploded."

This led to a second *Kiss* comic in 1978, which even came with a free poster and once again at the retail price of $1.50 sold equally as well as the first. At this stage there was talk of a regular Marvel Kiss monthly comic, although negotiations ended when Simmons was given some unpleasant news.

"We were told that by Marvel that they of course would own the characters because that was their philosophy."

Of course, Marvel were not dealing with a poor writer or artist, but one of the biggest selling bands in the world who knew the value of their own image rights.

"We basically told them – in the nicest legal way – that they could kiss our ass collectively and individually. That no-one was going to own Kiss and the characters, except Kiss. So we parted company. When Marvel came to their senses we tried again in the Nineties."

Indeed they did, and with Stan Lee undertaking the writing chores, Kiss met the X Men franchise within the pages of *KISS Nation* comic printed in 1996.

One wonders if Marvel actually came to their senses earlier than this. After the sales generated by the two Kiss comics, Marvel appears to have considered publishing other comics with a musical theme, and Stan Lee even told *Rolling Stone* in August 1978 that Marvel might produce comics featuring Elton John and the Rolling Stones. Although Simmons had walked away from the negotiating table and taken the Kiss characters with him, this did not stop Marvel producing a one-off 68-page 'Unauthorised' Beatles comic biography in 1979. Similar in size, format and price to the Kiss book, it was excellent and should be sought out by all Beatles collectors.

Marvel also explored the option of turning another visually attractive pop star into a comic book character: Alice Cooper. Someone at Marvel had the genius idea of featuring Alice Cooper in *Marvel Premier 50*, a monthly title whose brief was to introduce new heroes or act as a forum for Marvel one-shot stories. It was an obvious fit, not only did Cooper have some previous superhero experience singing on two tracks of the deleriously wonderful concept album *Flash Fearless vs The Zorg Women Parts 5 and*

6 (1975), but Cooper had progressed from his early hard rock days to become a figure with a strong teen appeal. "Schools Out", "Elected" and "No More Mr. Nice Guy" were monster hits in the early Seventies. From this bridgehead, Cooper had invented the Alice Cooper horror persona, who wore make-up, and rather than boa's of the feather variety, hung real snakes around his neck. Cooper continued to record great music on albums like *Welcome to my Nightmare* from 1975, pre-empting Michael Jackson's *Thriller* by some years by employing the voice of Vincent Price on one track. Cooper also crossed over into mainstream culture with appearances on *The Muppet Show*, and by sending himself up he broadened his appeal. Even today he retains a huge following in America and England.

Cooper's appearance in *Marvel Premiere* 50 was a concept comic and based upon his 1978 album *Tales From The Inside*. Rather than turn the comic into a poor paper musical, it was well scripted and well drawn and even now is a compelling read. Great fun was had with Cooper's legendary image and pas-

sion for snakes and he was placed in a mental hospital under the heel of the domineering Nurse Rozetta.

Marvel appeared to have great hopes for a stand-alone Cooper comic, and an editorial even asked readers, "But what of the future? Should Alice be awarded his own Marvel title? Should we break him out of that asylum and send him blasting through the Marvel Universe?" Maybe Cooper's fans were slow writers, because it was not until twenty years later that Marvel produced a follow-up title – although *The Last Temptation of Alice Cooper* was radically different kettle of fish. Scripted by Neil Gaiman, it was a dark, mysterious and compelling horror story although – in keeping with his image – Cooper does change into a serpent at the end.

For most bands the passage of time takes its toll. The general demographic is a sharp rise to fame which peaks for a couple of years before sliding quickly downwards towards break-up, neglect or drug-induced implosion. Only a small number of bands have the staying power to keep going year after year after year and retain a loyal and devoted following.

During the mid- to late-Seventies as they were the biggest band in America, Kiss had further to fall than most. Hell, Simmons was even going out with Diana Ross for a while. Although not in the league of the Rolling Stones (though Simmons would violently disagree) and The Who (more violent disagreement from Simmons) and REM ("We are a rock and roll Brand. We can have Kiss comic books. What are you going to do, read REM comic books?") Kiss not only soldiered on, but kept a devoted army of fans. These fans remained loyal even when the band took off their make-up, peeled off their costumes and peered out from album covers just like any other rock band. They still bought Kiss product after there were personnel changes, after Peter Criss and Ace Frehley left the band to be replaced by a series of other musicians.

Simmons deployed a very canny business sense, spending time and effort to take care of his fans. This ranged from even more outlandish tours (there was even one in 3D) to a mind-boggling amount of Kiss merchandise. If you take a second to think about what can be made and branded with a logo, then somewhere in the last thirty tears Kiss have done it. Kiss fans could tee off with Kiss golf balls. Die-hard Kiss fans who, uh, die can actually be buried inside a Kiss coffin. Those

with a less morbid nature, but a growing family, can indoctrinate their kids into the Kiss Universe by giving them one of a vast number of action figures that depict Gene and the boys. Indeed – ignoring an unofficial Mexican outing – it was action figures that led to the next manifestation of Kiss in comic book form.

In 1990 Todd McFarlane was one of the hottest artists in mainstream comics. His eye-catching depiction of *Spider-Man* extended to re-branding the famous webs into something more organic than long pieces of twine. As in music, the cult of the artist (and writer) inspires intense hero worship in comic book circles and like Jack Kirby, Alan Moore, Frank Miller, Chris Claremont and Steve Ditko before him, McFarlane established a vast personal following amongst comic book fans.

Conventions are the rock concerts of comics and McFarlane was mobbed whenever he appeared. McFarlane's ascent coincided with a boom in comic book sales, helped in part by the establishment of the direct market and publishers mania for producing speculative collector's editions of comics with multiple covers. Saying that, it was no accident or hype that when Marvel re-launched *Spider-Man* in 1992 with McFarlane doing the artwork, the first issue sold over a million copies. But all was not well in the magic kingdom.

The entire issue of creator's rights had once again raised its ugly head. As we have seen, Steve Gerber challenged Marvel in the late Seventies but was unsuccessful in his legal challenge to claim authorship and ownership of *Howard the Duck*. By 1990, although Marvel and DC were still not in the business of allowing artists to own their creations, they had instigated a royalty system so that top selling artists and writers like McFarlane saw a hell of a lot more money that a flat page rate. Still dissatisfied, McFarlane and other leading Marvel artists – Jim Lee, Rob Liefeld, Marc Silvestri and Erik Larsen – did the unthinkable. They left mainstream publishing, and in what was perceived as a bold, and some might say foolhardy venture, set up their own company – Image. They appeared to have everything to loose.

For mainstream superhero titles Marvel and DC were perceived as the only casinos in town and if you were a writer, an artist – or inker for that matter – this is where you came to gamble. Although there had always been independent comic companies, they were small underground cellars, whist Marvel and DC were vast ballrooms with worldwide distribution to match.

Image though was lucky. The direct market meant that their comics could be solicited directly to comic book shops, and therefore the fans of the artists could get their hands on their hero's superhero work. McFarlane kicked off with *Spawn*. Hitting the shelves in May 1992, this lushly drawn story about a dead black soldier – Al Simmons (no relation to Gene) – resurrected as a Demon (no relation to Gene) to serve Satan, was brilliantly drawn and helped create the *Image* franchise.

Not content with being an artist, McFarlane not only later farmed out the *Spawn* pencilling duties, but also proved to be an astute businessman, forming McFarlane Toys to produce plastic action figures. Mcfarlane Toys were soon making the most detailed action figures – superhero, sports and rock and

roll – on the market and at a very affordable price. Of course, as the Kiss merchandising machine included action figures, it was only natural that Simmons and McFarlane would do business.

In 1996 Kiss were red-hot again, as the original line-up of Simmons, Stanley, Frehley and Criss had re-formed and embarked upon a globe-trotting tour. They also set about recording a new album.

"It was based around an idea I had," recalls Simmons, "our next album was going to be called *Psycho Circus* so way beforehand – six months before (it came out) – I sat down with Todd McFarlane and I made a deal for the action figures and the comics book, and basically told him that I wanted to do a comic book based on the *Seven Faces of Dr. Lau* or Ray Bradbury's *Something Wicked This Way Comes*. Sort of a circus coming to town and once you get inside the circus you have entered the twilight zone."

Like everybody else of his American generation, McFarlane was something of a Kiss fan, even if he admitted that he only listened to their albums after borrowing from his brothers as a youngster! I was made for loving you indeed!

McFarlane was receptive to Simmons' proposal, although as he recalls, "I had some ideas away from Kiss on some sort of weird, dark, bizarre circus scenario, so we struck a deal where I would take my ideas and combine it with the look and logos of Kiss."

Crucially, McFarlane was not interested in Kiss conforming to the traditional superhero styling that had graced the two Marvel Super Specials in the late Seventies.

"From my perspective, one of the things that had happened with Kiss was that every-

body was doing Kiss – and it is weird that I use the word comic book stuff – but the superhero kind of thing. It is like, here is Gene, here is the band. By day they play music and by night they sort of save the day."

McFarlane was interested transforming each member of the band into more elemental forces than real people, although McFarlane himself did not draw the book.

"I'm not doing any physical labour myself," McFarlane told me, "For want of a better word, I'm the ringleader if you will. It is my job to lay down the ground rules; what stories, what mood and what kind of ambience and atmosphere I wanted to have, and make sure that we stayed within the confines of that blueprint."

The ringleader was an apt description as *Psycho Circus* is set in a netherworld carnival atmosphere where things go bump in the night.

The first issue of the *Psycho Circus* comic book was published in August 1997. In many respects it laid down the template for what was to follow, with the circus ringmaster being transformed into Simmons' 'Demon' character, although he only appears briefly as some vast, powerful, fire-bellowing, supernatural force. Other circus characters like Stiltman, the animal tamer, and the clown were all hosts for the other Kiss band characters. As with most Image titles, the art was sumptuous and writer Brian Holguin's plots concentrated upon the dark and supernatural.

"I didn't want to be like Josie and the Pussycats where you solve a caper just in time to get to the stadium and do a show," he revealed in an interview at the time. "I said let's look at it as if we knew nothing about Kiss. Let's look at the images and what they represent. There was this sense of them representing internal aspects of humans or even more than that. You have Gene who is very dark and demonic. You have Ace who's very ethereal. Paul Stanley is sort of the emotional romantic character. Peter Criss is the old jungle essence."

In the comics the band were not depicted as real people, or even superheroes, but more as dark, mysterious and almost God-like characters.

Although initial sales were strong and the reaction positive, it took some hardcore fans a while to warm to the series, especially as the Kiss appearances were limited. However they could not complain about the artwork with phenomenally detailed renditions of the band. Even today, Simmons remains delighted.

"I love it," he told me, "every single page of original art is with me. It is a mature comic and certainly not for kids."

This was true with dark themes of damnation and redemption being explored. Image made sure to tap into the financial jugular of Kiss fans by also producing special format *Psycho Circus* magazines that along with reprinted stories also contained interviews, photographs and page after page of official Kiss merchandise including, of course, McFarlane's bestselling Kiss action figures.

Psycho Circus was published for three years and by the time it was cancelled in June 2000, Image had produced 31 issues. McFarlane pulled the plug when *Psycho Circus* was no longer making financial sense, "because of the contract I was having to pay royalties (to Kiss) and it was getting to the stage where it was getting to be a bit of a push, if you will.

Still, we had a good run on it. I guess that we could have kept going on it, considering where the numbers for comic books are today! Anyway, consider that most people go five or six issues; going over thirty with *Psycho Circus* was pretty impressive."

In some respects *Psycho Circus* highlighted some of the problems with mixing music and comics. For hardened Kiss fans, reading a monthly comic that featured their idols was cool and they bought it, read it, bagged it and collected it with an uncritical eye, along with their *Psycho Circus* album. However, the key to the magic kingdom of a successful comic book is building a wider readership, and as a monthly comic *Psycho Circus* needed to draw in readers outside the magic kissing circle. Although the stories were good, the numbers slowly declined.

Of course, in the comics business, if at first you don't succeed, you try and try again. Just take a look and see how many times Marvel have tried to re-launch the careers of Nova, Luke Cage, Doctor Strange, The Silver Surfer, Iron Fist and even Howard the Duck. DC has also drawn more than one bucket from the Mister Miracle well. It is a testament to Simmons energy, drive and love of comics that a mere two years after the demise of *Psycho Circus*, another monthly Kiss comic appeared on the shelves. It was, though, radically different from the dark, gothic Image comic.

"I have known Gene for a long time," Mike Richardson, President of Dark Horse Comics told me, "and we have talked about doing things in the past. As you know Gene is a terrific businessman and he is known as part of the rock group, but he is also very active in his various businesses. Because of a (film)

producer I know – Barry Levine – I got back in touch with Gene and went up and visited him and started talking about doing projects together. I learned that the Kiss comic was coming to an end at Image and so I thought let's try to do this more as a traditional Marvel-type superhero book."

Simmons' thoughts were running along similar lines and his basic concept for the new Kiss comic was "sort of the Fantastic Four meets Kiss."

As a concept this made sense. Although the Image books were well drawn, the guts of the stories were supernatural thrillers. McFarlane and Simmons were right to experiment with the look of Kiss, but as the band were not the central characters each month this made them somewhat peripheral figures. The two original Marvel books were great fun and signposted the way down a path that had not been previously explored in a monthly series: Kiss as bone fide superheroes.

When contracts were exchanged, Dark Horse gave the writing duties to Joe Casey, who had not only scripted *X-Men* and *Superman* comics, but was also a huge Kiss fan. Even so, Casey initially had reservations.

"Even before I knew that Gene wanted to go that route, I told (Dark Horse) editor Scott Allie that I wouldn't do the book unless that was the direction: Kiss depicted as straight-up superheroes."

The first Dark Horse Kiss comic was printed in June 2002 and received a strong reaction.

"It launched very big," recalls Richardson. Indeed, Simmons even appeared at the famed San Diego comic conventions to help publicise it. Writer Ian Carney, whose credits include *Bob The Builder* – "Can you fix

it!" – was in town promoting his *Sugar Buzz* comic, which in issue 9 (May 2002) featured the adventures of a fictional "fab power pop group" Bachelor Speedbump. Being a Kiss fan, he was fortunate enough to run into The Demon.

"I was only there for about twenty minutes and this huge guy with sunglasses walks in with two pneumatic girls following him," he recalls. "I thought, 'I'm sure that is Gene Simmons!' I followed at a crafty distance and saw him and said, 'Gene! Gene! Can I have my photo taken with you?' He said, 'Of course you can, it's my job! Do you want me to stand next to you, or pretend that I'm your best friend?' I said, 'Best friend, please,' and he put his arm around me."

In fact Simmons put his arm around a lot of people that day as he was besieged by requests for autographs.

The premise of Kiss being like the Fantastic Four was sound. Crucially, for the first time there was an attempt to flesh out the characters.

"His name is Gene Simmons and this is his life now. Board meetings. Quarterly Fiscal Reports. Stock prices. Weekly itineraries and business trips. First class air travel and twenty-four hour limo service."

Iron Man's Tony Stark with a good heart and no passion for alcohol! Of course, having pots of money is not enough for Gene and it was not long before the old Demon in him not only comes out, but climbs swiftly onto a motorbike that the real-life Simmons designed himself. The Kiss team – The Demon, Space Ace, Star Child and the Beast King – are swiftly re-united, and despite some internal friction, ready to take on all-comers. Mel Rubi's pencils were superb

and for hardcore Kiss fans, this Dark Horse comic was manna from heaven. It sold well too.

"We have had three issues so far and they are gangbusters – they are flying out of the stores," Simmons told me in 2002.

Significantly as Kiss were depicted as a straight-ahead superhero team, this was the first comic where readers unfamiliar with their music or history could just turn the pages and enjoy the good slugfests. Of course, for the faithful there were all kinds of goodies, including two characters based on Kiss songs.

"Mr Speed is a character I created based on a song that Paul (Stanley) wrote that is going to be our version of Quicksilver or The Flash," recalls Simmons. "There won't be a Scarlet Witch, but there will be a Christine Sixteen who will be coming up later on."

Mr Speed was actually designed by artist Scott Kolins who had worked on one of DC's flagship characters, The Flash. He too was a huge Kiss fan, and so for him it was a commission from heaven. But was it hard to design a character based on a song?

"It was not hard at all," Kolins told me, "I know the song really well, but could easily understand how to reinterpret the song into a character with speed powers."

Kolins made sure to add some design elements that would push buttons with hardcore Kiss fans.

"I tried to include what I thought might be nice touches, like the two different sneakers on Mr Speed's feet. One was orange and the other red. As I understand Kiss lore, Ace Frehley showed up to audition for the band with one orange sneaker and one red sneaker."

GET UP, HUNT-STAFF!

So, there you go.

The Dark Horse Kiss comic worked well combining a tremendous mix of fast-paced action and humour. Mel Rubi really brought the characters to life and Casey too was inspired to write some great slugfests which are the life-blood of superhero comics.

"I wanted to see Gene kick the teeth out of a super-villain with one of his monster boots. That was the image that I always kept in my head and you can see it happen in issue #1!"

After six issues, Casey handed the writing reins to Scott Lobdell who scripted two issues. Then Mike Baron came on board. This was a nice bit of comic book synergy, because as a struggling writer Baron had inspired Casey on the stellar title *Nexus* drawn by Steve Rude. So Casey was more than happy to recommend Baron for the gig.

"I scripted two issues over Scott Lobdell's plots," Baron told me, "I wrote the third issue to finish off that story arc, then I did the next story arc over three issues – numbers eleven, twelve and thirteen."

Did Baron find it hard to write about characters that were based on real people with Gene Simmons in the background ready to breathe warm fire down his neck?

"No. It wasn't difficult. I had a talk with Gene and he made it clear that this was a comic book and the characters in the comic were mythical persons, so I'm not concerned about misrepresenting actual people. I'm just writing characters for a story, although my knowledge of the Kiss performers does inform my writing."

As with Casey, Simmons gave Baron a pretty free hand whilst setting obvious parameters.

"Gene said think about the Fantastic Four,

not literally of course, but in the sense that they are a team with four different and contrasting personalities which were suggested by their costumes. The Demon Simmons is a bold, and sometimes too brash leader. Ace Frehley – the Celestial – is more of a watcher, a guy who holds off, takes it all in and shows no emotion. Starchild is someone who absorbs all points of view and empathises with anyone. The Beast King is a kind of cross between the Thing and The Hulk, in the sense that his savage nature sometimes takes over."

As with Casey, Baron gave the comic a great flow and his issues are excellent, not only from the perspective of Kiss fans, but as great superhero comics. He even works in a reference to Simmons legendary prowess in the bedroom in one issue, with the tongued one dressed in a business suit bemoaning the crushing burden of running his business empire.

"I can't turn it off. It's with me 24/7. I started it, and now it's taken over my life." A ghostly woman in red appears to say, "Let me, Gene. Let me into your bed, into your heart." To which he responds, "You don't know what it's like. You might not like it in there."

Sadly, we don't get to see Gene in bedroom action although he would have probably insisted that the encounter lasted twenty-two pages and ended with a splash page that would give new meaning to the term.

The Dark Horse *Kiss* was cancelled after thirteen issues. Although the first issue sold in the region of 40,000 copies, each issue came with two different covers – cover art and band photo – to entice fans to buy two copies of each. However, subsequent months saw a slow decline in sales and it is estimated that the last issue sold in the region of just

over 11,000 copies. So, faced with the economics of the balance sheet like McFarlane before him, Richardson had to cancel the title. "It ran its cycle."

Matters were not helped by the fact that in general there was a slump in comic book sales; even a top-selling comic like the Jim Lee drawn *Batman* sold around 100,000 copies. Even the much-awaited JLA/Avengers crossover only hit a highpoint of 120,000. *Spider-Man 2* might have been a fantastic movie, but even that could not drag sales of the webbed wonder's five, six or seven monthly titles up into the stratosphere.

In an interview prior to cancellation, Baron probably put his finger on the reason why this last Kiss comic hit an iceberg.

"The only way a comic can succeed these days is if it offers a fascinating premise and great art, or it is a long-running franchise. Kiss is a sort of long-running franchise, but there has been so much disruption to the continuity. I think Dark Horse is the third label that they have been on, and none of them picked up the readership that *Batman* or *Spider-Man* has, because they came out month after month without fail."

As to whether there will be another Kiss title in the future, don't bet against it. Richardson and Simmons have already held discussions as to what to do next.

"There has been talk about doing Kiss manga and there has been talk about doing a magazine," says Richardson, "we will see what we come up with. Gene is a terrific businessman and a very creative guy, and we will put our heads together."

Simmons continues to stoke the engine that is the Kiss machine and has even personally branched off into cartoons with the series *My Dad Is A Rock Star*. That he and Kiss are etched into contemporary culture was confirmed in the comic *Bart Simpson's Treehouse of Horror* where Simmons plotted one story revealing that – gasp! – Bart Simpson was his illegitimate son, Bart Simmons! For the record, this comic also featured stories plotted by and featuring Alice Cooper ("Welcome to my nightmare! Welcome to my breakfast…"), Rob Zombie and – er – Pat Boone!

As for Simmons, whatever people think of their music, when it comes to comic books, Kiss are a band that are bigger than their guitars.

© 1996 Kissnation. Published by Marvel Comics.

X Marks The Spot

They say that sex sells, but when it comes to comic books it is X that marks that particular G-spot. The X-Men phenomenon really kicked off big time in 1975 and thirty years later is showing no signs of slowing down, even if the wheels and cogs of the monthly comics are getting worn and require regular squirts of artistic oil, best supplied by the magnificent Grant Morrison. *Ultimate X Men*, *Uncanny X-Men* and *Wolverine* comics are consistently in the top twenty superhero comic books sold around the world. Of course, two Hollywood blockbusters have hit the silver screen

in recent years and have done wonders for the visibility of the franchise, as well as help sell all manner of plastic toys. Hell, X-Men have even been given away with McDonald's Happy Meals.

Ironically when the X-Men first appeared in 1965, the comic had little momentum. Professor X's school for gifted mutants was a novel idea, but the adventures of Cyclops, the Beast, Iceman, Angel and Jane Grey was equivalent to non-alcoholic lager when set against other super-teams like The Avengers, Fantastic Four, the Justice League and The Bash Street Kids. I read somewhere that the Sixties incarnation of the X-Men was groundbreaking, as the persecution of these mutants was a metaphor for racial tolerance in America. Personally speaking I don't think that this theory holds much water, as at that time afro-Americans were fighting for basic rights to sit where they liked on buses, eat in restaurants and generally enjoy basic human liberties. White mutants wandering around in blue and yellow costumes looked as conspicuous as Mick Jagger and Keith Richards searching for aspirin in Walmart, and re-reading the stories they were certainly not the Malcolm X-Men. The life stories of Charlie Parker, James Brown, Sam Cooke, Little Richard, Jimi Hendrix and other black performers were full of incidents where success in the entertainment business did not guarantee them a hot meal. Not one X-Men story shows them fighting any battles in segregated diners or buses.

Getting off Stan's soapbox, The X-Men's fortunes changed in 1975 when Len Wein invented a whole new batch of X-Men and X-Women. Unlike the original team, this bunch really looked like mutants. Storm – who was black – could control the weather; Colossus – who was Russian – was silver, and Wolverine – drafted in from Canada and veteran of occasional spats with the Hulk – seemed to inflame comic readers' imaginations and sales took off. When Chris Claremont took up writing duties, the X-Men became a comic book religion and as time passed there were spin-off X-Men comics galore and numerous Wolverine ministries. Readers, collectors and even some pop stars could not get enough X into their lives.

"I have got a stack of X Men comics," Gary Lightbody of hip rock band Snow Patrol told me when asked if he had ever been interested in four-coloured adventures, "but my favourite comic was *Wolverine*. I bought so many *Wolverine* comics it was ridiculous! I still have some that were never taken out of the bag, I don't know why (laughs). I thought that they would be ultra, ultra, ultra rare and I'd have a little bit of a pension there. Maybe some sad comics freak would buy them off me – and I say that in the nicest possible way, because I am a comics freak myself!"

One consequence of the X-Men's monster success was a procession of mutants in and out of the team, although Paul McCartney probably shed a tear when Magneto never teamed up with Titanium Man against them. Saying that, he did once meet the artist who first drew Magneto backstage at a Wings' gig in 1975 – none other than Jack Kirby. Anyway, in musical terms, the most interesting mutant recruit was a character called Dazzler.

Ah, Dazzler, aka Linda Blair, who had the unusual mutant ability to transfer sound into light. She first appeared in *X-Men* 130 (February 1980) and the Marvel office quickly deemed that she should get her own title. Not only that, but *Dazzler* was one of the first Marvel comics to be offered to the direct market – mainstreaming into comic book shops only – and sold an impressive 300,000 copies when she hit the beach in March 1981. In her private life, Blair was an aspiring singer trying to make it in the music industry. In order to employ her powers, she would carry a pocket radio at all times to generate music to give her power.

The scene was deliciously set in the opening pages of *Dazzler* 1. Fleeing from a gang of four men, our heroine runs down an alley into a dead-end.

She turned her back on a promising law career to follow her heart and become a singing star! But Alison Blaire is different than other singers for she is also a mutant, gifted with the ability to convert sound into dazzling light... light she can use to thrill an audience or subdue a gang of thugs. Fate has chosen her to be different. This is her blessing... and her curse.

STan Lee PRESENTS:

DAZZLER

DANNY FINGEROTH • FRANK SPRINGER • VINCE COLLETTA • DON WARFIELD • JANICE CHIANG • JIM SHOOTER
SCRIPT — PENCILS — INKER — COLORS — LETTERS — EDITOR-IN-CHIEF

the ABSORBING MAN WANTS YOU!

IT'S NOT EVERY DAY THAT THE SOUNDS OF MUSIC EMANATE FROM THE FANTASTIC FOUR'S BAXTER BUILDING HEADQUARTERS. BUT THEN, IT'S NOT EVERY DAY THAT THE DAZZLER COMES TO VISIT...

TOO BAD MR. FANTASTIC DOESN'T JOIN IN. ALL HE EVER SEEMS TO THINK ABOUT IS HIS SCIENTIFIC WORK.

THIS IS SUCH FUN! THE TORCH AND THE THING MAY NOT BE THE BEST MUSICIANS WHO EVER LIVED, BUT THEY'RE FRIENDS I CAN RELAX WITH WHO THINK MY ABILITY TO CONVERT SOUND INTO LIGHT IS NEAT-- NOT FREAKISH!

"I'm a singer not a fighter," she says quoting Michael Jackson from his duet with Paul McCartney on "Ebony and Ivory", "but sometimes a girl has to take a stand!" So whilst the gang leer, she slips on a pair of roller skates and turns on a small box, "reverberating wildly, a Pink Floyd song blares from the miniature radio." As she has the ability to turn sound into light she uses the power supplied by the music to beat up the villains.

Things take a turn for the worse when one of the hoods shoots her radio – no fan of Floyd then, or maybe a die-hard Barrett fan – but Spider-Man then swings in to save the day. When he asks why the thugs are after her, we get a lesson in music economics: "Actually, my latest manager, the owner of a posh disco, was also an underworld heavy. He offered me a contract with a 0% royalty arrangement. The goon-squad is his negotiating team."

A 0% royalty rate! My God, she's being treated like an old jazz or blues player, segregated from eating with white Americans in the bad old days! Maybe there *was* something about fighting racism in those old X-Men comics after all!

Dazzler tries to get her singing career off the ground, although concert appearances were abandoned or interrupted as she took on a stellar array of Marvel's villains. To be brutally frank, Doctor Doom and Galactus probably sacked their booking agent after getting the Dazzler gig.

What made Dazzler so bad – and it sucks big time – is the fact that the writers didn't seem to have a clue about music. The fact that Dazzler was the only performer in the world who could roller-skate around the stage, generate her own light show and sing at the same time, can be accepted – after all, this was comics. But how anyone could be a wannabe disco diva in 1981 or 1982 with a backing band of three white guys on guitar, bass and drums is beyond me. They actually looked like a bad version of the Maniaks, a fictional band put together in a DC comic for three issues in 1967. Where was that all-important synthesiser, played by an attractive, mincing New Romantic type? And what disco drummer worth his salt'n'pepper didn't have a Syndrum? Maybe he spent all his money on doughnuts, because this boy was fat.

One can only imagine how much fun Dazzler would have been in the perverse hands of someone like Steve Gerber who knew his music and pop culture inside out. As it was, the good moments were few and far between.

At one point Dazzler plays Devo's "Whip It" to fuel her powers. Wow! As the series progressed, the disco connection was played down and Dazzler became a rock singer, taking her personal light show to wow audiences with cover versions like Talking Heads' "Psycho Killer", The Boomtown Rats' "I Don't Like Mondays" and a "hot Elvis Costello number".

Of course, what I say means nothing. *Dazzler* ran for five years – albeit at one time bimonthly – which meant that she did attract a loyal, if perverse following. I've read them all, and believe me, perverse is being kind. Even when Marvel decided to have some fun with the music connection they fumbled the ball. A story called 'Chiller' in *Dazzler* 33 revolved around Blair acting as an extra on a video-

shoot for Teddy Lingard who was soooo obviously intended to be someone else.

"I will not accept the use of clones in these stories," wrote in an angry reader in a letter in the following issue, "If you want to use Michael Jackson in a story – fine, use him, but no more of this Teddy Lingard nonsense. This is a Marvel comic."

Of course, I can poke *Dazzler* with a sharp stick as much as I like, but in the last analysis this fiction has become fact. Britney Spears is a big-breasted blonde singer (I forgot to mention that Dazzler had breasts like a porn star, didn't I?) who not only went onto mega-stardom, but actually secured a deal promoting Sketchers' roller-skates. She might not generate her own light show, but Britney would be ideal to play Dazzler in a Hollywood feature film based, of course, on the graphic novel car crash that was *Dazzler the Movie*. Then again she could just join the gang in the next X-Men film....

11

Revolutionary Comics
"Unauthorised And Proud Of It!"

What has the late Gianni Versace got to do with comics? Was the Italian designer a fanatical collector of Silver Age Marvels? Sadly, the link is a mournful one. On the morning of July 15th 1997, Andrew Cunanen murdered Versace on the steps of his Miami home. There is now evidence to suggest that five years before, Cunanen may have murdered the founder of Revolutionary comics, Todd Loren.

During the time he ran Revolutionary Comics, between 1989 and 1992, it would be true to say that Todd Loren polarised opinion. Many perceived him as an arrogant

opportunist who began publishing comics to make a quick buck, whilst others saw him as a breath of fresh air, a visionary and a defender of First Amendment freedoms.

The same polarisation of opinion was bestowed upon the 'Unauthorised' comic biographies of rock, rap and pop bands that Revolutionary published, even today many mainstream comic book writers and artists see them as lacking in any merit or quality. On the other hand, for music fans and collectors they are an essential item of memorabilia, with back-issues still traded on eBay. Indeed, this visual form of biography flattered many musicians featured in the comics. When I interviewed Nick Mason of Pink Floyd about his vast car collection, I also asked him for his views on the five-part Pink Floyd mini-series that Revolutionary had published.

"I've seen them, wonderful!" he recalled, "Absolutely terrific and very funny. I've got the whole set of the Pink Floyd story. I was astonished when I saw them. I think that is something that is really odd – to see yourself in comic book form."

A similar reaction was expressed by Jimmy Page when once asked to sign a copy of Revolutionary's 'unauthorised' Led Zeppelin series. The legendary guitarist admitted to Scott Jackson, who drew many Revolutionary covers, that "he had signed a whole bunch of these and did like the book."

Todd Loren and Revolutionary Comics not only invented the unofficial music comic biography, but spawned a whole host of imitators who followed in their wake.

Todd Loren was not born with that name. He was born as plain old Stuart Shapiro on January 14th, 1960. His father, Herb Shapiro, studied music and played the trombone, but after getting married discovered that music could not generate enough money to support a growing family.

"As it happened, my hobby was photography," he recalls, "and I went to work in a camera shop. Eventually by saving and getting a second mortgage, I started my own camera store."

This was in America's Motor City, Detroit, home of Motown, the MC5 and Iggy and the Stooges. According to Shapiro, as a child Loren was "very overweight" and in the cruel schoolyard this led to all manner of teasing.

Revolutionary founder Todd Loren. © Herb Shapiro.

Like many American children, Loren began buying comics and trading them amongst his peers.

"I went through all the phases," he once related in an editorial, "The Archie/Richie Rich phase, the *Mad/National Lampoon* phase, the Horror phase, the Marvel phase, the DC phase, the underground phase."

Like any serious collector, Loren was soon spending all of his available cash on his hobby which, as a teenager living on an allowance was never going to be enough, especially when he began attending comic conventions. His father saw a more practical way for his son to acquire more comics.

"I suggested to him one day when he was around sixteen that he should put on a comic book convention himself, that way he could not only get the comic books that he wanted to buy for his collection, but he could make money as well. And he just took up the ball and ran with it."

For this first convention Loren's father loaned him the money to hire the hall. As for promotion, although Loren could not drive at this time, he roped in a friend to ferry him all over the Detroit area dropping off flyers announcing the upcoming convention.

"Come the day," recalls Shapiro, "it was a huge success. Not only did he pay me back the couple of hundred bucks, but he made a couple of hundred bucks and booked the hall again. From there on there was no stopping him."

Loren put his energy into setting up more comic conventions and with the relentless drive of a natural entrepreneur, soon moved his operations outside Detroit.

"I expanded the conventions to Chicago, Pittsburgh and Cleveland." He then moved into record conventions and "by 1984 I had put on over 500 of these small swap meets all over the country, including places like Boston, Toronto, New York, Washington DC, Baltimore, Atlanta, Philadelphia, Dallas, San Diego, LA, San Francisco, Minneapolis, Milwaukee and Indianapolis."

Not only did he get the comics that he wanted but began to make some serious money. As his father proudly states, "By the time he was eighteen he had accumulated enough money to buy his own home." Through a strenuous exercise regime Loren had also shed excess weight and had a firm, toned body.

An insight into Loren's ability to stage successful conventions is provided by artist Don Simpson, best-known for his nuclear-powered Megaton Man character who parodied

many of the usual superhero conventions. In an interview with Jon B. Cooke for the publication *Comic Book Artist* in May 2000, Simpson related how he received his first commission as an artist by Loren, who paid him to design flyers his early comic conventions.

"This would've been like '76, '77 when I was in junior high school. It was my first professional exposure. I'd get five bucks a shot doing the flyers."

Simpson also related how Loren speculated on the first issue of *Howard the Duck* literally buying every copy of the comic in the Detroit area, "in a hundred mile radius." Thus when he staged his next monthly convention, Loren attracted fans by offering ten copies of *Howard the Duck* as free prizes. Of course, he actually paid Simpson for his work designing the flyer for this convention, not with hard cash, but with one of the ten copies of *Howard the Duck* 1!

Loren was a huge fan of *Howard The Duck's* writer Steve Gerber and arranged for him to appear for a signing at one of his early conventions, by phoning him up and offering a free airfare. Gerber was delighted to accept the offer, as well as do a personal signing session for Loren.

From conventions, Loren expanded into the mail order business. Initially he sold through his company, Comicade, and would advertise in the back pages of Marvel Comics. This rapidly grew into a large operation with an inventory of between 70,000 to 100,000 comics. In 1984, he moved to San Diego where he also set up a company called Musicade.

"I had the idea to take all the "rock souvenir" type merchandise which was sold at

© Larry Nadolsky.

First Amendment rights, censorship issues as well as banging the drum to increase sales. He also opened a retail outlet near the San Diego sports arena.

Although Musicade was doing well financially, Loren was restless to do something creative. He later told Scott Jackson who was responsible for the majority of rock'n'roll comics covers that "his dream was to have his own product that he did not have to buy from somebody, that involved this thing he liked which was rock music."

Loren had apparently thought about publishing unauthorised comic biographies of rock bands as far back as 1986 and touted the idea to artists at the San Diego Comicon "and was pretty much laughed out of the place." His inspiration was an unauthorised black and white spoof comic about Bruce Springsteen called 'Hey, Boss' written and drawn by a Canadian artist called Larry Nadolsky. Musicade actually distributed this comic and it had sold very strongly.

A few years later, Loren decided to try again. This being 1989 Loren decided to target Guns 'N Roses as the subject of his first biographical comic. With their bad boy image, punk metal music and a lead singer whose adopted name was an anagram of 'Oral Sex', they had won a huge fanbase as testified by the monstrous sales of their stunning debut album *Appetite for Destruction*. When he could not find a writer to take on the task, Loren scripted a couple of stories himself and approached Larry Nadolsky to illustrate them in black and white. The first Guns 'N Roses story related how the band formed and took the saga up to the point where their first album topped the American album charts. There was also a hilarious back-

concerts, and put it all together in one super catalog."

Loren was soon selling items like T-Shirts, promotional photographs, posters and sew-on patches. Building a new life as well as a new business, he decided to change his name from Stuart Shapiro to Todd Loren. As he once wrote in an editorial, "I guess I thought it was a rebellious thing to do, and I always liked the name 'Todd'."

Over the next few years Loren built his Musicade business to the point where its retail and mail order operations employed between 35 – 40 people. By now Loren was producing 64-page catalogues of his merchandise – "7,000 items!" – and used his editorials in these catalogues to vent his feelings on a range of issues from collecting,

© Infinite One.

up story with Loren writing in a *Mad* comics vein, which was in keeping with an editorial contention that "we plan on making satire an important part of Rock 'N' Roll comics." Loren actually showed his father the proofs of this first book when they met up on a family holiday in Florida, "we went over them together," Shapiro recalls, "I thought the idea was genius."

Loren invested around $2,000 to have 10,000 copies of the first Guns 'N Roses comic printed. His timing was perfect. Not only were Guns 'N Roses hot, but the direct market for comic book distribution ensured that an independent comic by a new publisher like Loren could get straight into comic shops. When the comic was published in April 1989 it quickly sold out. Matters

were helped by Guns 'N Roses apparently being none-too-pleased with the somewhat crude and unflattering artwork, which led to threats from their lawyers for Loren to "cease and desist" publication. This only made Guns 'N Roses fans and comic book collectors even more desperate to buy Loren's first Rock 'N' Roll comic. It might become valuable in the future! With the first run selling out, Loren was quick to reprint a second edition and by the time the dust had settled he ended up going through seven printings in just under a year, with the Guns 'N Roses comic finally selling a phenomenal 175,000 copies.

Crucially, such large sales and the delightful whiff of controversy around the comic showed Loren that there was an untapped market for more unauthorised comic biographies. After the first printing of Guns 'N Roses had disappeared from the shelves, he was quick to produce an unauthorised biographical comic on Metallica, charting their rise from the leaders of the San Francisco Bay metal scene to world conquest, with albums like *Kill 'Em All* and *Master Of Puppets*. Once again Loren wrote the script and Nadolsky took care of the art duties. Metallica was published in June 1989 and sold strongly. At this stage Loren began to consider going into publishing comics full time. He was prodded by his father who had sold his camera shop and moved to San Diego to work with his son at Musicade.

"The mail order business that Todd was running and I was helping out, started having labour difficulties with threats of union organisation and lots of internal problems. We were doing so well with the publishing that I suggested, "Listen, why should we keep aggravating ourselves with this business – even though it was fairly successful – why don't we just go into the publishing business?"

Loren decided to call his new venture Revolutionary Comics which was – apparently – based upon a favourable press review of the first Guns 'N Roses comic, which hailed the entire concept "revolutionary". However, when it came to an "unauthorised and proud of it!" biography of Bon Jovi, it was not third time lucky and Loren was hit with a legal restraining order after the first printing. Then the entire 15,000 print run of the fourth Mötley Crüe comic was confiscated and destroyed. Both artists had merchandise deals with a company called Great Southern who contended that Loren's comics were bootleg material and also infringed upon copyright. Great Southern threatened legal action against any comic distribution company handling these 'bootleg' comics, which led to two of Loren's main distributors deciding to no longer carry his fledgling line.

"We were very new to the comic book world, and the distributors didn't want to risk it," recalled Loren.

This lack of distribution threatened to end the journey of Revolutionary Comics before it had properly begun. Fortunately for Loren, Musicade was still in business and served as a lightning rod for comic shops who wanted Revolutionary product to contact Loren, and in the short-term he was able to ship comics directly to them through that company.

Although Loren railed against the threats of Great Southern, he eventually backed down and agreed to withdraw the biographies of Bon Jovi and Mötley Crüe from circulation. As they were also under the Great Southern

umbrella, a Skid Row book pencilled in – and inked – as issue 8 never appeared. To be fair, Great Southern were playing hardball to protect their own business interests, to turn a profit selling official merchandise for which they paid bands a licence fee and royalties on items sold. Loren saw it from a different perspective, "licensing rights that Great Southern owns do not entitle anyone to censor First Amendment protected free speech."

Winding down Musicade and liquidating the entire stock of comics and music-related merchandise, Loren moved Revolutionary Comics into a smaller office space in the upwardly mobile Hillcrest region of San Diego. Somewhat like San Francisco's Castro area with a large hip gay community, Revolutionary occupied a former bank building and a small suite of three offices on the third floor, reached by an ancient lift. In addition to Todd, his father, and his mother who undertook administrative duties, there was also someone to handle computer chores and "that was pretty much the staff. We wound up with five or six people running the whole shebang," recalls Shapiro. Writing and artistic duties were farmed out to a growing number of freelancers like writer Robert Conti and artists like Nadolsky, Greg Fox, Blackwall, Scott Penzer and others.

Whilst negotiating the potentially fatal bump Great Southern had placed on the road, Loren continued to print new comic biographies with the Rolling Stones and The Who receiving the Rock'n'Roll comics treatment. With his background in memorabilia sales, Loren knew that comics on established bands with a hardcore following would guarantee sales. As with his previous Musicade

catalogues, each comic contained an editorial that appeared on the inside of the cover and as well as giving details of Revolutionary's mission to deliver unauthorised biographies in comic book form, Loren also challenged writers and artists to make submissions.

One who took him up on this challenge was a 16 year-old kid called Dean Hsieh who wrote in to say how bad the first Guns 'N Roses comic was: "The script was shaky, the lettering left a lot to be desired, and well, the artwork just plain sucked." Hsieh included some of his own sketches, "These aren't my best work, but they do show you, I hope, the kind of quality art a comic should have, especially a comic featuring Guns 'N Roses."

For the adversarial Loren this was meat and drink and he challenged Hsieh to "put your pen where your mouth is" and "let's see what you can do with a little effort." The results were published in the destroyed Mötley Crüe comic that was re-printed in 1990 after the band broke their ties with Great Southern.

Hsieh's six-page story about bass player Nikki Sixx trying to cure his drug addiction after a heroin overdose was pretty crude, but very much in keeping with Loren's brief to produce comics and stories that reflected the hard edge of rock'n'roll. Attitude was more important than art. Artistically Hsieh was at one end of the spectrum, but at the other was someone like Ken Landgraf.

Landgraf was a superb artist with a track record at Marvel, DC and independent comic companies. A huge music fan, he had even published his own independent rock'n'roll comic as far back as 1979, so could appreciate what Loren was doing.

"I answered an ad in the *Comic Buyers Guide* that Todd Loren had placed," he recalls, "he got hundreds of replies. I was one of the artists he picked."

Landgraf's first work for Revolutionary was an excellent six-page 'Who Cares!' story in The Who biographical comic. Written by Loren, this was a *Mad* inspired strip depicting Roger Daltrey, Pete Townshend, Keith Moon and John Entwistle as a group of rocking babies who naturally sing "Hope I die before I'm weaned!". They also pen a Rock Opera called *Mommy* – "Mommy can you hear me?/Can you feel me near you?/ Mommy can you burp me? Can you wipe my rear too."

It was great fun, especially Landgraf's one-page splash depicting the band's high point at the 'Woodblock' festival.

With the dust settling on the Great Southern action, business returned to an even keel for Loren, who even regained some of the distributors who had left him after the threat of legal action. Loren continued to target bands he thought would generate sales and it was no accident that *Rock'N'Roll* comic 9 featured Kiss, famed for the devotion of their fans. That bass player and main tongue-man Gene Simmons fought hard to protect the trademark of the band name and any merchandise from bootleggers, was a calculated risk for Loren. Ironically, when he saw the comic, Simmons loved it and later actually contacted Revolutionary with a view to collaborating on further comics.

Sales of Revolutionary comic books were strong, being quickly snapped up by fans of the bands featured. As for the comics industry at large, there was a generally negative response. Attention was drawn to the poor quality black and white artwork, and as Loren's biographies were "unauthorised and proud of it!" he was generally perceived as someone who was trying to make a fast buck.

Then again, Loren was not trying to build a franchise to rival DC and Marvel Comics where art was at a premium. His operation was somewhat similar to the underground comics that emerged in the late-'60s whose attitude was to publish what they liked in black and white and damn anybody else. Also, his market was outside the traditional wagon train of the comics fraternity; music fans enjoyed not only this unique way of documenting the careers and excesses of their heroes, but also the parody that was generally missing in an industry dominated by image and slick promotional video. You could not

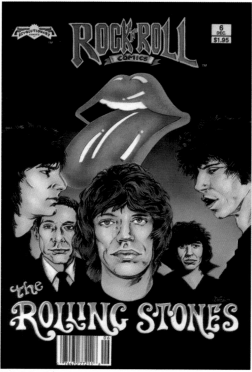

© Infinite One.

fail to be amused by a Loren/Landgraf four-page *Mad* satire on the Rolling Stones which showed Keith Richards saying, "Hey Mick, I've been wondering about something. Who stuck all these needles in my arms?"

In comics the glossy cover art is a crucial selling-point. A well-drawn and striking cover not only attracts sales but, in the direct market, is used as pre-marketing tool to attract orders from comic retailers. For his first covers Loren had turned to people like Lyndal Ferguson, who had done a pretty good job – although Loren was always looking for new talent. Scott Jackson literally stumbled across Revolutionary comics.

"I chanced upon a comic store on my way moving from the Midwest to California. My girlfriend saw these rock and roll comic books sitting in the store and I must admit I took them lightly, but I still bought them for her. I think it was the Guns 'N Roses and the Bon Jovi issues."

Once in California, Jackson found work as an assistant manager in a record store and one weekend finally read both comics: "and no offence to any of the artists – and they probably know who they are – I thought to myself that this was a gig I could get involved with." There was a phone number inside the comic and Jackson made a call and found himself talking to Todd Loren.

"Whatever I said must have been a pitch to the angels, because the next thing he said was, "OK Scott, go ahead and make me a Rolling Stones cover."

Typically Loren did not ask to see a portfolio of Jackson's previously published work which, at that time, only extended to a couple of album covers.

Jackson did the cover in two days and took it down to San Diego to hand it into Loren. Typically, Loren was not only impressed – he ran it on the front of the Rolling Stones issue 6 – but signed Jackson to a one-year contract. Jackson was soon able to stop working in the record store and live his dream of becoming a full-time artist. Over the next four years he was to produce over 150 front covers for Revolutionary.

"It was an overnight thing," he recalls "and the next thing you know I was going from one cover to probably three or four a month when they started doing some of the Experience books like Pink Floyd and so forth."

Although he initially handled most of the writing chores himself, as the line expanded Loren brought other writers to the table. One was Jay Allen Sanford, who ended up plotting and penning more Revolutionary comics than any other writer. Sanford had met Loren through the latter's mail-order business, "when Todd was selling off his Comicade catalogue back-stock, someone told him that they knew a guy who ran a comic shop, knew a lot about the market and could unload them for him."

This was Sanford, who helped Loren liquidate the stock. Discovering Sanford to be a music fan, Loren, in these pre-internet days, had asked him to not only research material on bands, but write for Revolutionary as early as the second unauthorised biography on Metallica. At that time Sanford refused.

"I wasn't interested in writing comic books. I found it ludicrous to count the words to fit in a word balloon, especially when writing a story that has already been told about a band and there's no chance to fictionalise it at all. I thought the idea was incredibly boring so I wasn't interested. But then he started to do these little short stories and I thought those would be much more interesting. It would be cool to see if I could tell a whole band story in three to four pages."

Sanford soon began scripting short backup stories for Revolutionary before gravitating to writing full-length biographies. Although Sanford was a rabid music fan, when it came to what bands were covered Loren exercised total control.

"At that point Todd was a real chart watcher and he had total say," recalls Sanford, "there were only three writers there; Todd, myself and a guy named Rob Conti, who went on to work briefly for a company called Rock-it Comics that sucked horribly and went out of business. But we had no say – Robert and I – as far as the subjects. Todd would watch

the charts and then try to guess who would be hot. It was not a matter of throwing darts or anything like that, he really wanted to be the guy with the comic book out when the band were at the peak of their sales. And he succeeded quite often in those early days, he got pretty lucky with his choices."

This was true. Well-established rock acts like Def Leppard, Whitesnake and Aerosmith soon joined the 'unauthorised' biographical ranks. This being 1990, the New Kids On The Block were also riding high with white boy pop/rap hits like 'Please Don't Go Girl', 'You Got It (The Right Stuff)', 'Didn't I (Blow Your Mind)' and 'Cover Girl'. Typically Loren decided that they were a suitable subject for an 'unauthorised' comic biography. Loren felt the need to defend his decision in the Aerosmith issue which came out prior to publication:

"Some of you have been dreading it, and here it comes, the New Kids On The Block issue. It's true, this issue is a departure for us, in that it stretches the meaning of 'Rock'N'Roll Comics'. Those of you who dislike New Kids might also enjoy the book. As is our tradition, we pull no punches in our satire."

When the New Kids comic was finally published in April 1990, it was pretty a tame affair, charting their rise to the top from their first concert performing to inmates of a State Prison, to their *Hangin' Tough* album and monster success. There were three backup stories; the four-page Loren-penned 'New Kids On The Rag' poking fun at the clean-cut boys in a very *Mad* magazine fashion and 'The History of Teenybopper Stars' charting the rise of teen idols from cavemen right up to New Kids in 1989. The final story took an amusing look at the conflict between a rabid New Kids' fan and her mother who has no idea "where these kids get their ideas that their lives should revolve around their idols." The mother then sits down to read about Elvis, next to her Elvis lampshade and framed Elvis poster. All in all, Loren's New Kids comic was affectionate fun rather than biting satire.

THIS IS AN UNAUTHORIZED BIOGRAPHY

NEW KIDS ON THE BLOCK

A NEW TEEN SENSATION!

| ROBERT V. CONTE WRITER / EDITOR | MITCH WAXMAN PENCILLER | GREG FOX INKER and LETTERER |

© Infinite One.

Of course, the comic nearly never saw the light of day. At their peak, as well as having three singles in the American top ten singles charts, the New Kids were also a marketing and merchandising phenomenon. When their management and their merchandising company, Winterland, got wind of Revolutionary's intent to publish a biographical comic, they swiftly went to their lawyers to seek an injunction to prevent its publication and distribution. Of course, Loren had been here before with Bon Jovi and Mötley Crüe and had backed down in the face of a legal threat. This time he decided to defend what was perceived as a First Amendment right to publish biographies or offer parodies of famous people. Lawyers were instructed on both sides.

The New Kids' injunction to prevent publication was defeated by Loren's legal team, who argued that the comic was "part biography, and part satire". Bookstores are filled with biographies of public figures – both authorised and unauthorised. And, while the subjects of such biographies may be offended by the publication of their life stories, they generally have no claim for trademark infringement.

Judge Rhodes, who heard the case in the San Diego Court, agreed with Revolutionary.

"An unauthorised biography of a public figure is covered by the First Amendment. The main point here seems to be the use of pictures to portray such a story. It is perfectly reasonable to expect that telling the story of a public figure, be he a New Kid or an ex-President, would require pictures. I recently saw an unauthorised biography of Lyndon Johnson, and of course, his picture was on the cover. There is no difference."

We're getting legally technical here, but Revolutionary was also under the cosh for using the New Kids' logo without permission – hence a trademark infringement suit. There was also another significant card face-down on the table, as one arm of the vast money-spinning New Kids' hydra was a deal with Harvey Comics to print New

Kids On The Block comics. Apparently Harvey had paid the New Kids in the region of £100,000 for the pleasure, and such was their appeal, made their money back on the first comic they printed. Although it cost him over $20,000 in legal fees, Loren defeated the New Kids' injunction and was allowed to print and distribute the *New Kids* comic, although the New Kids' legal team were still determined to sue for trademark infringement.

At this stage the New Kids agreed not to pursue any further action against Revolutionary Comics and according to Loren's own press release, "recognised and acknowledged their right to publish biographical material in comic book form as being protected by the First Amendment of the US Constitution."

Naturally, the New Kids' lawyers had conditions, one of which was that Revolutionary could not use the New Kids' logo, or print further books on them. All of this was hammered out around a conference table where the New Kids' legal team suddenly found themselves on the receiving end of both barrels of Loren's verbal shotgun.

"They said, 'OK we've decided that we won't sue you so long as you don't publish anything more about New Kids On The Block'," recalls Herb Shapiro who was at the meeting. "To my way of thinking that was very good, that was very equitable. Todd looked them right in the eye and said, 'What did you think this was all about? It wasn't about whether or not we were going to publish anything about you, this was about whether or not we can publish anything we damn-well please to publish!' He looked them right in the eye and he said, 'Go to

Hell! Just for that I'm going to do another book on the New Kids On The Block,' and laughed. He said, 'I'm going to call it the *New Kids On The Block Hate Book!* He says, 'I'm going to draw a bulls-eye on the cover, and their faces are going to be in the centre with pins sticking out of them.' He just had a tirade against them, and I never saw so many high-priced lawyers curl up and be cowed. I thought to myself this kid has balls the size of a bull!"

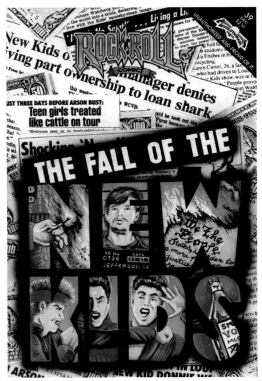

© Infinite One.

True to his word, Loren did later publish a biographical comic called *The Fall of The New Kids* in December 1991, which covered their fall from grace and was written by Jay Allen Sanford. "That was the dirtiest comic that I ever wrote," he laughs, "and I'm the

NEW KIDS VS. REVOLUTIONARY

WRITTEN BY TODD LOREN
DRAWN BY STUART IMMONEN
LETTERS BY MABEL WONG

HI FOLKS! I'M TODD LOREN AND HERE'S THE STORY ON HOW WE WERE SUED BY NEW KIDS ON THE BLOCK. IT'S LATE MARCH 1990. ISSUE 12 OF ROCK N' ROLL COMICS HAS JUST ARRIVED AT THE OFFICES OF REVOLUTIONARY COMICS.

TODD, THE NEW BOOKS ARE HERE!

I'LL BE RIGHT THERE.

WELL, IT LOOKS LIKE WE SURVIVED THE GREAT SOUTHERN CRISIS. NOW WE CAN FINALLY GO BACK TO SENDING OUR BOOKS TO THE MAJOR COMIC BOOK DISTRIBUTORS WHO HAD CUT US OFF.

WHO WOULD'VE THOUGHT THEY'D CUT US OFF JUST BECAUSE A LAWYER MAKES AN EMPTY THREAT ON THE PHONE?

I WAS SURPRISED BY IT, BUT WHEN THEY SAW THE INDIVIDUAL STORES BEGINNING TO ORDER MORE BOOKS DIRECT FROM THE PUBLISHERS, THEY DECIDED TO REVERSE THEIR DECISION.

BUT WE MAY NEVER REGAIN THE MOMENTUM WE HAD. ROCK N' ROLL COMICS WAS THE HOTTEST COMIC IN YEARS! THEN IN ONE FELL SWOOP, OUR DISTRIBUTION WAS ALL BUT GONE!

WELL, HERB, NOW WE CAN WORK ON REBUILDING. IT WAS A MAJOR SETBACK, BUT WE'VE GOT TO KEEP ON MOVING FORWARD. THIS NEW KIDS ISSUE WAS A MAJOR RISK FOR US, MOST OF OUR READERS ARE INTO HARD ROCK.

IT'S JUST A GOOD THING WE HAD THESE FACILITIES TO SHIP OUR OWN BOOKS.

WITHIN A WEEK, ALL OF THE BOOKS ARE SHIPPED. THEN...

UH-OH.

BAD NEWS. WE'RE BEING SUED BY THE NEW KIDS.

I'LL GET RUBEN BROOKS ON THE PHONE.

guy that (went on to) publish porno-comics! There were condoms draped over the bed-head and everything." Tales of blow-jobs from fans and the like was, of course, all based on stories in the public domain. Loren even appeared himself in a back-up story about the New Kids versus Revolutionary court case.

When the dust had settled on the New Kids' legal action, Loren expected to finally win some respect in the comics book industry. None was forthcoming. The general view was summed up by a Gary Groth editorial in the respected *Comics Journal* in October 1990, where, under the headline, 'Todd Loren, First Amendment Advocate or Lying Sack Of Shit?', Groth laid down his views on the matter. "Todd Loren is the latest in a long line of vulgar, self-promoting buffoons that make the comics profession such a sink-hole of shoddiness and opportunism."

Typically, Loren loved it.

"Todd thought that was the best headline he had ever seen," recalls Sanford. "If any-body wrote that about me I would be morti-fied. He was very P.T. Barnum in that way."

Loren retaliated by writing a response to the *Comics Journal* published in December 1990, called 'Gary Groth: Lying Sack of Shit or Lying Sack of Shit?'.

Of course, Loren's father who worked with him on a day-to-day basis saw things from a different perspective.

"Reaction from the industry was always negative. For some reason they did not like us and the more they were not liking us, the more Todd got his back up and the more ar-rogant he became towards them, considering them to be short-sighted and blind. They would criticise us for our lack of ability to put out great artwork, because we would hire artists who were not of the first rank. They failed to understand that the biographies were unlike regular comic books, in which artwork is an extremely important compo-nent. In our particular case the artwork was merely a means to an end in order to tell the story. So it seems almost as if the entire industry deliberately failed to understand what we were trying to do and criticised us for things that were not really important in the books. They criticised us for the artwork, criticising us for not being, I guess, the way they were. Even though Todd put on a front as if this did not bother him, it really did hurt him. He really wanted to be accepted by the industry and I don't think he ever achieved that."

Back to the business of pumping out com-ics. Revolutionary had begun to issue two ti-tles a month from November 1990, and even went colour using a company called Imagi-Nation that employed a technique which used a computer to colour panels. This may have not only been an attempt to look slicker, but also head off competition, as other new publishers sought to produce their own 'unauthorised' rock comics. One of these competitors was Rock Fantasy Comics who, like Revolutionary, targeted big rock bands. Despite interesting cover art, the interiors of these Rock Fantasy comics were dreadful. Aiming to mix together "rock and roll with Fantasy/Science Fiction for the printed page" they produced comics that looked more like traffic accidents than art. For example, in their Led Zeppelin comic they could not even be bothered to ink the pencilled art-work! Then again, perhaps the inker refused to waste his talent on such poor work.

Saying that, the artistic anarchy of Rock Fantasy was ideal for a quite-tolerable Sex Pistols book, although is it my imagination or does the front cover pull off the amazing feat of showing a line-up featuring Glen Matlock, Johnny Rotten, Paul Cook and Sid Vicious? Other Rock Fantasy offerings on Pink Floyd, Def Leppard and the Rolling Stones were little more than soiled toilet paper. When people badmouth Revolutionary, it is probably these books – or some of the Personality comic books – that they remember, which had nothing to do with Loren's company at all.

The Revolutionary experiment with colour did not last long. "It was not what we wanted," recalls Shapiro and Rock'n'Roll comics

returned to glorious black-and-white "for the time being" Loren stated in an editorial in May 1991.

In truth, the plain black-and-white look suited Revolutionary, with the colour being provided by the antics of the rock and pop stars featured in the comics. A prime example was part II of the Black Sabbath/ Ozzy Osbourne story that depicted Ozzy's famous bat-biting episode. The power of Marc Erickson's art conveyed the moment perfectly and it is amusing to read Ozzy state, "aaarrgghh, Jeezus…that was a real bat! And the bugger bit me tongue!"

Despite issues with colour – which aptly included colourful acts like Prince/Funkadelic, AC/DC and Madonna – the quality of art and writing was getting better and better. Although Robert Conti left Revolutionary after a dispute with Loren over monies owed and ownership of the original Kiss art, there were many other writers willing to climb aboard the Revolutionary bandwagon.

Spike Steffenhagen was one of them, and like Sanford was to plot and script many Revolutionary titles. Typically Steffenhagen got through the door because of the size of his balls. Like many people involved in music, Loren had been appalled by Tipper Gore's Parent's Music Resource Centre (PMRC) which, from 1985, lobbied hard for censorship in music. This led to those famous stickers that adorn so many albums today warning parents and listeners about foul language. Loren had railed against the PMRC in his Musicade editorials, and once Revolutionary was up-and-running, began to publish the satirical *Tipper Gore's Comics and Stories*. When Steffenhagen saw one of the early issues he got in touch with Loren.

"I told him that it sucked and I could do better." Typically this led to a face-to-face interview where Loren asked Steffenhagen to read his own *Tipper Gore* script out aloud; he got the job.

"After it folded Todd gave me Anthrax – not the disease, the band – to write up."

Steffenhagen loved music with a passion and lived the rock and roll lifestyle to the full, and so like Scottish football journalists, was literally a fan with a typewriter. It was no accident that in his superb Led Zeppelin ministry we actually see someone receiving oral sex in the background of one panel.

© Infinite One.

Like many significant bands, the story of Led Zeppelin was impossible to shoehorn into one 32-page comic. Therefore Loren decided to publish mini-series of bands like Zeppelin, the Beatles, Elvis Presley and Pink Floyd. This was not only a great idea, but also helped generate steady monthly sales for Revolutionary, as fans of each band would want the complete series for their collection.

Each of these extended comic biographies was brilliant, and Revolutionary deserve credit for the care and attention that went into them. Loren himself scripted seven issues of the eight-part *Beatles Experience*, which really was an excellent history of the band, weaving their musical achievements and cultural impact into the times in which they were active. It was nice also to see that in the first issue, a back-up story featured a six-page biography of Little Richard, who was not only such an early influence upon the Fab Four but apparently – according to writer Loren – once suggested to Chuck Berry that they sleep together!

Steffenhagen got to take on Pink Floyd in a five-part epic. As a writer he not only got beneath the skin of the story, but the complementary art by Ken Landgraf was superb. Cover artist Scott Jackson also went to town on these books.

"I was beginning to see the set as a whole, and created covers that fitted well when put together."

This led to glorious fold-out covers, as well as experiments with florescent inks. One of Jackson's most striking covers was for part four of the eight-part Beatles' series. As the story centred on the *White Album* period, he wanted a plain white cover with the Beatles' faces embossed onto the front with the corner stamped "just like the original album". Loren did not understand the concept. Who was going to buy a comic with nothing on the cover? Jackson had to explain it further.

"I told him that when someone walks into a comic store on Friday there is going to be a stone-white comic book. They will wonder what it is, and when they look up close, they will see that it is the *Beatles Experience*, and

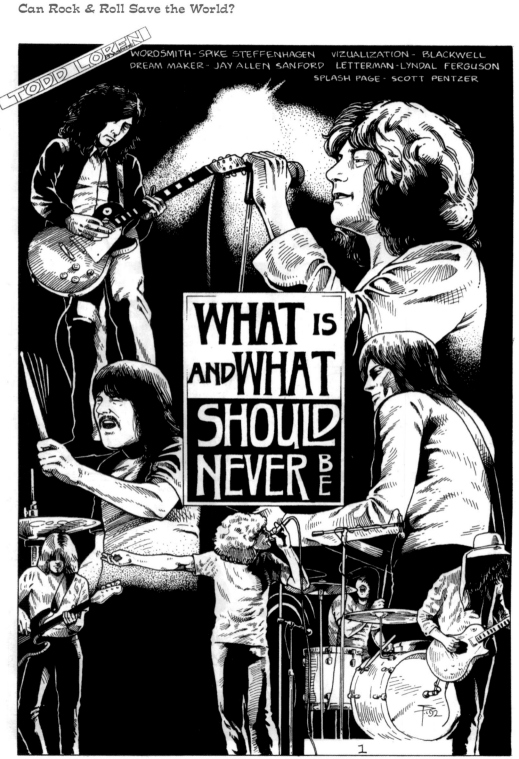

A pages from the Led Zeppelin series. © Infinite One.

understand that it is about the *White Album* as it will replicate that feel."

By the time Loren agreed it was too late, but the cover that Jackson did was equally stunning with the embossed faces of the Beatles printed in silver.

"I received calls from my colleagues commenting on the 'stand out' property this issue had on the comic racks."

Despite the early legal hassles, in general, many musicians enjoyed seeing themselves depicted in comic book form. Jay Allen Sanford began to receive personal feedback,

"I was really the first person in the company to start interacting with the musicians. Todd was very much apart from the music industry (being based in San Diego) but because I was living in different places and still working for other magazines. Virtually every month I would meet two or three bands we had written about in the context of doing things for the magazines I was freelancing for. I was surprised how many were supportive. The guys from ZZ Top were really into it, and Anthrax ended up ordering copies of theirs to sell through their fan club."

Of course there were some negatives, a spelling error once landed Sanford in hot water.

"I think I can only remember getting one negative comment and that was the guy from the Byrds whose name I can't remember now [Roger McGuinn] but he played the twelve string. I met him and he goes, 'You are the assholes who spelt my name wrong in your stupid comic book!'. He had been mentioned in one of the Sixties issues; I think it was the Dead. I looked it up and his name *had* been spelled wrong, and he was very upset."

On the other hand Ice T was so happy to be given the Revolutionary treatment in issue 27, that he invited Sanford backstage when he was supporting Guns 'N Roses on an American tour. The backstage area between the Ice T and the Guns' N Roses camps was divided by a curtain and things were going swell, until someone told Axl Rose that the writer of Revolutionary's second unauthorised comic book was standing less that ten feet from him.

"He started yelling at me," recalls Sanford, "He was saying that he was going to kick my ass if I came over to their side!"

What Sanford did next went down in the annals of fame at Revolutionary.

"I actually waited until they were on stage doing their set and I took about thirty cop-

© Infinite One.

THE AUTHORIZED BIOGRAPHY OF
MOJO NIXON!

STORY: TODD LOREN
WITH ADDITIONS
FROM AN INEBRIATED
MOJO NIXON

ART BY:

© Infinite One.

ies of the Rock and Roll comic – which he had badmouthed in *Rolling Stone* magazine about a month before – and spread them all out on the backstage catering table on their side." Rose's reaction was related to Sanford nine years later by none other than Guns 'N Roses guitarist Slash when they met at a gig.

"I told him that I was the guy who did the comic spread backstage," recalls Sanford, "and he almost fell over laughing as if he was going to have a heart attack. 'I thought Axl's head was going to explode when he came off stage and saw all of those comic books everywhere!' Slash told me, but had been totally gassed by it."

Although Revolutionary preached the mantra of "Unauthorised and proud of it!" Loren frequently challenged bands to come forward to give permission for Revolution-

ary to do authorised books "as long as they let us do it our way!" He even offered to split profits 50/50. Ironically the first 'authorised' Revolutionary biography was of folk singer Mojo Nixon, which appeared as a back-up story in the ZZ Top biography. Nixon was best known in America for hits like 'Elvis Is Everywhere' and 'Debbie Gibson Is Pregnant With My Two-Headed Love Child'. Nixon also put in a personal appearance in the Revolutionary comics booth at the San Diego comics convention that year.

As for more established bands, "the first ones to really co-operate with us were Kiss – of all people," recalls Herb Shapiro. "What happened is that Gene fell in love with the books. He liked them so much that he co-operated until – I guess – the Gene Simmons thing clicked back into his head, and he went three-hundred-and-sixty degrees on that and went the other way."

Before the fallout Revolutionary published a comic called *Kiss: Tales From the Tours* "which was literally dictated over the phone by Gene Simmons." The comic sold well, helped by Simmons appearing in videos and photoshoots – and even on the cover of the album *Kiss Alive III* – wearing Hard Rock and Rock'n'Roll comics T-Shirts. Revolutionary were to later publish three comics of the 'Kiss Pre-history' story

Loren himself did not really mix with musicians and was more interested in keeping the publishing company afloat. Although writers like Spike Steffenhagen and Sanford would not have looked out of place in a speed-metal band, Loren looked like a clean-cut businessman. Even when he tried to look rock and roll. It did not come off.

"I remember him coming to a convention once in a Levi jacket just covered in music patches and buttons (badges)," recalls Scott Jackson, "but he never seemed to fit that image."

Saying that, Loren knew how to make an impression.

"At one convention he took me and Spike Steffenhagen to the Hard Rock Café in San Diego on a Saturday evening," recalls Jackson. "As you can imagine, there was a line around the building on a Saturday night to get in. He said, 'Guys, watch this!' He walked up to the *maitre d* and he was obviously telling them who we were and they just snapped their fingers and we had front row tables. Todd had a way – a way of acquiring what he wanted."

What Loren wanted most of all was strong sales to keep Revolutionary in long-term business. To this end he had already experimented with expanding his line with the short-lived *Tipper Gore* comics, as well as a humour title, *Barf*. As with the music biographies, he literally stumbled across another market niche.

"The creative juices were flowing in him all the time," recalls his father. "There was nothing that could stop him once he had an idea from implementing it. One day he was at a shopping centre on one of those days where none of the stores are doing anything. He notices that one store in particular is just teeming with people, they were practically lined up to go in there, crowds going in and out. Out of curiosity he walks over, and it turns out to be a sports memorabilia collectibles store. He looked around and then started asking questions about the people who were collecting baseball cards and sports

memorabilia. He came into the office the next morning and said that we had to put out a series of comic books for people who collect sports memorabilia."

Typically after some quick research, Loren discovered that the baseball pitcher Nolan Ryan had just set a record for pitching his seventh no hitter game. So Ryan was to be the first comic and Loren quickly got an artist to draw up a front cover to send to distributors to let them know that the book was coming.

"The phone started ringing off the wall immediately so we knew we had something," recalls Shapiro.

To save time, Loren got his father to research and write the story, "then we got it out to one of our artists and our initial printing on that book was fifty thousand copies, which was for us a big deal."

This was the start of the *Baseball Superstars* and *Baseball Legends* series, which published around thirty-eight separate issues. There was also *Sports Superstars*, which embraced subjects like Michael Jordan and Mike Tyson.

This diversification may have been inspired by the need to widen Revolutionary's cash flow, but did show some vision. Loren even extended the line to include Bio-Graphics of famous people. In a nice piece of synergy, the first bio-graphic featured Marvel Comics supremo Stan Lee. In the accompanying editorial Loren not only related how important Marvel comics had been to him as a teenager, but the story of a close encounter with Stan the Man at the 1991 San Diego Comicon.

"I went up to him and said, 'Stan! I'm going to be publishing a comic book about you!'"

Like any good salesman Loren actually had a mock up of the cover in his hand to show a pleasantly surprised Lee. When asked for an interview 'to make sure we get all facts right', Lee was not sure if he could talk, in case Marvel might not approve of the comic.

At that point Lee called over Tom De Falco who was heading up Marvel at this time. De Falco wanted to know if Loren had permission from Marvel to do the comic, at which point Loren informed him that it would be an "unauthorised biography". De Falco spoke about checking with his lawyers and getting back to Loren. As De Falco walked away Lee took Loren aside and said, 'Even if they say no, do it anyway!'

Of course Loren went ahead with the comic biography, which really does give a flavour of Lee's contribution to comics. Typically there was a *Mad Magazine* backup satire with Lee instructing artists "How to Create Comics the Marble (sic) Way". Others in this biographical series were Boris Yeltsin, Gene Roddenberry, Pee Wee Herman, David Lynch and Spike Lee.

This line of comics may havebroken new ground, but of course they did not sell very well.

"People were not looking for that from us," recalls Shapiro, "although I still think that it was a wonderful idea."

Loren also produced a couple of Porn Comics. Unsurprisingly, when he launched the first issue of *Carnal Comics*, Loren could not resist firing a shot across the bows of Gary Groth's Fantagraphics that had also started an adult line – *Eros Comix* – to help finance their more art-related projects.

It is hard to work out how financially successful Revolutionary were. Staff levels increased, and like many independent publishers it was a case of working through peaks and troughs. A comic on Madonna would sell well, but one on white rapper Vanilla Ice would do poorly, especially as it appeared after the bubble of his popularity burst and subsequently sold around 3,000 copies.

"It was always rocky," recalls Shapiro, "We would put out one comic book that would sell an enormous amount. You had to sell say, ten thousand books minimum to break even and sometimes we'd only sell three or four thousand and other times we would do very well. It kind of levelled out to the point where we weren't doing much more than making ourselves a salary. Although I will tell you that we were having so much fun."

This fun involved Loren "kidnapping" his parents some days and taking them down to Disneyland or out to a new restaurant he had found for lunch. The relationship between father and son had improved to the point where they could be classified as close friends. Matters had been helped by working together to remove the areas of conflict from their past.

"When I went to work with him in San Diego," recalls Herb, "we did something that was at first difficult, but we worked together to get all of that crap from the past out of the way. We worked with a psychologist who helped, but it was mostly both of us willing to meet each other half way. As a result of that I can say that he became my best friend and vice versa."

Although as their working relationship grew one remaining trait of his father's drove Loren mad.

"I was trying to become what Todd called 'an elderly hippy'. I had grown a ponytail and he teased me unbearably about it. One day I guess that he couldn't stand it any longer and he came into the office with a pair of scissors and while I was on the phone cut the ponytail off! I could not think of anything to do to him. He was wearing a shirt and tie at the time so I went back into his office and cut his tie off. That was the only thing that I could do in retaliation."

Outside the father and son wagon train, Loren could be difficult to know. He kept his private life to himself to the extent of rarely inviting people over to his house. Jay Allen Sanford, who knew him better than most, believes that behind the adversarial publishing gladiator, was someone who deep-down was shy and withdrawn. Loren was also gay and no doubt liked to keep his personal and professional lives in separate boxes. Sanford only found out that Loren was gay through a spelling mistake.

"I didn't really know until I mis-spelt something sometime. Instead of 'Amalgam' I think I put 'Analgram' or something and he called me up giggling and saying, 'Was that Freudian, Jay? Do you want to send me an analgram?' After I hung up I thought that was a very gay joke. I thought, 'I guess Todd's gay!' I never thought of it before."

When it came to business meetings with freelancers, Loren could be downright cryptic. Ken Meyer Jr. who began to do covers along with Scott Jackson recalls having to meet Loren in a Subway sandwich bar in the Hillcrest region.

"I met him there because he did not want me to know where the offices were for some reason."

This probably had less to do with paranoia and more to do with the fact that Loren was probably avoiding process servers in relation to his ongoing disputes with Great Southern, New Kids and some former Revolutionary workers.

With things running smoothly, Loren was soon crossing swords again. This time his adversary was Denis Kitchen. Kitchen was a legend in underground circles and his Kitchen Sink publishing operation had printed a whole host of essential underground books. He had also managed to stay in business as an independent publisher – no mean feat. In 1991 he negotiated what seemed to be one sweet deal. In return for a licensing fee, Kitchen Sink were to publish an authorised comic on the premier underground band: the Grateful Dead. The first issue of *Grateful Dead Comix* appeared later that year. Of

Son (without tie) and father (without ponytail).
© Herb Shapiro.

course, Kitchen was horrified to discover that in January 1992 Loren intended to publish his own unauthorised biography of the Grateful Dead.

© Infinite One.

"I was paying a licence fee to the Grateful Dead when he was doing a Grateful Dead comic without a licencing fee. When I brought it up with the Grateful Deads' attorneys they said, 'Well we don't know if we can sue him and we don't know if we want to spend money to sue him.' I said, 'Here you are licencing something to me exclusively and then you allow someone to compete against me.' It was a very awkward position in a way, because I also understood that there is this tradition of unauthorised biographies.

I remember my first thought was, 'Christ, I could have done these; he did and I didn't.'"

Sparked by Kitchen, the legal offices of the Grateful Dead wrote to Loren demanding that he "cease and desist from your current or future use of any unauthorised mark associated with the Grateful Dead in connection with your comic publication." The Dead's manager even rang up Revolutionary, although could not see the joke in his conversation with Loren's father where they discussed whether the Grateful Dead were copyrighted characters in the same way as the Muppets or Ninja Turtles.

"So, are they Muppets or Ninja Turtles?" asked Herb.

"I can't comment on that," replied the manager.

Loren not only went ahead with his three-part Grateful Dead series, but also engaged in a fax war with Kitchen. In many respects Kitchen was caught between a rock and a hard place. Although he had paid the Grateful Dead a fee and royalties, his own comix were hamstrung by very little co-operation from the band. That the Dead did not legally take action against Revolutionary felt like very much a kick in the teeth. Revolutionary produced a three-part history of the Grateful Dead and Loren – of course – included much of his correspondence with Kitchen in the editorial pages.

Although he was always willing to fight his corner, Loren's feeling of self-importance could also be downright amusing. When Guns 'N Roses recorded a song called 'Get In The Ring' Axl Rose went through a list of people who had pissed him off during his career and who he'd like to, well climb into a boxing ring with. Todd Loren and

Revolutionary comics were not cited. So in one editorial, Loren took Rose to task for not only for being hostile to the press, but not requiring Loren to start learning the noble art. "Hey Axl, I dare YOU to get into the ring! I dare you to write me and answer these charges!" Rose never rose to the bait in writing although perhaps his backstage threats to Sanford could have been big fight preliminaries.

On June 18th 1992, Todd Loren did not show up at the office. Was he sick? He did not phone in and several calls were made to his home in an effort to speak to him. Eventually Herb Shapiro drove to his son's house and noting that the garage was open and the car missing, called a locksmith to open the front door. In the upstairs bedroom he saw a sight that no father should have to see. His son had been murdered – stabbed to death.

To this day the case remains unsolved, although there has been speculation that the killer was Andrew Cunanen, who later found sick fame as the man who killed fashion designer, Gianni Versace. Cunanen targeted rich and successful gay businessmen and was living in San Diego at this time. There is speculation that Loren met Cunanen through an exchange of gay videos. Loren had also told his parents of a affair shortly before his death with a man whose description appears to match that of Cunanen.

Of course playing detective after the event is a waste of time; for Herb Shapiro and his wife who worked with their son on a day-to-day basis it was a terrible, terrible blow.

"It struck so deep… there is hardly a way to explain it. There is no way to explain something like that unless you can experience it, and God forbid that you would have to experience it," recalls Shapiro.

When the writers and artists of Revolutionary were informed about Loren's death they were shocked.

"I thought it was a joke at first," recalls Sanford. "The exact kind of thing that Todd would do to drum up publicity. After he was told that he could not produce any New Kids comic books using their logo, Todd completed *The New Kids Hate Book* and released a press release saying that the art had been stolen from his car, hinting that the New Kids had hired agents to do it. He loved these weird publicity stunts, and I thought it would be very Todd-like to fake his death. I was away in Connecticut at the time, so I flew right back to California expecting it to all end up with him sitting up in his coffin and laughing. But the police met me at the airport and interviewed me there, so I knew it was pretty serious and was for real."

Spike Steffenhagen, who had enjoyed a combative but fruitful working relationship with Loren, was also totally shocked. He knew that Shapiro had called for a locksmith to open the door of his son's house.

"I don't know why, I was watching the news – I don't know if I was looking for something about Todd. The news was on and there was this grisly discovery by a father that was the discovery. Then it comes on and the victim's name is believed to be Todd Loren. I just started screaming, 'Why?' And crying."

At the burial service, Elvis Costello's version of "What's So Funny About Peace Love And Understanding" was played again and again as it was Loren's favourite song. As an elegy, his father, Herb Shapiro also read out a history of Revolutionary that Loren had penned himself.

When it comes to the violent death of a loved one, dust never settles. It can't, it hangs in the air like memories. Amazingly, as his son had worked so hard to build up the company, Shapiro thought it would be a fitting legacy to carry on running Revolutionary Comics.

"I wanted to keep it going which was a mistake. At that time what I should have done was close down the operation, but I wanted to have some kind of monument to him so I approached Jay."

Jay Allen Sanford attended the funeral and was as close to Loren as anybody. Shapiro asked him to take over from Loren and run the creative side of the company. Sanford agreed, although it was a daunting task. "It probably should not have been attempted and the fact that we pulled it off and managed to keep it up for a couple of years is pretty amazing, but we did some really great stuff.

However, for Shapiro these were lost years.

"Ah… well… after Todd's death… if you were to have looked at me or dealt with me you would have thought that I was just proceeding in a normal way, but very frankly for the next two years I was just on auto pilot. I just did things. Got up and went to work and went home. I appeared to be functioning well but I can hardly remember those two years."

Sanford had the troubled experience of having to occupy Loren's former office and pick up the reins of the business. The first priority was relocation.

"We had to move our offices up to Northern San Diego because that old office down

in Hillcrest was absolutely haunted by the ghost of Todd. Not literally, we did not hear him, but we could see him and feel him virtually everywhere. And the fact that the murder was unsolved made it even more nerve-wracking."

At this time there was even speculation that Loren had been 'hit' by people in the music or comics industry who had a grudge against him. New premises were found and around six months after Loren's death the company moved to the Mirimar section of San Diego.

One person who thought that he would get lost in the shuffle after Loren's death was Spike Steffenhagen. Steffenhagen had enjoyed an adversarial relationship, especially when Loren would give Sanford assignments that he wanted.

"I was leaving. I can't do this anymore! A big part of it was that I didn't know what to expect from Jay except from what Todd had told me. Jay said, 'I'd really like for you to stay on, can you come to the meeting?' I said, 'Yeah, I'll do what I can to help you guys out until you are stable.' Then we had a private meeting and he said, 'I have Todd's list here of things you were supposed to do this year, what do you think of it?' I told him that they were simply compromises. He ended up okaying the Pantera book, which was a big thing, because he had worked in

Revolutionary's second office. © Jay Allen Sanford.

Jay Allen Sanford. © Jay Allen Sanford.

record stores and stuff and was a rock fan, so he knew they were about to break. 'That is a good call!' I was like 'Whoooa! He gets it!' They have not sold a million albums, yet but they are about to and their fans are loyal. The other one was the punk book that I did. He said, 'How are you going to put a band like the Ramones in a book, because they are so influential?' I said I would do a brief overview, a history of punk and kick it off with Iggy Pop, the MC5 and that scene, then have the (New York) Dolls and the Ramones and then I would take it to England because after that pretty much everyone knows the story. He said, 'Yeah! Excellent.' After that we were pretty much up and running."

Musically Sanford had different tastes to Loren, and whilst he maintained the old policy of trying to produce comics that would shadow successful bands, he also brought his own judgement into play. Letting Steffenhagen take over the Hard Rock Comics line was a good call, as Steffenhagen began to explore threads of music that had Loren had previously rejected. Therefore there were books on artists like Jimi Hendrix, the Dead Kennedys. Megadeth, Motörhead and British Heavy Metal. Sanford also green-lighted comics on some of his own favourite artists, like David Bowie and Kate Bush, which also helped shift comics in England where Revolutionary had opened up another line of distribution. Although Sanford used many of the artists that Loren used, he also brought in some fresh blood.

"My goal was to bring in more famous names that comic fans would recognise." This even extended to writers. "We talked to Neil Gaiman before the Alice Cooper comic about doing a Cure comic. He was interested but we could never meet his price."

When it came to business, Sanford had no intention in trying to maintain Loren's adversarial position and was keener to work with bands and the comics industry at large, rather than against it.

"I decided that our goal should be to chronicle the entire history of rock and roll, rather than the history of what sells in rock and roll. I didn't see how we could do any more flash-in-the-pan books like the one on Vanilla Ice, that came out three months after his fall from grace, and it sold so poorly. I thought that if you did a book on the birth of punk then you had a book with a twenty-year shelf life.

"So I started chronicling strands like the San Francisco Scene, as opposed to single bands or hot bands. I was going for a very different type of company from what Todd had run. A lot more friendly to the musicians. Write to them first, ask for interviews and getting them usually, send them the comic and make deals where they could take the comic on the road with them. Try to work it as something that was part of the music industry, rather than being something always looked at as the bastard child of both comics and music."

© Infinite One.

This new policy began to reap dividends with the Ramones being interviewed for the *Birth of Punk* issue and former Hendrix sideman Noel Redding for the *Best of British Invasion* book.

Sanford also had to deal with the expansion of the company. Shortly before his death, Loren had negotiated a deal to improve the nationwide distribution of Revolutionary comics. He had signed an agreement with a Chicago distributor called Harvey Weinstein to get Revolutionary titles placed on the news-stands across the country. This was a major breakthrough and gave Revolutionary the opportunity to potentially tap into a thicker artery of cashflow. Anybody going into a 7-11 or similar store would see Revolutionary product.

Of course to close the deal, some compromises were made on Loren's part. One was that Loren had to start a new title aimed at a young audience, and to this end the *Starjam* line was introduced into the Revolutionary stable. The focus of the magazine would be on popular TV shows like *90210* and more teen-orientated pop stars like MC Hammer and Janet Jackson. Amazingly Loren even agreed to censor some of his comics in order that they would not cause offence. In some cases this meant sanitising images and speech in some already-published titles.

Spike Steffenhagen was furious when one of his Kiss comics was softened, changing Gene Simmons' reference to female "pussy" to a comment about a cat! His title for a Red Hot Chilli Peppers' story "Our Cocks Smell Like Sock, But Our Music Rocks' was changed to 'Our Music Rocks Down To Our Socks'. The upside of this deal was that 175,000 copies of each comic would be placed on newsstands across the country. At the time of Loren's death, some of the figures were beginning to come in and they made impressive reading, as Jay Allen Sanford confirmed.

"The Nolan Ryan issue of *Baseball Superstars* was number three of all comics carried by that newsstand distributor all month. It

Spike Steffenhagen and Sanford. © Jay Allen Sanford.

was ahead of *X-Men* and *Superman!* I can't remember what was ahead of it, maybe *Archie* or something. Number three of all comic books. It was a huge success!"

Another of the initiatives under Sanford's stewardship was the production of compendiums, which featured sections of previously published comics. The acorn that spawned this oak was Tom Potts, who started at Revolutionary as a general factotum.

"A few months into the job I was checking out the stock and thought about how the first Queen book had a great centrefold spread, but it was in the wrong spot of the book," recalls Tom. "So I suggested to Jay that he rework both of the Queen books into one, with the centrefold in the right spot."

This led to several other compilation titles on Guns 'N Roses, Metallica and The British Invasion, which were ideal for news-stand distribution. Sanford gives Potts full credit for these compilations.

"It was a great way to recreate older books into a new format – we'd cut the lame material, jam together art from various books, rewrite dialogue and captions – I even changed entire scenes! I recall creating an all-new *Backstage at Monterey Pop Festival* comic by taking art of Jefferson Airplane from a Doors comic, pasting it with a drawing of Hendrix from *Hard Rock Comics* and a drawing from Genesis, where I painted hair on Phil Collins to turn him into a member of Big Brother, with Janis Joplin (cut out from the Janis comic) standing next to him demanding a belt of Jack Daniels!"

Ken Meyer Jr drew most of the covers for these compendium issues.

Even under Sanford's stewardship, Revolutionary was dogged by imitation. Although Rock Fantasy were below par, Personality Comics trod similar water in their choice of bands, and the covers looked so much like Revolutionary comics that some retailers and consumers thought that they were published by the same company.

"They hurt our sales immensely," recalls Sanford, "because they were so bad. They were not comic books *per se*. There would be a drawing on one page and text on the other page just like copying something out of a rock and roll encyclopaedia and retelling it."

Bigger fish were also beginning to swim in the same waters. Fish with deeper pockets. One was Rock-It Comix. Financed by Malibu Comics, the general editor was Rob Conti, who had previously scripted for Revolutionary in the early days and then left after a dispute with Loren. With money behind them, Rock-It could afford to secure collaboration

© Infinite One.

and participation from musicians by paying licensing fees. Under the banner of 'Music for your eyes' they produced magazine-type publications on Metallica, Lita Ford, World Domination, Santana and Pantera. To be fair, the Santana comic was wonderful, based on an interview that Carlos Santana gave artist and writer Timothy Truman. The production values were sumptuous, with full colour throughout.

A Rock-It book on Ozzy Osbourne was written by Englishman Mike Carey, whose working methods were similar to those employed by the Revolutionary writers.

"For the Ozzy book I was given a vast amount of research material – huge albums full of press clippings, painstakingly arranged in chronological order, plus the 'Don't Blame

Me' video and a whole bunch of old concert recordings and stuff. For Pantera, by contrast, I was pretty much left to my own devices. But I think that reflects the different flavour of the two books. The Ozzy comic was biographical – it was a retrospective of his career. The Pantera book was just a vampire story that just happened to have the band Pantera as characters."

Interestingly, Carey was given a basic plot by Pantera singer Phil Anselmo.

"Basically, he wanted the clash with the vampires, the scene where the band are captured and tortured, and a finale involving the fans as well as the band. I wrote a story around those stipulations."

Typically Revolutionary was not impressed with Rock-It. At the 1984 San Diego Comicon Spike Steffenhagen and cover artist Scott Jackson took the competition to an amusing level.

"They had a booth there, and this thing was monumental, they had video screens! Lita Ford was signing books on their stand!" recalls Jackson, "and we had one called *The Runaways* with Joan Jett and Lita Ford, which had just come out as well. Rob Conti comes right up to us saying, 'Look guys,' and he is showing off this fortress of a booth they have with Lita signing comics for them. 'Maybe you guys can come to work for me, you know?' So me and Spike go and grab a couple of issues of our book and we stand in line. The guy right in front of me slaps her right on the butt, and I kind of looked twice for a second, but she turned around and she obviously knew the guy real well, 'Hi Jim, going for a drink in a little while, ok?' We get to the booth and Spike throws his issue down and I throw my issue down. She

© Infinite One.

is writing on this unauthorised comic book and she goes, 'What the hell is this?' Spike goes, 'I wrote it!' and then I said, 'I drew it!' I could hear Rob Conti on the other side of the booth saying, 'Don't sign that!' but it was too late, and Spike and me were jumping up and down with the crowd looking on."

Rock-It Comix did not last very long, as Malibu were bought by Marvel Comics, who swiftly shut down Rock-It as they had plans for music comics of their own. According to Mike Carey some interesting ideas got left in the pipeline.

"There was a storyline that Geezer Butler (Black Sabbath) had come up with, and they wanted someone to co-write it with him. It would have been somewhat like the Pantera book, in that it was a mixture of rock and horror themes."

That competitors like Rock Fantasy, Rock-it, Personality and – as we will see in the next chapter – Marvel Music got involved, was a testament to the power and potential profitability of Loren's original vision. Ironically, when Revolutionary went out of business in June 1995 it was partly due to competition and partly to do with their own line of sports books.

The deal with Harvey Weinstein was something of a double-edged sword. Although Revolutionary got news stand distribution, Weinstein made certain demands in order to deal with competition offered from quarters like Personality's own line of sports books. He insisted that the Revolutionary sports books change from black and white into full colour.

"We did that," recalls Sanford, "and the sales remained the same – spectacular – but costs have now doubled on four books a month. Then he says, 'let's do more sports books, let's do Baseball Legends!' Now we've got six to eight sports books a month. They are grossing really good money but the costs for those books are astronomical for the colour."

Weinstein next insisted that Revolutionary included free trading cards with all of the sports comics. This was a take it or leave it offer.

"So now we've tripled the cost of the books from our original budget and yet sales did not increase one whit from having the cards in them, they stayed exactly the same. A monster success by any standards, except

for the fact that the margin on these books was heavily eroded. The work was incredible, because in a full-colour book all the players' pinstripes have to be the right colour, as did the stadiums. For research alone, we had to hire two staffers just to get the facts right. That was what sucked us dry. Everything else remained a success, we were probably outselling the Todd years two to one, and getting tons more press and tons more respect, but that sports line literally just sucked all the money right out of us, and increased all the work and all the effort."

Despite the problems, it looked for a time as if Revolutionary was going to be taken over by DC comics. Sanford had a meeting with Paul Levitz at the 1993 San Diego Comicon and there were meetings between DC and Revolutionary in an attempt to hammer out a deal.

"We went to New York to the Time Warner Building on a couple of occasions," recalls Herb Shapiro. "In their offices and we saw stacks and stacks of our books on people's desks and they were, going through our books trying to figure out a way to do them." Of course, the proposed deal floundered because a company like DC could not put out books the Revolutionary way – 'Unauthorised and proud of it!'

Even though DC backed out of the deal, Sanford believes that it was a missed opportunity.

"They had access to Time Warner who had all the contacts at the record labels to line up the licences they needed. In fact, they came to the table with about twenty bands they had tentative agreements with to do comics. Certainly more than Marvel ended up doing at Marvel Rock. But it just came down to

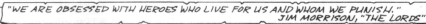

"WE ARE OBSESSED WITH HEROES WHO LIVE FOR US AND WHOM WE PUNISH."
JIM MORRISON, "THE LORDS"

| JAY ALLEN SANFORD | GREG FOX | TODD LOREN |
| WRITER | ARTIST | EDITOR |

numbers. I thought that the numbers looked attractive for everybody to make money, but DC never found it attractive enough."

Saying that, DC did dip a toe into the waters with a Prince comic, which must have sold well, because the following year they did another one.

Revolutionary Comics wound down in June 1995. Although the cost of the sports books was high, Herb Shapiro had also had enough.

"I didn't have the heart anymore," he recalls, "my drive had just evaporated and I got fairly despondent about it. My other son lives here in Florida, and he and his wife asked us to move from San Diego to Florida to be near them and the grandchildren and all that. I thought, well this is the time to give it up and I did."

Revolutionary went bankrupt and closed its doors. The last comics published as far as Sanford could recall, "were *Rock'n'Roll* 64 (Sixties San Francisco) and 65 (Sci Fi Space Rockers) which comprised mostly reprint material. There had never been a 61 on Yes because I hated the art so much, there were a couple of decent pages that I stuck into the Sci-fi rockers book."

Some of the comics that did not see the light of day included the Spin Doctors, Stone Temple Pilots, Depeche Mode, The Jam, John Cougar Mellencamp, the B52s, the Smashing Pumpkins, Meat Loaf and the Allman Brothers. Whilst Shapiro and his wife retired to Florida, Sanford bought the rights to Revolutionary's *Carnal Comics* line and started a career as the world's most successful publisher of authorised biographies of porn stars.

The legacy of Revolutionary was important. Loren created a market for comics that had not existed before and his fight for First Amendment freedom has, in the long term, had a major impact in the comics industry. The recent Nirvana and Eminem graphic novels were certainly unauthorised and proud of it. Also, as time has progressed, the comics that Revolutionary published have worn well, remaining sought-after and collected by fans of the bands depicted. Indeed, Mötley Crüe recently licensed and reprinted a Revolutionary comic book in a recent four CD boxed set. Finally, the proof of the pudding is in the reading – and they remain fun to read.

12

Make Mine Marvel....music!

Mick Jagger and Keith Richards are one of the greatest song-writing teams of all time. The number of classics that they have written are an alpine range of peaks that include "Satisfaction", "Brown Sugar", "Jumping Jack Flash", "Sympathy For the Devil", "Paint It Black" and "Start Me Up". Of course, despite the richness and density of their songbook there are lesser-known riffs. One of the backwaters from recent years is "Voodoo Lounge" credited to Jagger/Todd.

I know, I know, if you are a Rolling Stones' fan then you are scratching your head. Af-

ter all, you know that *Voodoo Lounge* was a Stones' album released in 1994, notable for not only being pretty good fare, but the first recorded without long-standing (and barely moving) bass player Bill Wyman. And a guy with the surname Todd was not the bass player on that record…

Of course the Jagger/Todd credit does not refer to the title track on the album, but the concept comic based on the album of the same name. Yup, in 1995 Marvel comics published a 48-page full-colour fine art paper beauty based upon the album, which could not only be found in comic shops,

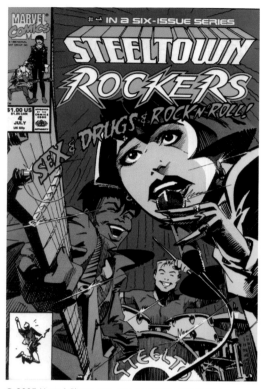

© 2005 Marvel Characters, Inc. Used with permission.

but also sold on the *Voodoo Lounge* tour of America. The Todd in question was not a resurrected Todd Loren from Revolutionary comics, but Mort Todd, the editor of a line of Marvel Music.

Although best known as the home of superheroes Marvel comics had toyed gently with the loins of music comics in the past. Two *Kiss Super Specials* had sold a million copies each in the late-'70s, and a superb *Beatles Super Special* had been published in 1978, with the same standard of art and attention to detail. A *Sgt Pepper's* special was also produced to tie in with the awful movie starring the Bee Gees and Peter Frampton, although it was withdrawn from distribution. There were whispers about a comic featuring Elton

John – as Captain Fantastic or the Brown Dirt Cowboy? – it never progressed beyond preliminary negotiations. As we have seen in the Kiss chapter, *Marvel Premiere* 50 was dedicated to Alice Cooper.

At the dawn of the 1990s, Marvel began to dip their toes into the waters again. Whether this was influenced by the emergence of companies like Revolutionary and Personality is unknown, but like DC, Marvel must have seen the glut of authorised and unauthorised music biographies and thought that there must be money in it. Like all businesses, when someone bakes a pie in your backyard and it smells nice you tend to get baking yourself.

One of the first experiments with music was a promotional comic for Cheap Trick's 1990 album, *Busted* and no doubt paid for by their record company Epic, with Marvel supplying the talent, it was an eight-page black and white biography that was well written, well drawn and well, Revolutionary in Marvel team colours. Another interesting animal was a six-part series called *Steeltown Rockers* (April – September 1990) which followed the formation of a young band and their struggle to get gigs and keep everything together. Although some of the graphic riffs were taken from the Hernandez brothers *Love and Rockets*, it was a pretty good jam session, and the band ended up playing at a comic convention.

Next up was *Nightcat* published in April 1991, and this was a very strange beast indeed. A singer called Jacqueline Tavarez had appeared on the music scene. Someone, somewhere at Marvel, thought it would be a dandy idea to turn her into a superhero and put her into a comic that would tie in with her debut album, also called *Nightcat*. Indeed, according to the comic, it was Stan Lee himself. He pops into the recording studio just after she has laid down a vocal track and introduces himself. "The name's Lee, Jacqueline! I like your style! How'd you like to be Marvel comics' newest superhero? We can do a *Nightcat* comic faster than you can say 'Excelsior'." And so they did, a full 46-page monster. How it sold I don't know.

My personal view on *Nightcat*? It's awful. Dross. Crap. Piffle. Whether Tavarez was seen as a new Madonna, or mutton dressed as lamb is open to question, although these days she is filed under 'where are they now?' Back then her leather costume made her look like the main course in a porn film. But Marvel were back in the music comics business.

Things got serious when Marvel decided to establish a specific 'Marvel Music' branch that would be the umbrella under which all of their music comics would shelter. The man chosen to steer this ship out of harbour and onto the high seas was Mort Todd.

Todd was by his own admission "a punk rocker in High School", and as an artist in his own right, illustrated many album covers "most notably the *Back From the Grave* series of 1960s garage punk rock bands from Crypt records." He also edited *Cracked* magazine, "which in case you're not aware, was a fifth-rate *Mad Magazine* rip off. I was proud to evolve it into a third rate rip-off and quadruple the sales."

Todd got the job at Marvel when, like Marvin Gaye, he heard something through the grapevine.

"I learned from an editor at Marvel that I was on the short list of people to run the line

so I called them, was interviewed and must've impressed them enough to hire me."

Looking back today Todd recalls that, as such, he did not have a mission statement for Marvel Music, but in general "was hoping to attract a wider audience to the comics medium and have people who would never pick up a comic book buy the Marvel Music titles."

The plan was also to produce music comics with great artwork and with high quality card covers.

"As I found out in my *Cracked* days that some people would pick up comics if it was in a format different from the traditional comics format."

Todd also recalls that Terry Stewart, president of Marvel comics at that time, was also

Marvel Music Man, Mort Todd. © Mort Todd.

a big music fan "and committed to expanding the medium and was of great support". Of course it was not all champagne and roses, as "the traditional Marvel editorial was against it and couldn't understand what I was attempting."

What Todd was attempting to do was apply Marvel's famed art and storytelling panache to music acts. However, unlike companies like Revolutionary, Personality or Rock Fantasy he could not go down the route of publishing 'unauthorised' biographies or stories. As Marvel was a large company – gargantuan at the time, driving sales through multiple covers and various collector's issues – they had to do things by the book. Or the cheque book.

"I had a rough idea of some of the major artists I wanted to do books on," recalls Todd, "and as we talked to record labels and management they would also try to get us to sign up other acts."

Marvel paid licensing fees of between $15,000 and $45,000 to each band against royalties in the region of ten per cent. As well as receiving cash, all bands and artists were given input into the finished product.

"Each book was unique in its development. Mostly, after we did a deal with a band's licensing company, we would talk to the band and they would tell us what they wanted to do in the storyline."

The first comic to be published under the Marvel Music imprint was another Alice Cooper title. As luck would have it, writer Neil Gaiman was already working with Cooper on a comic book concept based around Cooper's latest album, "and since

Marvel had already done an Alice book in the '70s" recalls Todd, "they approached us. It was just synchronicity that we were developing a music line and to launch it with a Gaiman book that would (supposedly) ensure that traditional comic book fans would come on board."

At this time – as he is today – Neil Gaiman was seen as one of the greatest writers in the medium. His Gothic *Sandman* series had won a legion of loyal fans who bought and read his work with all the avid enthusiasm that music fans give their favourite recording artists. Gaiman had even been in a punk band in his native Croydon in the late Seventies, although unlike the Damned he never had the pleasure of cleaning out the toilets at the Fairfield Hall venue.

That Marvel Music had great hopes for *The Last Temptation of Alice* was reflected in the fact that Cooper and Gaiman went on the road to promote the title. In an interview with the independent UK publication *Comics Forum* Cooper ruminated on the appeal of Stan Lee's outfit.

"Marvel's good. Marvel's really good. See, they draw you with a better body that you've got; bigger pecs and stuff. I like that. I like that lots."

Gaiman offered some insight into the collaborative process with Cooper.

"After I agreed to do it, I worked on a first draft plot, which I sent to Alice. He went through it, commenting on it – saying things like, 'I like this, can you expand on that. I don't want to cover this'. That kind of stuff. After the second draft, I went to Phoenix where he was writing the album and we worked on it together. It was a pretty organic experience; there was a lot of give and take

between us, we both contributed ideas, and it was personally very refreshing to work like that."

The end result was published in three parts, with art by Michael Zulli and is an interesting summit between comics and music. Whether it is – as some say – one of the greatest examples of the mixing of the two forms is open to question. The plot is classic Gaiman, dark and gothic with a young boy entering a 'Theatre Of The Real' where Cooper is some kind of top-hatted soul stealer who tempts the boy with eternal life, "…you stay here. With me. In the theatre. And you never leave, and you never grow older. And there's no danger at all." Of course there is danger aplenty, especially when the boy tries to rescue a young girl who, like many other children, has been lured and trapped in the theatre by Cooper. Typically at the climax Cooper transforms into one of his trademarks – a snake – and although the boy rescues the girl she proves to be a ghost. The story is an excellent read and was probably equally enjoyed by fans of Gaiman and Cooper. Saying that, it was probably Cooper fans who bought *The Last Temptation* album that was released at the same time as this three-part deluxe comic book.

Although *The Last Temptation* went down a road that Marvel had already travelled, Todd intended to feature artists from a wide variety of music genres, ranging from Rap to country. And he did. One baffling title was devoted to country music star, Marty Stuart, called *Marty's Party is Space*. As the title suggests, it involved Stuart in a suitable cosmic adventure. I'd like to say more, but the comic is impossible to track down. Whether there was an untapped market of comic book buy-

© 1994 Nightmare Inc. and Neil Gaiman. Illustrations © 1994 Michael Zulli.

ers in the country music demographic is open to question, but fair play to Todd for trying to find it.

One title that did sell well was a comic about the Woodstock festival, produced to tie in with the second festival of August 1994. Surely a marriage made in marketing heaven, as Marvel's *Woodstock* comic could also celebrate the famed 1969 Festival. The finished result, based around a science fiction story scripted by Todd and illustrated by many artists, was graphically lush, although it looked more like a piece of memorabilia than anything else. The cover art, by the late Martin Emond was a tribute of sorts to famed psychedelic artist Rick Griffin. Sadly what was inside did not live up to the promise:

"Indeed, one generation passes the torch to a different, and yet not-so-dissimilar group, and everyone today knows that you don't have to be tweaking on a neuro-pacifier to appreciate the stratospheric thunderings of the Red Hot Chili (sic) Peppers. Aerosmith, Metallica, Cypress Hill, Nine Inch Nails and their ilk."

In fact, there is a distinct absence of musicians from the 1969 Festival on display. Surely Hendrix playing his famed version of 'The Star Spangled Banner' would have been an obvious moment to capture, as were the performances of The Who and Joe Cocker. But they are not there. The performers on show are generic representations, including a two-page splash depicting what might be the Grateful Dead.

According to Todd, permissions were not a problem, "but it would have been a headache. Basically we got the Woodstock licence to tie-in with the Woodstock II event, and to use band likenesses would have involved having to license every group separately."

The *Woodstock* comic became one of Marvel Music's bestselling titles as it was sold through MTV and at the festival itself. As with the Alice Cooper comic, the production values were high, with a soft cover similar to a paperback book.

"There were a few reasons for the format," recalls Todd. "One was to add to their collectability but also, as I said before, to appeal to non-comic book fans. I found out in my *Cracked* days that some people would pick up a comic if it was presented different from the traditional format, which they wouldn't be caught dead with. And, with a classier format we could have a higher price point which would make the retailers happier."

Sales aside, Marvel music did cover some new ground. *Break The Chain* was a unique concept where artist Kyle Baker illustrated the lyrics to a song by rapper KRS-One.

"The idea was you'd play the record and read the book and learn to read," Baker later told *The Comics Journal*. "I used to have a *Little Red Riding Hood* book that came with a little 45rpm record, and I'd turn the page when I heard a bell which helped me to learn to read. So we did one with some cool rap stuff."

Each comic came with a cassette tape that could be played as the child read the story. "Yo, check this out. Let me introduce you to four kids living in the city. But before we go into that, listen to this: WORD! Every time you hear WORD! You turn the page, like now. WORD!" Not only was it intended to encourage young Afro-American children to read, but also explore their own culture and examine the works of people like Malcolm X, rather than use the name as a cool soundbite in conversations.

In order to generate interest from music TV channels, Baker also created an eye-catching promotional video based on his artwork, along with 'Break the Chain' CDs and 12-inch vinyl which were also pressed up and marketed. The concept was good, the intent was good, the music good and Baker's artwork was superb, but at Marvel many wondered what the hell was going on. What was the Marvel logo doing on a rap record? Todd certainly felt the breeze of criticism,

"At Marvel itself there was a negative reaction amongst other staffers because we had a large budget, no real deadlines (unless it was tied to a CD release) and I got to travel an awful lot."

Despite internal politics, the jewel in the crown of Todd's Marvel Music empire was a biography of Bob Marley.

"Although I'm into 'alternative' stuff, I wanted to cover the legends of music (for commercial and creative reasons) and Bob was a talent that crossed the spectrum of all music fans. The more I learned about his amazing life and the world around him, the more excited I got about doing the book."

As with all Marvel Music titles, Todd went to town.

"The writer Charles E. Hall and I spent two weeks in Jamaica doing research including spending a night in Trenchtown. The experience was very enlightening and gave us the proper awe of the life of Bob to do the book justice."

Todd also took pains to give the look of the story the required realism, by asking one of the great Marvel artists to do the pencils. "Gene Colan did not know much about Bob Marley, but with enough reference material he was the perfect choice for the story. The finishes of his art were painted by Tennyson Smith, a Jamaican Rasta artist that would make the representation of Bob's life truer."

The life of Marley was conceived as a three book series of which, before Marvel Music's demise, only two were published. The first two parts are excellent. Not only did it detail the rise of Marley from poverty to worldwide success, but also put him in context, by including a ten-page history of Jamaica and the development of Rastafari as a creed and religious grouping. Even the copious marijuana smoking was not avoided and well handled:

"The Rastafari know Ganja as the wisdom weed that grew from the grave of Solomon. Many credit its use with helping them perceive the wickedness of the Babylon system. The Rastas smoke the herb while "reasoning" with their bredren."

Sure, this may sound somewhat pompous, but much better than Marvel walking the typical American line of, "Boy! Those black guys down in Jamaica sure smoke a lot of dope!"

The first volume had a foreword written by Bono from U2 – "I know claiming Bob Marley as Irish might be a little difficult, but bear with me…". Todd is currently attempting to secure the rights from the Bob Marley estate to publish the entire three-part biography.

Most of the Marvel Music titles were published in 1994 and 1995. Billy Ray Cyrus was fortunate to have his own comic books, as were rap act Onyx. Also, as we have seen,

Mick Jagger agreed to allow Marvel to produce a comic book inspired by the *Voodoo Lounge* album. In this case Todd was looking to generate synergy. Hence the Jagger/Todd collaboration.

"Mick Jagger was not much of a comics fan," recalls Todd, "but after we did the deal, he did a lot of research visiting comic shops and such, and was very involved in the creation of the Stones' comic."

Personally speaking the *Voodoo Lounge* comic is a major disappointment. Artist Dave McKean produced his famed collages which occasionally featured the band and snippets of lyrics from the album. This might sound cruel, but it looked like page after page of front cover ideas. *Voodoo Lounge* was little more than a fine art exercise with the Rolling Stones' name attached. It can be read in two minutes and forgotten in three.

Of course, when it came to music and comics there was no way that Kiss were going to stand on the sidelines. Todd was quick to re-package the two original '70s *Kiss Super Specials* into one book. After negotiation with The Demon, it was also agreed to do a new Kiss book. As always, the Kiss frontman knew exactly what he wanted.

"Gene Simmons was adamant that they party with the X-Men so he could impress his son who was a fan of the mutants," recalls Todd, "we even sent out actors dressed as Marvel characters to his son's birthday party."

Simmons got his wish and in *KISSNATION* – with dialogue by Stan Lee – the four Kiss characters got to tangle with the world's most favourite mutants. It was a throwback to the days of Kirby and Lee, with a great story and plenty of action. Great fun.

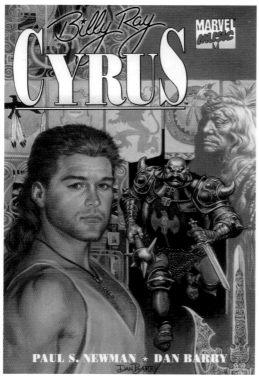

© Billy Ray Cyrus.

KISSNATION was released after the demise of Marvel Music. Due to poor sales Marvel pulled the plug in 1995. Looking back with hindsight, Todd believes that lack of sales was less to do with the quality of the product, more a distribution problem.

"Alternative distribution was one of the things that attracted me to heading the line. We were promised all kinds of new (for comics) distribution that I felt would energise and expand the market. Some books were sold at concerts (with the *KISSNATION* book selling at the Kiss reunion tour), packaged with CD releases (Alice Cooper) and even toll-free over MTV (the Woodstock book). Ultimately when they couldn't get the books into record shops and book stores,

I chose not to renew my contract. They were only getting them into comic shops, and since most of them (Marvel Music books) didn't have muscley, rubber-suited fightboys they weren't too successful. The sales department told me that they couldn't sell Elvis or Bob Marley books to this market. Every day you can't go more that a few feet without seeing Elvis or Marley merchandise… I told them that you could sell Elvis tampons if you wanted – so that admission from them told me I was beating my head against the wall.

"We were probably ahead of our time, and I think they would sell much better now."

In many respects, Marvel Music *were* ahead of their time, although some of the titles were baffling. Then again, Todd was looking at the long as well as short term "and create books that would be 'evergreen' and sell forever, like the bands they were based on."

When Marvel Music folded its tents, there were a number of tantalising projects in the pipeline. One was a three-part series on the King of Rock'n'Roll himself, "the Elvis book was an incredible story of spectral Elvis travelling on a mystery train making stops through his life. The artwork would switch from ghostly-painted art (over Gene Colan pencils again) to straight biographical sequences drawn by that giant of comics John Severin."

A proposed AC/DC comic sounded like great fun and, although some art appeared on the *Ballbreaker* CD, fans missed out on storylines like "the band (with Brian Johnson) go to hell and party with Bon Scott!" White Zombie, House of Pain, Public Enemy, Snoop Dog, and even that famed coun-

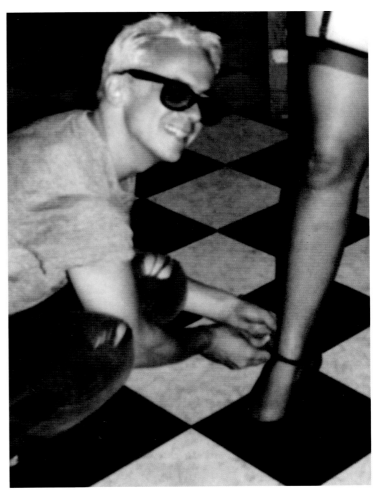

...and finally, Mort Todd as a punk playing thigh chess! © Mort Todd.

try music showcase, Grand Old Opry, never saw the light of day.

Looking back, Todd admits that he delighted in his time running Marvel Music.

"I got to travel. I had to hook up with the bands… it's not like the other editors had to go out to Los Angeles to rap with Iron Man. My expense account was larger than the president of Marvel's, and one editor personally blamed me for bankrupting the company."

This was patently not true, but Marvel Music, although a failure in terms of sales, was an interesting diversion, although since Todd left the company, Marvel have steered clear of any sailing waters that might contain rocks.

13

"Sgt Rock Is Going To Help Me"

I have before me a random copy of *Comics International*. This is the monthly bible of the UK comics industry, giving news, gossip and information on the scene, as well as details of upcoming titles, graphic novels and the like. The American equivalent is *Previews*, and is as thick and colourful as a porn star's dick after a visit to a master tattooist. But I digress…

Examining the list of upcoming publications in this June 2004 edition of *Comics International*, there are some titles obviously influenced by the sound of music. *The Darkness*, *Waterloo Sunset* and *Life During Wartime* are just three comics whose titles are garnered from the name of one hot band and two classic songs.

Song titles have always been mined, pinched, borrowed and employed as titles of comics and stories. On the other side of the fence, Marc Bolan once told Marvel UK scribe and future West End Boy, Neil Tennant in 1976 that he had talked to Stan Lee "about the possibility of me creating a superhero for him. Something along the lines of *Electric Warrior*, a twenty-first century Conan." So, if he were alive today Marc Bolan would have relished talking about a comic

Secretly, he digs on Top 40 more than any-thing, but he's trying to impress Bleu, who got him started into being a Mod. Bleu is all over the place, but she's especially fond of all New Wave, Britpop, Mod, Power Pop, Motown, Northern Soul, Garage etc. Victor in the other hand is a full-blown Rudeboy, and though he's into Goth and still secretly listens to it regularly, he's absolutely obsessed with Two-Tone and traditional Ska. He'd give anything to say he was born in the West Indies."

Blue Monday has also included guest ap-pearances from musicians. Damon Albarn ("I was wondering if you'd like to dance wiff me") and Paul Weller ("I'm old enough to be your..) appear in a dream sequence fighting over Bleu's affections, although neither can compete with the 'King Of The Wild Fron-tier' period Adam Ant! Indeed, the entire plot of 'The Kids Are Alright' story revolves around Bleu moving heaven and earth to see the solo Ant play live. She fails – amazingly the gig is sold out! – but meets him backstage after the show. Stand and Deliver, Bleu!

Did Chynna have problems drawing a more, ahem, mature Adam out of make up?

"The book takes place in the very early-'Nineties, around the same time as *Manners and Physique* (Ant solo album) came out. So, to me, it was in the right context and wasn't an issue. I drew him as accurate as I could for the time period it takes place in."

Adam saw the story and was suitably flat-tered.

"Marco Pirroni (Ant's former guitarist, foil and friend) and I talk regularly now and are developing a project," says Chynna, "He read the comic and dug it, and through him Adam saw it. Apparently, Adam was cool with the book, so that's good."

So, at least he won't be throwing spare parts of engines through her windows.

Although each issue of *Blue Monday* is named after a song, Chynna sometimes gives individual pages a soundtrack, which lends the artwork a cinematic feel, but again reflect her own listening tastes.

"I just wanted to put as much of myself into this book as possible. That, and I have a habit of promoting my favourite things like a madwoman. I want everyone to know how great these guys are… you won't read this book and automatically know everything I'm into, but you'll get a great initial grasp on it. I really do obsess over English bands, though… it's kind of disturbing."

More disturbing was the Vertigo Pop series *London* (2003), where writer Peter Milligan penned a delicious music-related story.

"I was interested in doing a story about the ageing process – lost dreams and lost hopes – using a wacky body-swapping plot device," he told me. "From there I got the idea of how great it would be to set it around the rock music world. A world where you are, in a sense, always seeing these guys, these rock dinosaurs desperately trying to be young, whether it's by the kind of wife they have on their arm, the music they play, or the guys they hang out with. That seemed to be the perfect way in which to explore this very interesting stuff."

It was. The four-part story revolves around a sixty year-old rock star called Rocky Lam-ont, who has a stack of hits and a mountain of cash, but lacks the most important coin-age of all – youth. He gets around this prob-lem by swapping bodies with a young busker

called Sean Cody, who he envies for having: "So little talent. So little to say, and so long to say it in."

Typically Rocky treats his new body with great care by indulging in an orgy of sex, whipped cream and drugs while re-launching his career with a new name and a new face. It is great fun, sporting a host of name-checks like David Gray, Noel Gallagher, Bono and – uh – Engelbert Humperdinck. The story has a more serious side, especially when it comes to drugs. "I think it is quite clear that the way drugs are used is very key to the story. I was drawing parallels to the high society drug use of Rocky and Trixie (his wife) – the cocaine on a silver platter with a glass of champagne – and the alternate, nasty end of the spectrum, watching Cassie (Sean's girlfriend) freebasing. In any investigation of the world of rock and roll and its sisters and cousins, you can't ignore a degree of drug use."

This is true, although you would not get away with it in any comic book line other than DC's mature Vertigo imprint, or something from the modern underground press. Of course, what makes Milligan's *London* work, is that when it comes to music he knows what he is talking about, being a big music fan who even name-checked the Neptunes in the X-Men/pop culture parody *X-Statix*.

When comic book writers and artists get a comic involving music wrong, it is best to look away. An example of car-crash music comics is *Shangri La*, published by Image in January 2004. As with *London*, the theme re-volves around an old rocker, Correy Stinson, who agrees to pretend he is dead in order that his back catalogue can be re-marketed. When he backs out of the deal, the record company hire a hit woman to make the deal a reality. She is a fan and can't do it, so a hit man obsessed by and dressed like Hank Williams is employed to kill them both. It's a pretty bad party all round, and readers are advised to steer clear.

The same almost applies to Mike Baron's *Sonic Disruptors*, published by DC in 1988.

"It was an attempt by me to meld rock and roll with comic books and was about a bunch of rock and roll rebels fighting a repressive government in the United States in the future," he recalls. "The government had taken over all forms of broadcasting and kind of homogenised it. Rock and roll rebels were setting up illegal radio stations in satellites circling the earth and broadcasting loud, brash, rock and roll, which by its very nature is anti-authoritarian."

It was an interesting idea, although the six issues printed contained too few good riffs – despite Clash and Aretha Franklin references – to call it a decent song.

"*Sonic Disruptors* has the distinction of being – I think," recalls Baron, "the only limited series that was cancelled by DC in mid-run."

It must be said that the highway between the cities of music and comics does have two lanes with traffic going in both directions. Eric Clapton was caught reading a copy of the *Beano* on the front of the seminal *John Mayall and the Bluesbreakers* album (1966), although he has yet to write a song about Dennis The Menace. Indeed, former Yes man Rick Wakeman still runs an occasional eye over the adventures of Desperate Dan.

"One of the reasons bands like comics," he told me, "and one of the reasons why *Viz* became hip is because being a musician, and part of the music industry is a wonderful excuse not to grow up. We still stop at service stations and buy *Dandy* books just to crack up laughing when we're going to shows. I'm

fifty-four and I am sure that there are a lot of fifty-four year-old businessmen, workers and van drivers who would love to be able to walk into a shop and buy a *Dandy* and a couple of comics but they sort of can't. We can!"

Other songwriters have borrowed freely from the comics world and name-checked characters in their lyrics. *Superman* has been widely quoted, most famously in Laurie Anderson's "O Superman", which got to number 2 in England in 1981. 'That's Really, Super, Superman' as Andy Partridge of XTC would sing, or even Donovan who boasted that "Superman and Green Lantern ain't got nothing on me." The Flaming Lips are still "Waiting for Superman" as far as I'm aware.

Batman has been best served by Sean Ryder from Black Grape who delightfully sung "Jesus was a black man/Jesus was Batman/No, that was Bruce Wayne" on the single "Kelly's Heroes" in December 1995. The theme from the Sixties *Batman* TV series has been covered by artists as diverse as Paul Weller's Jam and avante-Jazz artist Sun Ra. In fact, Ra recorded an entire album under the name of The Sensational Guitars Of Dan & Dale in 1966, where he instrumentally serenaded the world of Wayne on tracks like "Joker Is Wild", "The Riddler's Retreat" and "Batman And Robin Swing". Ra even recorded a single – with Buddy Guy on guitar – called "I'm Gonna Unmask The Batman" which swung like a well-oiled James Brown band.

Moving to Marvel, Chrissie Hyde of the Pretenders wrote an entire song based on *Howard the Duck*, and Paul McCartney penned a story about two villains, Magneto and Titanium Man, "who were involved in a robbery that was due to happen at a quarter to three on a main street". Marvel literally

Sun Ra's aural homage to Batman.

wet their pants in gratitude that one half of the world's greatest songwriting team had given them so much free publicity. McCartney was apparently inspired as he was sitting around in the studio in Jamaica reading Marvel comics whilst recording with Wings.

Getting back to Marvel, they were less pleased in 1972 when a British band called Icarus released a concept album based on people like Spider-Man, Captain America, Thor and other Avengers called *The Marvel World Of Icarus*. Maybe they objected to lyrics like "Hulk Kill! Kill! Kill! Kill!" and "Hulk is on the rampage doesn't understand that underneath that thick green hide is a very mixed up man." It must be said that the track 'Fantastic Four' is wonderful, and sounded like the Captain Beefheart band in full flight during his *Clear Spot* period.

Like The Teardrop Explodes, Massive Attack and The Avengers, American electro-punk outfit Suicide took their name from a reference in a Marvel comic book.

"I liked a lot of the older Marvels," singer Alan Vega told me, "*Ghost Rider* was my favourite, then there was *X-Men*. I wasn't into too many of them. As a kid I got into other stuff, so I didn't read comic books for years, then I started up again. I really fell in love with *Ghost Rider* because it was a spiritual thing in a way. There were two worlds there so I really got into that. That is how we got the title of the (first) album, there was an issue of *Ghost Rider* that said, 'Satan's Suicide'. I said, 'Marty (Vega's keyboard playing sidekick), that's it!' Because for weeks we had a blast trying to come up with names, man! We were laughing our heads off because it was the funniest few weeks I've ever had just trying to get a title for a band. Didn't we do one gig as 'Nasty Cut And The Band Aids' or something like that? Anyway, Marty said, 'NO! Let's just use Suicide.' It just came straight off that front cover!"

Moving closer to home, the Human League saw fit to sing about *Judge Dredd* in the aptly

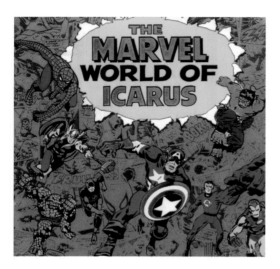

named song "I Am The Law", although the Clash were not thinking of *Mega City One* when they performed a cover version of "I Fought The Law and the Law Won". Also, contrary to popular belief, Black Sabbath's "Iron Man" has bugger all to do with the Marvel character of the same name. Just listen to the lyrics. With typical perversity, Serge Gainsbourg recorded a song whose lyrics were based partly on comic book sound effects, 'Biff. Pow. Zing!'

The most obscure reference in music I found is awarded to Dee Long who was one-third of Klaatu, who people mistook for a re-formed Beatles in the Seventies. On one of his solo albums he wrote and performed a song about his love of *Mad* magazine. Finally, the biscuit, cake and cream doughnut is taken by metal artist Thor, who sung about a comic book character based on himself, "My name is Thor ....ROCK WARRIOR!"

Speaking of Thor brings us to another clearing in the wooded landscape inhabited by the crossover between music and comics. There have been a vast array of album covers

illustrated by comic book artists. In many cases the musicians are fans of comics and request that their record company try and get a particular artist to illustrate their cover. Thor, for example, was a huge fan of artist Neal Adams who – amongst others – drew *Batman*, *Superman* and *The Avengers*.

"I had a management company at the time and they contacted Neal Adams to do this in collaboration with my upcoming album," recalls Thor.

Thor was photographed like a superhero for the cover of *Keep The Dogs Away* (1977) and Adams agreed to draw a four-page biographical comic to be included as an insert inside the cardboard sleeve. For some reason, it was never slipped inside the album jacket, although Adams enjoyed the experience and later wrote a song with the Rock Warrior.

"The Thor stuff was very cool stuff," he recalls, "and I loved to work on it."

There are too many instances of comic-book artists illustrating record covers to list here. Thousands; as diverse as Charles Burns, Adrian Tomine, Mobius, Richard Corben, Hunt Emerson, Rick Griffin, Gary Panter, Jaime Hernandez, Jamie Hewlett, Dave McKean, Joost Swarte, Robert Williams, Mort Drucker and Savage Pencil all lending their talents to help brand or sell music.

Indeed, Joe Petagno has not only illustrated Motörhead album covers, but was also responsible for their famed logo.

"I met Lemmy in '74," he reveals, "while I was doing some work for Hawkwind. A few months later he got the sack and asked me to do a logo for his new band called Motörhead. We discussed the ideas over generous helpings of vodka and orange, the drug of the day, at the local pub. Two weeks later the Head was born and the rest is history."

Famed *Watchmen* artist Dave Gibbons has done artwork for the likes of Jethro Tull and Madness.

"The final thing I was involved in was an album cover for Kula Shaker," he recalls. "I was in America at the San Diego comics convention and I had taken my teenage son over there with me. My wife called and said that a guy had phoned about doing an illustration for a band called Kula Shaker. I went "Kula Shaker?" My son went, "Wow! Kula Shaker! Do it! Do it!"

And so he did the cover for their debut album in 1996, making sure that his son got some concert tickets and backstage passes as part of the deal.

One of the most famous album covers is Robert Crumb's cover for Big Brother and the Holding Company.

"How many times have I told this story?!" the legendary underground artist wrote to me. "Janis Joplin and all the other members of her band lived around the Haight-Ashbury neighbourhood where I was living then, in 1968-69. Janis had seen my Zap comics and liked them and asked me directly – or was it Dave Goetz? – don't remember exactly – maybe they both came to see me together. I was flattered, and I needed the money, so I did it. Simple as that. Of course they needed it, like the next day, so I took some speed and worked all night on it, finishing it in the morning. Originally I did a front and a back cover. They decided that they didn't like my front cover design and ended up using the back cover for the front. I got paid $600 from CBS."

Another well-known example is Neal Adams' cover for the 1972 album *Who Will Save The World? The Mighty Groundhogs*. Led by Tony McPhee, the Groundhogs had been through some personnel changes during the Sixties, but by 1972 were a three-piece blues outfit with progressive music leanings and a popular following in England. McPhee was not only partial to writing concept albums like the 1970 offering *Thank Christ For The Bomb*, but was also a fan of Marvel comics.

"I picked up on them in the late-Sixties," recalls McPhee. "Before that when I was a kid I used to get *Mad* magazine and the book collections. I had the whole set of Marvel Comics and when Neal Adams began drawing the *X-Men* and others, I could not believe how someone could draw that well!"

When it came to preparing a new album, the Groundhogs manager Roy Fisher, suggested that they get Neal Adams to design the cover.

"I would write the music to whatever the design was," recalls McPhee.

Adams was approached and agreed to the commission. He had fun doing this cover,

although had to redraw it, as the original art-work was lost when he fell asleep on the New York subway system and his bag was stolen. Email enables artists today to be commissioned and submit their work electronically, but back in 1972 it was not so easy for an English band using an American artist.

"Remember, you are over there and I am over here so we did it across the ocean," recalls Adams. "It was before faxes and stuff, so it was a little harder in those days to do this. They generally told me what they wanted to do and what they wanted it to be. Of course, they wanted to be superheroes and beat the bad guys. They gave me some rough little drawings and some ideas of what they would like to have, and I sat down and worked it out." When Adams finished the sleeve design, "you opened the album up and you were reading a comic book," recalls Adams, "only it was twelve inches by twelve inches."

McPhee was delighted with the artwork as well as being flattered.

"He was very kind to us. He gave me more hair that I had at the time!"

McPhee then set about writing the songs to go with the images on the album comic.

"He came up with the idea of *Who Will Save The World?* I think he knew that we were interested in the environment and things like the *Silver Surfer* comic, which was environmental comment. It was his idea to make the Groundhogs a superhero group so we could right wrongs. It saved me a job really, as before I always had to think of titles. With the title in front of me it was easier to realise the songs about the environment and what man was doing to it and things like that."

The resulting music was as good as the cover, especially the opening track "Earth Is Not Room Enough", and remains one of the Groundhogs most popular albums.

Neal Adams later designed a 3D cover for Grand Funk Railroad, and even received a platinum album for the cover of an LP by a group called Extreme. The most interesting story concerns a comic book Adams drew for Eric Burdon.

"Eric, to me, has always been a very talented person but obviously he has had his troubles!" recalls Adams. "When I met him, he had been through the Animals and he had been through War, and I guess you know enough about Eric Burdon's history – or maybe you don't! Well, War was a great group, but they ended up kicking Eric Burdon out (laughs). I don't know why. You don't know. Since the tape recorder is on I can't say! But obviously without Eric Burdon, War just fell apart. It seemed to me that they took their most valuable commodity and got rid of it for whatever reason – right or wrong. War, what is it good for? Absolutely nothing! (laughs).

"Anyway he called me one day, and I had never spoken to him before, but I had been doing a lot of stuff for *National Lampoon*, so we got together in a coffee shop and he told me what he wanted to do. He was working on a new album and it was going to be all Eric Burdon. He wanted to do a 16-page comic book that would appear in the album. So that was cool. I said, 'What do you want the script to be?' He said, 'I want the script to be the words of my songs on the album.'

"Okay. So, my job was to do the words of his songs on the album as a comic book. That is what I did. I interpreted his words. Some of them were about American Indians that got slaughtered, including Gerinimo; some of them were about Vietnam; some were very heavy about space and astral things. None of it was really beyond me, it was really a trip-and-a-half to do it, so I did 16 pages, which have since been reprinted in various magazines around the world.

Anyway, I finally got the tape from Eric, who was living in California at the time, and the words were good. I loved the words to the songs, they were really very different and very powerful and wonderful, so I couldn't wait for the tape (with the music on it). So when I got the tape, I listened to it was Eric reciting the words to the songs…as a new way to do it! So pulled out a gun and shot myself and I'm dead now, and have been dead for a while (laughs).

I did not know what the hell to make of it. I mean, I wanted to call Eric and say, 'Eric you can sing the Lord's Prayer, you can sing anything. Maybe you know what you are doing man, but it does not make any sense to me.' Well, the album never came out."

Of course, in 1986 the soundtrack album to the film *Recruits* was released and featured a song that Adams co-wrote with rock warrior Thor, who also appeared in the movie. A prime example of a poacher turning gamekeeper. As the next chapter shows…

Heroes and Villains

Typically, it was Stan Lee who started the ball rolling.

Sometime in 1965 he dragged as many Marvel comic book artists, writers and staffers as he could find into a recording studio. It would be delightful to report that the Marvel Bullpen arrived after midnight as drunk as skunks and, accompanied by bored session musicians, took a vocal Cossack-ride across territory like "Strangers In The Night", "Wooly Bully" and "Hound Dog". Basically, giving us a comic book version of those awful albums that William Shatner and Leonard Nimoy went on to record when

off duty from *Star Trek*. It's crap Jim, but not as we know it!

Sadly, this was not the case. Rather than Sinatra or rock and roll, Lee took his cue from Slim Gaillard. Never heard of him? Well, Slim was a jazz man and well-known for his hip patter, and once laid down a monologue called "Slim's Jam" backed by musicians including the legendary Charlie Parker and Dizzy Gillespie. Well, like Gaillard, Lee laid down a monologue of hip Marvel-speak – "ad-libbing the whole thing" as he recalls, with interjections from the legendary artist Jack Kirby – "What are we doing here anyway?" – and others. There was no music on the five-minute recording, but great fun was had by all, especially the adoring Marvel fan club – The Merry Marvel Marching Society – who received this flexi-disc in the American postal system some time in 1965.

There was another flexi-disc in 1966, that featured the self-glorifying anthem. "You belong… you belong… you belong… you belong… you belong to the Merry Marvel Marching Society!" Thor, The Sub Mariner, Captain America, The Hulk and Iron Man were all drawn walking forwards like an early prototype of the Village People. Years later Devo ("we accept you/we accept you/one of us/one of us") and Adam and the Ants (Marco! Merrick! Terry Lee! Gary Tibbs and yours truly!") mined similar self-glorifying material with greater chart success.

Joking aside, since those two Marvel broadsides, a number of comic book artists, writers and cartoonists have dragged themselves into the recording studio to lay down tracks for posterity before getting back to the drawing board! Most famous of all is Robert Crumb. Despite carving his initials on the tree of culture at the end of the Sixties, when psychedelic rock, pop and folk was going ballistic, Crumb was – and remains – devoted to old jazz and blues, preferably played at 78rpm.

"I started out playing a plastic ukulele at age 12. I had a mindless, instinctive urge to play music," he stated to me in a delightful letter. Along with knocking out artwork for *Zap*, *Fritz the Cat* and other muses, Crumb began playing in public in the early Seventies with like-minded individuals, such as Al Dodge and Robert Armstrong. The Keep on Truckin' Orchestra – with Crumb on lead banjuke and vocals – eventually went into

the recording studio to lay down two tracks to be released by Kitchen Sink Press in 1972. Typically, "River Blues/Wisconsin Wiggles" and a later single were pressed at 78rpm.

"I liked that idea, reviving the 78," he stated, "But those two 78s did not sell well. We had overlooked the fact that, by 1972, almost nobody possessed hi-fi with 78 speed on the turntable anymore!"

But this marked the beginning of Crumb's recording career, and soon trading under the name of the Cheap Suit Serenaders, even ventured out on tour.

"It was always kind of fun travelling with the Cheap Suits. They were an interesting and wacky band of eccentrics. We had a few ego problems, but so it goes in the band business. Decent food?? Soft pillows?? Ha Ha… Those guys would eat anything – donuts, hot dogs, whatever. And we slept anywhere, under a kitchen table, in a hallway… we were young, and our 'tours' were anything but deluxe affairs… But yeah, it was an adventure, free of responsibilities, a good way to meet girls. Of course only the truly odd and crazy females were attracted to us. We had no groupies, but there was the occasional odd-ball girl that would take up with us, or one of us. I got my share. I can't complain."

Crumb and his Cheap Suits also got their share of studio time, recording and releasing three albums in the early-Seventies although, like many musicians, he found that getting the right sound was hard work.

"The recording studio is a brutal situation. It causes nervous breakdowns and bands to break up. It is real hard work. It can be devestating to hear yourself during playback. The engineer will isolate your part and turn the volume way up for all to scrutinize. Also,

most of the recording engineers we had to work with did not seem to understand how to record a group of acoustic string players. They always wanted to put a microphone right up against your instrument, which produced an awful, unnatural sound. It took us years of bitter experience with these lordly fellows with their big soundboards, to have the confidence to argue with them and convince them to let us record with just one or two microphones placed several feet away from us, which produced a much more natural and pleasing sound. It is amazing to gradually realise that, with all their fancy multi-track equipment, they did not grasp this simple equation about string band music."

Crumb's music is delicious fun and all fans of his work are ordered to seek it out in order to obtain a fully-rounded picture of this most-famed of underground cartoonists. Pick up the recent *Robert Crumb Handbook* which also comes with a compilation CD.

Another underground artist who played live and made it onto vinyl was Peter Bagge, who defined Seattle-slacker culture through his adventures of Buddy Bradley in *Hate* at the beginning and high watermark of the grunge movement. Indeed when Buddy managed a friend's band – Leonard and the Love Gods – it led to a brilliant comics and music crossover. Typically, Bagge got involved in music by accident when a band came together out of Fantagraphics publishing house responsible for his work. The core of the group was Eric

© Peter Bagge. *Hate* is published by Fantagraphics Books.

Reynolds (guitar/vocals) and Andy Schmidt (bass/vocals).

"It was one of those things where the guys had taught themselves their instruments a couple of weeks before, and had the audacity to play in front of people," he recalls.

Bagge – who learned to drum in junior high school – made the mistake of feeling sorry for them as they toiled away at their first gig during a Halloween party "and after a few beers I kept the beat for them. For one song." As Bagge still had a set of drums in his garage, he was asked to join the band.

"I was reluctant, but said that I would only play with them if they could get a paying gig. Then just to humiliate me, somebody offered us fifty dollars to play in a bar. So I was stampeded (laughs)."

Thus began the career of the Action Suits.

Bagge originally intended to play a few gigs and quit. He was prevented from jumping ship by a miracle.

Art: Peter Bagge, Music: The Action Suits.

"All of a sudden Eric was writing really good songs, the type that very much appealed to me, with a Beatles' poppy lilt to them. I suddenly liked this band I was playing in and I had never expected to like it. Then we had a new mission – simply to become competent enough to clean up the songs enough so we could record them."

This involved practice and building up chops in the Seattle live circuit.

"I think that we might have played six or seven times in front of people and I hated it. I couldn't stand it. I'm not a slamdancer and here in Seattle at the time there was that punk ethic where anything goes and its cool and *de rigueur* to make noise and throw stuff. For me, you practice and you practice and you think that you sound good. So when you get on stage I want people to hear what we have been working on (laughs). To me, in my mind this is a recital! So when I'm up there playing, every time I see some drunk up front screaming and hollering I feel like slinging my drumstick right at his fucking head! 'Hey! We're playing up here!'"

The Action Suits released three singles in 1996, all with Bagge cover art. They're not bad, especially "Visualize Ballard". At that stage Bagge took a bow and left the stage, "by the time we had made a handful of recordings that was it for me. I was way too old to be in a rock and roll group (laughs) so I had to quit." Still, it was fun whilst it lasted.

Other comic book artists and writers who have made it into the recording studio include Alan Moore, Grant Morrison and Mike Allred, who had the audacity to record an entire soundtrack with his band The Gear for a film scripted and directed by Mike Allred! When asked why he formed a band his answer was pert and worthy, "like any rock'n'roll entity – ya just GOTTA!"

Joe Quesada, who as Editor In Chief helped revive Marvel's fortunes after near bankruptcy, had a musical past. "I was a struggling New York singer/songwriter musician almost as long as have been in comics," he confided to my tape recorder in a transatlantic call.

"It literally is a whole other life that I led before actually becoming an artist in the comics industry."

Quesada was in a band called Idle Chatter, taking care of lead vocals and rhythm guitar.

"It was very pop-rock towards rock and roll stuff. Two-and-a-half- to three-minute songs and then out! Nothing very complicated but very hooky stuff. It was a lot of fun to watch, to hear and to play."

When it came to getting a record contract in the Eighties, record companies never got past the Idle Chatter phase themselves.

"This was way back before the time when independent labels became really a very important and viable option for bands, so we were playing when arena rock was very, very big and we were more a sort of underground pop act. We were recorded quite often, but we were auditioning for the big guns like Columbia and Capitol and all those sorts of labels. That we were the world's greatest unsigned band is the way I look at it now!"

Some artists have combined both careers. Jeffrey Lewis has not only recorded two albums for London's Rough Trade label, but also produces self-published comics like *Jeff's European Travel Diary* of 1999, *Come To My Show*, *Trip To Key West*, *The Worldwide Comix Scavenger Hunt* and *Reflections On Tomorrow Thus A Yesterday Flower Shall Doom*.

"It is almost a hand-made item as I am still putting them together myself," he told me. "I staple each one myself and all that sort of thing, so it is similar to my music before I was signed, when I would put my music out on homemade cassettes. Each one would come with a little comic, so it was basically a homemade item."

Like the personal work of Robert Crumb or Joe Sacco, Lewis's comics document his life, travels and his experiences as a lo-fi musician. Lewis injects his comics with frank autobiography, such as a novel method of masturbation that involves penetrating the space between the mattress and base of a single bed. When questioned on this, uh, stiff subject, he replied:

"If the whole point of these comics is full disclosure of what my daily life is like then everything has got to be in there otherwise it will not be a worthwhile project."

To promote his musical career Lewis has even produced promotional bubble gum with a comic strip hand-drawn on each individual wrapper.

235

© Jeffrey Lewis

"It was probably more effort than it was worth, but I think that people appreciated it for that aspect of it."

Musically, Lewis has been bracketed in a movement called Anti-Folk, and his first Rough Trade album *The Last Time I Did Acid I Went Insane* (2001) is recommended, especially great tracks like "The Man With The Golden Arm" and "The Chelsea Hotel Oral Sex Song".

On the subject of oral sex, no one has captured the rock and roll touring experience better than Joe Sacco. This artist, whose *Palestine* (2001) raised art as autobiography and social comment to new levels, acted as a member of the roadcrew and T-shirt seller for an American independent band touring Europe in 1988. The resulting thirty-page strip is a compelling insight into the mo-

notony, fun and pleasure of life on the road inside the small empire of a transit van.

Rather than draw from the perspective of a fly on the dashboard, Sacco is right there in the trenches with the boys, capturing details like the smoking, bitching, backstage catering and "even the dish who gets laid in Heidelberg knows to smile for the soft lead pencil."

That Sacco does not get laid during the entire tour is a point of great amusement to the band, especially when he defends himself by stating, "All the ones I liked had boyfriends."

He is then reminded of one of the rules out on the road that is probably followed by bands as diverse as the Strokes, Velvet Revolver, Interpol and Aerosmith:

"Didn't we tell ya? You ask, 'Do you have a

boyfriend?' And if the answer's yes, you ask… 'IS HE HERE?'"

At the other end of the musical spectrum is scratch DJ Eric San, aka Kid Koala. On his two excellent albums *Carpal Tunnel Syndrome* (2001) and *Some Of My Best Friends Are DJs* (2003) he has created tracks by scratching together snippets of hundreds of different records to arrive at compelling sonic melanges. If you like DJ Shadow you'll love this guy. Comic art is as vital to San as his music, and therefore each CD is packaged with small comic books.

"It's all about telling a story," he told me, "I can tell stories with drawings and I can tell stories using bits of vinyl records. I like to do both."

San has a delightful graphic style and that rare ability to tell stories without words. The 38-page *Carpal* comic features the adventures of a small, music-loving robot who falls in love with a girl. This story was expanded on San's third release, *Nufonia Must Fall*, a 339 page graphic novel that, once again without words, details this unlikely and ultimately unfulfilled love affair. San would work on this book whilst out on the road.

"When you are out on tour you spend a lot of time waiting around or travelling, so I just worked on the book during this time."

Not only is *Nufonia* recommended to all as a graphic novel, but it comes with a soundtrack CD which can be played when reading the story or enjoyed as stand-alone music. This is a brilliant marriage of music and comics. Although San's work as a musician has received critical acclaim and seen him supporting Radiohead, as well as collaborating with the Gorillaz, it is hoped that his excellent work as an artist will receive more attention in the future.

One of the most unusual artist/musicians is Mike Hoffman. As a comic book artist, Hoffman has a highly elaborate painted style which has drawn favourable comparison with the legendary artist Frank Frazetta, best known for his brilliant fantasy artwork and *Conan the Barbarian* covers.

"All classical artists go to fine art museums to see paintings of Hercules and Greek Gods and things like that," says Hoffman. "Frazetta comes out of that tradition, even though he did work in comics, which I do not think is a bad way to practice setting up scenes and putting figures in scenes. I like doing figures like that and have them in as little clothing as possible so you can see what is going on with the anatomy. So subjects like mythology and pre-history, or ancient history, lend themselves better to doing that."

As well as lushly illustrating and self-publishing comics like *Tigress Tales*, *Octavia*, *Lost Worlds* and *Madame Tarantula* in recent years, Hoffman has begun to record and release his own CDs.

"I have been doing music for almost as long as I have been doing art," he recalls with pride. "I got into it when I was about fifteen years-old. I stole a guitar out of an unlocked car and that is how I kind of got started. I was in a punk band in the Seventies called the Semantics, in South Carolina. We were sort of more intellectual than punk, wrote all our own songs. At the time I think we were the only band in the whole state who wrote their own songs."

When the band split up, Hoffman dedicated his playing hands to comic book art and illustration, but in recent years has returned

© Kid Koala / *Nufonia Must Fall* is published by ECW Press.

to music. This journey began when Hoffman contacted John Mikl Thor with a proposal to draw a comic about the metal superman. Agreement was reached resulting in *Thor The Rock Warrior* which came out in 2001.

"At some time we thought it would be a good idea to do a second comic book," recalls Hoffman, "and the idea – *Beastwomen From The Centre Of The Earth* – was obviously a sort of B-Movie title. I went ahead and released it, and it did fairly well in the comics market. Then later, I got the idea to do a concept album based on it."

Thus Hoffman wrote and recorded six tracks, as did Thor, and the resulting album

not only captured the feel of the comic, but also stands up as pretty good music in its own right.

"A lot of it was Mike's ideas too," recalls Thor, "it was just an adventure of Thor, what happens to him after falling into the moon pool (at the end of the first comic) that goes to the centre of the Earth. He then goes into the Mushroom World, so I wrote the song "Mushroom World", where the lyrics start 'Where am I? What place is this?' He tries to find out where he is and comes across all these different creatures."

There is not only talk of a film and electronic game based on the *Beastwoman* comic

© Mike Hoffman.
www.mikehoffman.com.

and album, but Thor and Hoffman under-took a brief tour of Canada to promote the album which Hoffman found to be great fun. Even more fun was releasing his own solo albums.

"The first one I did was a Spaghetti Western album, and since then I have done a sort of Tikki Polynesian album. The latest one is a monster album, a bit like Spike Jones. Some of it is overt comedy stuff, but other songs are regular rock songs based around monsters."

This last CD, aptly called *Monster University*, is great entertainment, with tracks like "Bad Brain", "Jekyll and Hyde", "Goodbye Transylvania" and "Kid Frankenstein".

Although several comic artists and writers have made music, there are a number of musicians who have written and drawn comic books. Glenn Danzig is best known for musically exploring some of the more interesting caverns of Hell, including Lucifer's fall from grace, on the 1993 album *Black Aria*.

He set up his own comic book company in the mid-'90s called Verotik, and began to personally script and publish several comics. *Death Dealer*, *Jaguar God*, *Verotika* and the deliciously named *G.O.T.H.* are just a few of his works aimed at mature readers, containing cracking stories combined with rich, compelling art from the likes of the legendary Frank Frazetta, Mitch Byrd and Simon Bisley. Bisley incidentally, was an English artist who drew a brilliant Batman and Judge Dredd team-up in 1991, called *Judgement In Gotham*, that featured Judge Death impersonating Mick Jagger at a rock concert and running through his own peculiar version of "Sympathy For The Devil". Come to think of it, Bisley was also a pretty good metal drummer himself, but I digress…

Shock-rocker Rob Zombie's love of horror has also not only seen him enjoy a vastly successful solo career, make delightfully gory feature films, and write comics with a suitably horror-based theme.

"I was always a big comics fan," he told me. "I started reading them back in 1972, mainly classic Marvel Comics stuff, *The Fantastic Four*, *Spider-Man*, *The Hulk* and all that. There were not as many comics at that point as there are now. I pretty much read everything as there was only about twelve different titles."

Although his band, White Zombie, and then his solo career took up his energies, comics was a medium he was interested in working in, especially as he was a fair artist himself.

© Mike Hoffman

"I can't remember if I got a letter or an email or phonecall, but someone at Crossgen contacted me and asked if I would be interested in doing a comics project," he recalls. "I had been wanting to do one for a long time, and previously the timing had not been right, but when they called it was the right time, so that is how it started."

The resulting comic was called *Rob Zombie's Spookshow* and the first issue was pub-

Artist Simon Bisley. © & ™ Rebellion A/S. All rights reserved.

lished in November 2003. Although Zombie does appear in the comic, the thrust of this series was more a showcase for his writing talents.

"A band like Kiss are more like characters. I don't think the band write the stories or anything in their comics. I am more of a behind-the-scenes guy."

Spookshow was an excellent comic with each issue containing four ongoing horror stories penned by Zombie, drawn by different artists.

"That was my idea," says Zombie, "I liked that because that way I could have a lot of different storylines and I thought it would make it much more interesting to the reader."

Thus, *The Return Of Screaming Lord Zombie* was illustrated by the legendary Gene Colan, who had enjoyed a memorable stint on Marvel Comics' *Iron Man* and *Tomb Of Dracula*.

Although Crossgen hit an iceberg, *Spookshow* continued to be published, and the stories that mixed gore, horror and humour began to attract a following.

"I think at first people were confused because they thought it was supposed to be serious, and they did not get that it was supposed to be funny," recalls Zombie, "but now they have got into the groove, people are really digging it."

To be fair, it is hard not to enjoy the wrestler El Superbeast's stories, especially in issue 4 in a story titled 'Night Of The Living Ringos', or 'Deadbeat Beatlemania!' As you might guess, it features a horde of zombies based on the former Beatles' drummer. Their attempts to kill El Superbeast's girlfriend are foiled when she distracts them by pretend-

ing to see original Beatles' drummer Pete Best behind them! "This is not good! I can't go back to Rory Storm and the Hurricanes!" moans one of the Ringos before they are decapitated and slain to rest.

The stories in *Spookshow* also involved characters like Doctor Satan and Captain Spaulding, drawn from Zombie's first feature film *House of a 1,000 Corpses*. This film is totally hardcore stuff – not for the faint of heart – and Zombie transferred a similar X-rated style to a comic called *The Nail*, a four-part series published in 2004 by Dark Horse comics.

"I had already written the idea and was going to try pitching it as a movie, but when they came to me and asked if I had any ideas for a comic, I thought it would be great for a comic because it is pretty over-the-top."

This is putting it mildly. The first issue starts with a guy receiving a blow job from his girlfriend, having his head lopped off by a chain-wielded by two demonic bikers, and ends with a young girl walking out of the woods in nothing but her white panties splattered with blood.

"It's not really for kids," says Rob, "there is so much nice superhero stuff I did not want to do that. That does not interest me. I figured out that whatever I found entertaining was what I would do."

In this instance the girl's father, a wrestler called the Nail, takes on the biker gang with bloody consequences not seen on a page since EC horror comics were banned back in the Fifties.

Although comics and music are different mediums, Zombie believes that they are "interconnected because the fans of the music are basically the fans of the comics. They

very much crossover into one big amalgam. The people who like the kind of music I do, like comic books or like horror movies. There is a lot of crossover and it works out beautifully."

Another crossover that worked beautifully emerged from the world of Hip Hop. In 1993 the Wu-Tang Clan released a brilliant debut album called *36 Chambers*. What made the album compelling was the fact that the music and beats were underpinned by samples culled from old kung fu movies. Over this backdrop, Method Man, Old Dirty Bastard (RIP), Ghost Faced Killer and U-God delivered spectacular raps, singing their own praises and spouting the Wu-Tang philosophy. The production was master-

minded by Wu-Tang supremo The Rza, who was not only into kung fu movies, but comics fan as well.

"Not every member of the Clan is a comics fan," he told me. "The only true comics lovers – the TRUE comics lovers – is me and Method Man. Method Man had the biggest collection, and I had the biggest collection, but I got robbed of my collection. We were the two guys who would go out every day and spend our lunch money on comics."

So, what comics did Rza buy in the Statten Island area of New York? Well, they were mostly the superhero output of DC and Marvel.

"Some of the first things I got hold of were the 1977 issues of *Spider-Man*. The story with the Green Goblin and Mary Jane, before they started coming up with the clone story and all that shit. I had those issues. I collected every issue of *Daredevil*. Also *Shang Chi Master of Kung Fu* I had every issue, as well as *Luke Cage Hero For Hire*, *Power Man* and *Iron Fist*. I had twelve cent issues of *The Fly*, the *Karate Kid*, *Superman*. *Moonknight*, *Rom the Space Knight* I had the whole collection. My favourites, of course, were *The Fantastic Four* and *The Silver Surfer*. The earlier comics I was a fanatic for. Once they got into the *X-Factor* and all that, it got too crazy, but I had all the *X-Men*, all the classic Marvels up to the year 1990. I could go on and on and on and on and on and on and on with comics man!"

In 1999 this love of kung fu and comics reached a logical conclusion when Rza was contacted by writer Brian Haberlin, whose credits included writing for *Spawn* as well as *Kiss Psycho Circus*.

"He had a comic deal with Image and reached out to some people inside the company to have a meeting with me, and we formed a partnership to put out comic books," recalls Rza.

The story of the *Nine Rings of Wu-Tang* began in the present day, with a black archaeologist discovering an ancient sword full of antique scrolls detailing the adventures of "the 'fabled' Prince Rakeem (the Rza) and his Wu-Tang Clan, nine Moorish warriors who were the supposed godfathers of a higher human awareness and spirituality."

Rza contributed ideas regarding the plot and characters to writers Haberlin and Aaron

Bullock. When the first issue hit the streets in November 1999, sales were very strong.

"The first issue was the number two selling comic book in the country," recalls Rza with pride. "The only thing that beat it was the *X-Men*. The first three issues of *Wu-Tang* were at the top of the charts. Seventy thousand units a month!"

Like Gene Simmons, Alice Cooper and Jerry Garcia before him, Rza got to see himself in comic-book form.

"At first I thought, 'What the fuck am I doing bald-headed? Why the fuck have I got an earring in my ear? I don't wear no fucking earrings!' I had to approve some of the drawings, and I also modulated my character. My character is bald-headed, but I wear a head full of braids. I said, 'Okay, I don't mind my character being bald-headed, but when he gets angry I want his fucking eyeballs to turn white!' There are certain things that you want to speak out on and there are other things you want to leave to the mind of the artist and the people making the comic, because you have got to realise that this is a comic book. This is not a biography or an autobiography. It is meant to be fiction."

The first five issues of the *Wu-Tang* comic fleshed out the nine characters based on the real-life Clan, as well as gently unfurling the flag of the plot. In a nutshell, there was a Shaolin temple of Monks who had mastered the 36 Chambers of the Wu Tang style, which involved fighting with weapons like swords. As each Chamber was completed, the monk would replace one of his natural teeth with a gold one, and those skilled enough to reach the 36th Chamber had platinum set into their gold front teeth.

Typically, an evil Manchurian Emperor had the monks killed, leaving just one Moor survivor who began to train a small band of warriors in Wu-Tang skills. This legendary band – each with a unique fighting style – then take on and knock several tons of shit out of the army of the Emperor.

Sadly, readers never got to see the shit fly. *Nine Rings* did not get beyond five issues due to artistic and business-related problems. An interesting story, but a can of worms best not to get into here. The important thing is that the comic book adventures of the Wu Tang may not be over.

"I think we will continue with it because now everything is reverting back," says Rza. "I have the story of the *Nine Rings* floating around Hollywood, and people are getting interested, so I'm sure it won't be the last you have heard of it."

With Rza having a number of soundtracks like Tarantino's *Kill Bill* under his belt, developing an acting career and with eyes set on getting behind the camera I imagine that this is true. After all, the Wu-Tang Clan 'Ain't Nuthing Ta Fuck With!'

Tank Boy, Tank Girl and Sunshine In A Bag

I'm standing on one of the rolling hills of Cheshire. This particular hill is a few miles outside of Macclesfield and down a long lane broken up by several cattle grids. I've been on this hill since mid-morning. From this elevated spot the view is fantastic, although the most impressive sight is not a prominent church spire, or the bald rolling hills, but a large tank that is no more than fifteen feet away from the end of my nose.

Sitting in the driving seat is Stephen Morris from Manchester's famed New Order. I'm here to interview Stephen about his passion for collecting military vehicles for *The Sun-*day *Times* motoring section. You might not know this, but Stephen owns four military vehicles whose previous one careful owner was the British Army. Technically speaking, the fifteen-ton beast whose diesel engine is growling in front of me like a lion at feeding time is not a tank at all, but an Abbot 105mm self-propelled gun. This piece of mobile artillery was the first 'tank' that Stephen acquired back in 1993. Bought from a dealer's forecourt, it was snip at just under £6,000.

"The great thing about tanks," he enthused earlier, "is that you get a hell of a lot of metal for your money!"

For photographic purposes, Stephen has taken the assault gun out of the barn it shares with the three other beasts of his collection and driven it into a convenient field next to his farmhouse property. That is where I am now.

Those who have enjoyed Stephen's celebrated drumming and programming skills with Joy Division and New Order, would have been equally impressed by the deft way he employs two steering rods to inch the tank through a very narrow gate and move it at speed up the incline of the field. However, the photographer is not happy. Like all of his profession, arriving at the optimum combination of light, background and subject matter is everything, and he is prepared to take time and effort to arrive at a satisfactory vista for his digital shutter.

Walking up to the tank he asks Stephen if he could swing the monster around backwards and have the tank facing the brow of the hill. This will improve the shot. Stephen is happy to accommodate the request, firing up the engine and getting busy with the steering rods. What happens next is farce of the highest order.

Rather than going up the hill to turn the tank around, Stephen decides to reverse down the hill, turn around and then drive back up. As he starts this simple three-point, turn the weight on the tank tracks cuts through the soft turf into the yielding wet soil beneath. After a lot of revving of the engine, the tank gets stuck. Stephen is not too bothered and sets about attempting to move the beast out of the morass. He is helped by

an ancient monument in human form who – I later discover – does odd jobs around Stephen's farm. This old geezer shouts at the famed drummer as if he is a hard-of-hearing sheep dog.

"Left track! Go on! Go on, you bugger!"

But we get nowhere. The tank tracks have removed so much grass that they cannot get a purchase on the soft earth below.

Things take a bad turn when, with Stephen trying to reverse back out of the mud, the tank begins to slide down the hill under its own momentum and bursts through the barbed wire fence encircling the field. The tracks chew through wood and wire with impressive ease. The photographer, who indirectly caused this mayhem in pursuit of the ideal snap, looks as if he has been informed that his fly is undone when he is wearing no underpants. The tank is none the worse for wear– and apart from a red face and a few beads of heroic sweat – neither is Stephen.

Personally, I am totally amused by the turn of events, but as this is my first full feature commission for *The Sunday Times* I dare not laugh out aloud. Unlike *Record Collector*, *Total Car Audio* and *Four Four Two* a little decorum is required. However, the old geezer next to me feels no such constraints and begins to cackle up a fit.

Thankfully, things turn out fine as, not having to worry anymore about hitting the fence, Stephen swings around and positions the tank at the bottom of the hill.

But is the photographer happy? Oh no. To get the ultimate shot, Stephen has to go back to the barn to drive out another vehicle and place it strategically next to the tank. This Daimler Ferret Mark IV scout car with its yellow desert camouflage looks fantastic.

Stephen informs us that it was a British Army white elephant, as the wheels are too big and without the benefit of power steering it takes forever to turn the wheel. When the photos have been snapped, it takes forty-five minutes and the employment of a jack and hammer to turn the wheels and get it back inside the barn. As I watch the old geezer and the photographer jack up the Ferret for the fourth time so we can heave the front wheels around, I get to see one of those rare sights of nature. To my right is a large stone building, and set in the side of its wall is a large, rectangular window the size of a telephone box. Through the window I can see Peter Hook, bass slung around his shoulder, furiously plucking the strings as he lays down a track for the next New Order album. Which, as this book goes to print has just been released.

Later, with the tanks back in the barn, I manage to catch fifteen minutes with Hooky who, like a professional comedian, gives value for money discussing Stephen's passion for military vehicles:

"I do believe that by the side of the bed – Gillian (Stephen's wife and previous New Order member) told me – he has a load of tank manuals. He actually sits there at night reading tank manuals. Don't tell him I told you that!"

Hooky also relates how, in typical rock star fashion, Bernard Sumner and himself delight in forcing Morris to give military fairground rides to visiting rock stars like ex-Smashing Pumpkin, ex-Zwan, Billy Corgan or Primal Scream's Bobby Gillespie. They all ask if the gun works and are dismayed to discover that it does not. So, they can't have a go, which is probably a good thing – because with friends

like these Manchester would probably be subject to regular shelling.

With Hooky in relaxed mood, the conversation turns to music and comics.

"I had every issue of *2000AD*," confesses the low-slung bass master. "I had that from Number one – about twelve years' worth of issues and my mum threw them out because they were all cluttered up under the bed. Mothers and girlfriends, they just don't understand. And wives."

New Order are not great lovers of intensive press campaigns, but he admits that he was tickled pink when, rather than take a photograph of him, *Deadline* magazine actually drew him.

"They did an interview and did a cartoon of me with Tank Girl which was amazing."

Which, after driving at length down that dirt track and over the cattle grids brings us to the subject at hand.

There have been very few attempts to publish magazines that mix music with comics. In America, Denis Kitchen first braved the waters in 1982 with a magazine called *Bop*, proudly proclaiming itself as 'America's first and only music comix magazine'.

"It was my hunch that we could reach an audience that read comic books and was also interested in music," he recalls. "I'm not sure that the premise was faulty, but I allowed a woman called Catherine Yronwode to edit it because she was both a big comics fan and a music nut. It was a real eclectic magazine and tried to be all things."

This is true. Despite a glorious front cover depicting two dancing jukeboxes, the editorial choices made by Yronwode were strange. Although a four-page story on Jerry Lee Lewis and Teen Beat 63 (with a brief cameo

© John Pound. *Bop* published by Kitchen Sink.

from Johnny Rotten) were excellent, other stories left a lot to be desired. Kitchen is the first to agree.

"There was a piece by an artist called Alex Toth. Now, Alex Toth is a genius, but he did this dumb thing about a guy tap-dancing in the dark for five pages which was just stupid."

In many respects, the problem with *Bop* was that the content did not reflect the current music back at itself, but seemed to be too interested in the past. To say that Kitchen took a bath on *Bop* is an understatement.

"I think that is the only book I ever published that I ever destroyed copies of as it was unsaleable. I could not give copies away and we literally ended up dumping scores of cartons into a landfill. I destroyed eight to ten thousand of them."

After one issue Kitchen halted production of a second which was a mercy killing. Looking back with hindsight he believes that *Bop* should have done the obvious.

"We should have focussed on rock and gone for a younger audience, or it should have had issues that were thematic. Have a 'Blues' issue and do everything from early blues to contemporary blues and have a blues cover. If we had proper distribution, anyone interested in the Blues would see it, although they would not necessarily buy the next issue on Rockabilly or whatever. That way we would find our audience and maybe after six issues the numbers would say to me, 'Jeez we've got to do another rocker or we're dead!'"

Although *Bop* was stillborn, in England a magazine called *Deadline* had more success. It was the brainchild of artists Brett Ewins and Steve Dillon, who planned a magazine that fused "comics, media, music and more"

into one publication. Tom Astor – who coughed up the cash to make the dream a reality – explained the concept to me.

"There was a real sort of feeling that British comics like *2000AD* were knocking at the door of more mainstream media. *Deadline* was an attempt to realise that, and we floated it to pick up on a broader interest, not to be just about traditional comic subject matter. There was always the idea that *Deadline* should not just be sold in comic shops but present itself more as a traditional magazine, although that was probably more of a statement of intent."

The first issue of *Deadline* was published in October 1988 and nailed its colours to the mast encompassing interviews with Jah Wobble, comedian Dave Allen and artist Brian Bolland. As for strips, Ewins drew 'Johnny Nemo' a hard-nosed futuristic detective story written by Peter Milligan. Dillon drew a strip called 'Sharp'. But the star of the first issue was 'Tank Girl' by Jamie Hewlett and Alan Martin. This five-page story of a beautiful, hard-drinking, tank-driving female bounty-hunter operating in the Australian outback on the trail of a gang of kangeroos was compelling. That she ended up getting off with the leader of the "foul mouthed marsupials" before blowing his brains out at the end of the strip, was the cherry on the cake. As with 'Judge Dredd' in *2000AD*, *Deadline* had its hit strip.

"I met Brett (Ewins) when he was invited to my college in Worthing," recalls Hewlett today. "One of my teachers knew him, and she approached him to do a lecture about comics, basically. I had been a big fan of his for years and after he had done his bit, I went down the pub with him and showed him all of my stuff. He really liked it, said stay in touch, finish out college and we would speak in the future. When he was getting *Deadline* together he contacted me and said, 'Have you got any ideas?'"

Ewins explained to Hewlett that there were going to be four strips in *Deadline*. One by him, and one by Steve Dillon and they were both going to be doing male characters.

"They wanted me and Phillip Bond (who did the other strip 'Wired World') to do a strip each with a female lead character," continues Hewlett. "That was the brief. I think I drew a picture of a girl with a tank in the background – 'Tank Girl' – that was it! It was as simple as that. We also knew a couple of girls that we used to hang around with at college. Two in particular – I have said this many times in the past – who were much like Tank Girl; always drunk, quite lairy and both very beautiful girls. We used to hang out and have a real laugh with them."

As this was his and writer Alan Martin's first break in comics, Hewlett spent a great deal of time and effort in drawing the first episode of 'Tank Girl'. With this attention to detail, the first and subsequent strips of his vibrant art was worthwhile. It was comics, Jim but not as we know it. In the third issue – Dec-Jan 1989 in a story called 'Bigmouth Strikes Again!', Tank Girl kills a bounty-hunter on her trail and gives two priests who drop out of an aeroplane a lift to the second coming of Christ on Earth.

"I think we were just grotty, snotty, little 21 year-olds enjoying ourselves," recalls Hewlett, "It seemed to hit a nerve and people liked it."

Of course, what made also made 'Tank Girl' a hit was that a certain proportion of people did *not* like it.

"We had some serious complaints. We had mothers writing in about the language and that. Brett and Steve used to just say, 'Oh we've had some complaints and then they would just laugh about it. They would never say, 'Can we tone it down a bit boys?' Brett was just bonkers anyway, so he was like 'Do what you like, I don't care.' But no-one pulled us off the shelves. I think W.H. Smiths threatened to stop stocking it at one point but they never did. So we got away with it."

Typically 'Tank Girl' was chock-full of musical references. As everybody should know, 'Bigmouth Strikes Again' was a Smiths' song. Some monthly strips even told readers what Hewlett and Martin were listening to at the time, as well as what films were assaulting their eyes.

"It seemed obvious to put those things in there," recalls Hewlett. "I was into comics and I had all of my favourite artists and stuff, but apart from bits of my drawing style, I think a lot of our influences were coming from films and music and weird shit that we thought was great – like having censorous things in there, or referencing *The Italian Job*. Also, we never wanted to do a serious heavy comic, we wanted it to be a bit of a piss-take, whilst at the same time do something that we felt was really pushing it. All the swearing and stuff; which we were always told was not allowed (laughs). We just kept using it because we knew it would upset somebody."

This desire to shock extended to Tank Girl having to consume a new beer called Spunk in one issue.

"G'day, I'm here to tell you about Spunk Beer," says a Mafia salesman on TV, "It's bloody lovely, I'm always drinking it and so is my wife... erm... and my barely-formed daughter and my dad... and they all say 'Drink Spunk Beer'".

The success of 'Tank Girl' saw *Deadline* promote the strip like mad. As well as the monthly outing in the magazine, there were all manner of posters, pull-outs, calendars and even T-shirts. Tank Girl was also generously splashed over the front page.

"*Deadline* would probably have been more commercially successful if, after the first issue, we had smelt the wind and changed the name to *Tank Girl Magazine*," recalls Astor.

Ironically another magazine called *Heartbreak Hotel* had launched just before *Deadline* aiming to fill the niche "where music and comics meet", but as they had nothing on board as good as 'Tank Girl' to draw in and keep readers, it hit an iceberg and went down pretty quickly.

Deadline continued to thunder out and Hewlett, of course, was having the time of his life.

"We had our little scene in Worthing," he recalls with affection. "Phillip Bond was there, Alan and me, and we had a big gang of mates and we used to sit, smoke pot and draw comics all the time. Like it should be really – very unprofessional!" (laughs)

Hewlett, Martin and many of the *Deadline* writers and artists enjoyed a rock and roll existence when they went on the road to undertake brief signing tours. *Deadline* was also quick to encourage female readers inspired by the 'Tank Girl' look to step forward. And with their shaved heads, clad in bras, leather jackets and little else, they did.

"It was good," Hewlett remembers, "We met a lot of them... some got the wrong end of the stick; they thought that being Tank Girl meant being really aggressive, get your tits out and drink a lot. I always thought it was a bit more than that, about challenging things, and sending up everything that was taken too seriously. We met a few that were unbearable, but then we met a few that were great. Not to say that it was the start of girl power, I'm not saying that it was, but it definitely blew away a few cobwebs in the comics industry."

It was also good mileage for *Deadline* to photograph and splash these girls on the cover, and as mini photo-features inside the magazine.

As the months rolled on, money became an issue for Hewlett and Martin. After all, dope and beer did not come cheap in Worthing-on-Sea.

"It was fifty quid a page when it started. Then we did one episode, part two of 'Bells End' it was, then 'Force 10 to Rikki Rikki Bay' and finally the story 'Half a Penny of Tupanny Rice' where me and Alan appeared in the strip and resigned at the end. We actually resigned for real, because they were not paying us enough, mirroring what happened in the story. We handed the story in and they said, 'Great!', and printed it. The next day we told them we were resigning because they were not paying us enough. They quickly upped the page rate to, I think, a hundred quid a page. Which was great! They kept paying us more!"

With brass in pocket, 'Tank Girl' and other strips inspired by their mutual muse continued to thunder out. Typically, as well as references to the music they were listening to, ranging from Ennio Morricone to the Wonder Stuff, there were eventually a few guest appearances by musicians in the strip. One was the Irish pop band the Undertones.

"The episode that we had the Undertones in?" laughs Hewlett, "Jimmy the drummer – I can't remember his second name – I could not draw him for some reason, so I put a paper bag on his head. And we got a letter from him – he's now a butcher in Belfast – and he said, 'I'm very dissapointed that I'm not in it.' So I think the following issue we put him in doing something."

Also featured were Pete Shelley and Steve Diggle from the Buzzcocks, who teach Tank Girl's kangeroo boyfriend Boogla how to play "Harmony In My Head" on the guitar.

"It was just all the people that we were really into. We used to end up hearing from them because they were reading it."

Saying that, unlike *Spider-Man*, *The Fantastic Four* or *Batman* the monthly production of 'Tank Girl', was not always as smooth as the gear change on an automatic gearbox. Hewlett and Martin would quickly bore of having to churn out 'Tank Girl' and so would try out other ideas. "We got into pirates for a while. We thought pirates were great, so let's do a pirate story." And they did for a couple of issues, sailing very close to the port of Incest before they got bored and stopped.

Fireball got much further down the track and ran for several months in 1991.

"*Fireball* was *Wacky Races* meets *Deathrace 2000* which I still think is an idea that should be remade as a live-action film."

Of course, at this time what the owner and various editors of *Deadline* wanted was not 'Pirates' or 'Fireball' or 'Boogla appearing in Arsky and Hutch', but 'Tank Girl'.

However the creative dynamics had changed. "When it started, me and Alan were living together but towards the end I had just got married to my first wife and suddenly you can't spend all day and night drawing without getting nagged at, so it was harder. The strips got better when I got divorced from her and moved back into a flat, and Alan used to come round and hang out all day. We reverted back to our old ways, sitting around all day watching telly, listening to music like the Pixies and drawing. It started going well again. We had a new spurt and got into it again and were really excited. I think the last five 'Tank Girl' strips we did for *Deadline* we were really pleased with. Things like 'Morning Glory', 'Bushman Tucker' and 'The Mount Mushroom Massacre' (co-starring Graeme Coxon)."

One reason why *Deadline* wanted as much 'Tank Girl' as possible in 1994, was because she had been optioned and green-lighted by the Hollywood machine. As co-creators, Hewlett and Martin not only saw some money but had serious fun.

"Obviously we were skint, we did not earn a lot of money from *Deadline*. We were very young and suddenly got the full Hollywood treatment – we fell into the shark pool really. They flew us over there and did the limos and all that."

As for the film, Hewlett recalls that the original script was awful, so he and Martin rewrote it, and in turn this script was rewritten and then toyed with further.

"For a while we were convinced that it might work – although we were young and stupid. We were out in America for the best part of a year, and when you are 22 or 23 years-old and hanging out in LA it is very

© Deadline, Hewlett & Martin.

easy to get carried away with it. We were going to see the rushes and it was looking really good, but when it came out it was…awful."

'Awful' is probably a polite word. It would be wrong to exhume the coffin and kick the corpse that was buried in 1995. Suffice to say Hollywood did the only thing to Tank Girl that she had not experience in the course of her comic adventures – she was anally shafted.

Saying that, she was in good company. Early *Spider-Man* films were dire, as was a Roger Corman version of the *Fantastic Four*. Alan Moore's *Extraordinary League Of Gentlemen* was extraordinarily awful. *Tank Girl* was just another comics-to-cinema conversion whose rough edges were sawn off to guarantee the right rating. Without the foul language, drinking, smoking, dirty underwear and in-your-face sexuality, *Tank Girl* lost her charm.

"I remember when it came out," laughs Hewlett, "we were doing loads of press in England about it and I just slagged it off. Then I got a phone call from the people at MGM just saying, 'Shut up! (laughs) You are not allowed to say that and if you keep on saying that there will be trouble!' So I had to shut up."

Whilst Hewlett and Martin basked in Los Angeles, *Deadline* continued to thunder out. There had been editorial changes. Brett Ewins and Steve Dillon had left the magazine after 18 months at the helm in 1991.

"I think that as *Deadline* developed over the months and years," recalls Tom Astor, "Brett and Steve found that they needed to get back to their comics careers, because they could not live doing comics at the *Deadline* page-rate whilst editing it."

At the same time, Astor took more control, and a succession of editors were employed to steer the ship out of port each month.

"I think I found that the obvious mix was more specifically music and comics. As I got more knowledge of the publishing industry, I knew that we needed to position ourselves on the shelves just to focus it a bit more. It was the obvious thing to link it up with music."

To this end, covers would feature musicians like Carter USM, Frank Black, Dee-Lite, the Smashing Pumpkins, Right Said Fred, Courtney Love and Kurt Cobain. In some instances, Tank Girl was used to help promote bands, as in September 1993 when Tank Girl proudly wore a Teenage Fanclub T-shirt. Along with comic strips, each issue usually featured two or three interviews with bands. Indeed, some comic strips even reflected music back at itself, with Jonathan Edwards regular one page strips in 1994 offering his delightful personal take on legends of rock.

Strips like 'Brian Wilson and His Amazing Pet Theremin', 'Kraftwerk at their Local Electrical Retailers', Nancy Sinatra & Lee Hazlewood as 'Jumble Sale Junkies', 'Phil Spector's Wall Of Sound' and 'Scott Walker and his Ace Bike'. Just to give you a flavour, the last strip features Walker riding around on his Chopper when he discovers that someone has been scrumping his apples. He tracks down Marc Almond and Julian Cope and tells them not to do it again!

With the *Tank Girl* film looming on the horizon, Hewlett's creation was splattered on the cover as often as in 1994 and 1995 in an effort to boost flagging circulation figures. When Hewlett was not availiable – or could not be bothered –*Deadline* drafted others to draw her, like Brian Bolland, Glenn Fabry, Mike McMahon, John Bolton or Nabiel Kanan.

"The *Tank Girl* film was very helpful, but it did not make up the difference," recalls Astor, "it lost some of its cult appeal without gaining any mainstream credibility."

The same song could probably be sung about *Deadline* itself. Repositioning itself as "The Style Mag For Underachievers" it ended up as neither fish nor fowl. The paper quality got better so that strips, like Savage Pencil's 'Dead Duck' and Dom Morris's 'Sadist' looked superb, although this was an attempt to attract more high-ticket advertising. But the thrill had gone. Even buying-in strips from America like *Love and Rockets* and Peter Bagge's *Hate* was a double-edged sword.

Brian Wilson And His Amazing Pet Theremin.

"The reason for that was that it was great stuff," says Astor, "but the sort of people who regularly bought *Deadline* and other comics, would have already known that stuff."

The last issue of *Deadline* was published in late 1995. Like a West End play, it had a good run.

The seed of the Gorillaz was sown when Hewlett and Bond conducted an interview with Blur published in the Dec/Jan 1992 edition of *Deadline*, when the Britpop giants were one hit album and single into their career. Hewlett had met Graeme Coxon a little time before *Leisure* had come out in 1991, when the guitarist was going out with one of his friends. At this time he also struck up a friendship with Albarn who, like everybody else, was a fan of 'Tank Girl'.

As always the interview was conducted in a totally professional manner.

"We just went out and got hideously drunk," recalls Hewlett and reading the two-page interview today, it is obvious that everyone around the table was spanked out of their brains...

JAMIE: "D'you know they reckon they've had people on Mars for about the last 20 years. Apparently the first thing Neil Armstrong said when he landed on the moon was "There's fucking hundreds of 'em". Apparently they had people on the Moon about twenty years before the official landing."

ALEX (JAMES): "Naaaa mate – They wouldn't have had the technology twenty years before."

ALAN (MARTIN): "I reckon so – It's the same way technology goes...which I can well believe... that it's twenty years in advance in Japan. It's all packed away in boxes just sitting on the drawing board."

JAMIE: "They reckon they've been on Mars for a long time, which I can believe, 'cos it's none of our fucking business. They can do what they want and they'll tell us when they feel like it."

Although Albarn and Hewlett became good friends, this was no time for collaboration. Blur would soon storm the towers of pop stardom as Britpop's golden boys, going toe-to-toe with Suede and Oasis, emerging bruised and battered, clutching at least one of the World Title belts and a vast loyal fanbase. With one tanked *Tank Girl* film and Blur albums like *Parklife*, *The Great Escape* and *Blur* under the bridge, Hewlett and Albarn ended up sharing a fridge.

"I had separated from my girlfriend at the time, and was hanging out in London with Damon. He had separated from his girlfriend, so we got a flat and lived together for a year. Obviously we used to sit and watch MTV and spit at the telly at all the manufactured crap. We talked about it one night and I remember saying, 'Why can't somebody manufacture a band properly, why can't it just be done right, why is it so shit? We should do an animated band!' He said, 'Yeah, fucking great idea!' We went to bed (not together dear reader) and I woke up the next day thinking this would be a great idea, as it had never been done properly before. There had been bands that had animation; there had been *Banana Splits* and the *Archies* and stuff, but it had never really been done properly. So I asked him the next day if he was serious about this and he said, 'Yes.'"

Up until this time Albarn's interest in the world of comics had been minimal.

"My only real experience of comics was when I could not think of anything to write for English homework," he confided to me, "so I copied something out from the speech bubbles in a comic and put it all together. I got found out immediately! I was aware of comics, but not really into it. I do love the idea – I still do."

He had reacted strongly to Hewlett's Tank Girl and the artist himself.

"Sharing a flat, we were getting on so well," he recalls, "we began to think how we could extend this into a working relationship, because we had such a similar take on everything. As he was a cartoonist and I was a musician there was really not much more that we could do than create Gorillaz."

From this acorn emerged a musical and visual phenomenon that in many respects is the perfect melding of comics and music in an equal partnership. For Albarn, after pop success and the forensic media intrusion that came with it, the Gorillaz was the ideal vehicle to explore musical ideas away from Blur.

"It was getting harder working in Blur. When it started out I had been able to, well, not dictate but drive the whole thing which was getting harder and harder – especially with Graeme because he wanted to drive more."

The Gorillaz was not only a creative outlet but also a project that did not require his face on an album cover, require him to do press interviews or open his mouth to sing before a live audience on yet another tour.

"We could get away with having these four characters representing the band and it also meant that he could do what he wanted to do musically and experiment," recalls Hewlett. "He did not have to be Damon from Blur making the sort of music that Blur make. He could do Hip Hop he could do whatever

he wanted to do and work with whoever he wanted. It was the four characters that were the band, so it was exciting for him and it was exciting for me."

The fictional band was discussed and they began to work on ideas.

"I went off and started mucking about and he went off to his room and started mucking about," recalls Albarn.

The line-up settled as Murdock (bass), 2D (vocals), Noodle (guitar) and Russel (drums).

"Murdock is Keith Richards," Hewlett laughs, "has to be Keith Richards! 2D is based on one of Blur's crew, a guy called Stuart who I've known for years, he works on their lighting and stuff and always makes me laugh. He has got a really good look and 2D is loosely based on him. The other two came out as they were. Noodle was originally Paula, a twenty-something bird with black hair and I could not get her right. Damon said, 'Look, you're are always drawing pretty girls. You are well known for drawing pretty girls! Why don't you draw something else for a change?' So I drew a little 11 year-old Japanese girl instead, it made sense really."

Although as he is at great pains to stress, "None of them are based on me or Damon."

With Hewlett designing and drawing templates for the animated musicians, Albarn set about exploring musical avenues for the band to explore.

"He did a few demos and it was very much like the situation I had with Alan. My studio was directly above his studio so we hung out together and he did – I think – three demos and I drew a whole bunch of pictures of the characters, and we took them to EMI."

Although Albarn had shifted millions of al-

GLYN.

THIS IS MY FRIEND GLYN, WE WENT TO SCHOOL TOGETHER, WE LIKED 'THE JAM' AND 'THE WHO' AND WE BOTH HAD SCOOTERS. WE BEAT UP ON SQUARES AND SMOKED VANGUARD CIGARETTES. I HADN'T SEEN HIM IN 10 YEARS, BUT I COULD TELL BY HIS TRANSLUCENT COMPLEXION, HIS DARK EYELIDS AND HIS SHIT CLOTHES, THAT WE STILL HAD A LOT IN COMMON. HE LIKES TOM WAITS, AL PACINO AND DRUGS. WE BOTH AGREE THAT 'SUEDE' ARE SHIT AND PORNOGRAPHY IS HOT. IT'S BEEN 10 MONTHS SINCE OUR LAST MEETING BUT I KNOW WHEN I SEE HIM NEXT HE'LL KNOW.

Tank Girl meets Damon Albarn © Deadline, Hewlett & Martin.

bums through Blur, at first the suits at EMI were somewhat confused by the idea behind the Gorillaz.

"It was hard to sell it to everybody really," recalls Albarn. "The hardest thing was getting them to understand that Gorillaz really were a cartoon band, not a cartoon band who existed exclusively in their own world, but one that had the potential to interact with our world."

Of course at the end of the day the project was given the green light.

"They gave us the money," says Albarn, "and work started in earnest."

When it came to making the music for the Gorillaz, this was Albarn's area of expertise. A prolific songwriter, he had no trouble coming up with material and relished the opportunity to let his muse run free.

"To start off it was quite a self-conscious thing to do, writing for cartoons, but then I realised that like any proper collaboration it did not matter what bit came first, because it is not about necessarily working together, because they are two different mediums. It is just about them feeling right together. So I did not pay any concern to Gorillaz because if I tried to create music for them it would be very limited or it would limit me. I decided to make the best album that I could and I used a lot of voices. If I was making a record of my own I would use only my voice, but here I used a lot of different voices, so there were options for Noodle and everyone to feature."

Hewlett only went down to the studio to hang out, although he did play on the first album.

"I played Jew's Harp on one song. He had this Jew's Harp laying around and I picked it up and went (mimes) 'wow, wow'. He says, 'Can you play that? I can't get a note out of it.' I said, 'Just go like this,' but he couldn't do it. So he recorded me playing Jew's Harp. There are some handclaps on there as well."

Albarn went to town musically, pulling in diverse threads like Hip-Hop, over which he laid skeletal arrangements or simply explored the possibilities offered by the recording process. This also extended to collaboration with other musicians.

"When we started doing Gorillaz, me and Damon went to America to meet rappers to work on the album," recalls Hewett. "We met up with the Wu-Tang Clan and D12 and they were all comic book fans. All these Hip-Hop guys are into comics and animation and king fu movies and, of couse, knew *Tank Girl*. With Damon they were like, 'Uh, yeah, uh we think we know your stuff.' With me it was, '*Tank Girl!* You're my man!' Because they all read fucking comics, it is so widespread. It was funny."

The same thing happened when comic book fan and famed scratch artist, Kid Koala came into the studio to add his technique to some of the Gorillaz tracks.

"I went into the studio and I was in awe," he recalls, "there was Jamie Hewlett. Creator of *Tank Girl*."

When word got out in the music business about Albarn and Hewlett's manufactured band, the initial reaction was scepticism. In England the words "manufactured" and "band" when placed in close proximity are seen as a terrible swearword. It conjures up images of boy bands, Minni Vanilli, good looking teenagers who can neither sing or write songs, but who get to the top on image and video.

© Jamie Hewlett.

"The music industry thought that we were taking the piss," recalls Hewlett, so he and Albarn took steps to help their fledgling band.

"Originally, originally, originally it was meant to be a total mystery who was behind it," recalls Albarn, "but it just proved impossible to do that, so to get it off the ground Jamie and I had to do quite a lot of press and stuff, which was okay, but slightly compromised the original idea."

Although Albarn had put the sunshine in a bag, recording fantastic songs like "Clint Eastwood", "Rock The House" and "Dracula" what broke new ground were the rich, lush, eye-popping visuals for the "Clint Eastwood" promotional video designed by Hewlett.

"I obviously directed them with passion and stuff, but the animation process was so slow; it is not until it is complete and they have lit it that you actually see it. You have to be patient. I remember when it was finished going to see it for the first time and being really, really blown away by it. I took a copy back to the office. Damon came up, and he was with Norman Cook (Fatboy Slim) – 'Come in upstairs and meet Jamie' – and we watched it about twenty times in a row. We were all screaming, 'Again! Again! Again! Yeah Man!' So, it was extremely exciting, it was a really good moment to see it come alive."

Come alive is an apt description, as the video is astounding. The opening credit shows the Gorillaz name tagged with spray paint, before the band are introduced playing the song. The ground opens up to reveal an army of Gorillaz, who at one stage dance like zombies in a cheekily visual quote from Michael Jackson's *Thriller* video. Words fail to communicate the vitality of the music and visuals, which still look and sound fresh today.

"I think our trade secret is the colours that he uses are very much the colours of my music," states Albarn. "It is hard to put into words because music is a colour! It is what it does to you emotionally and that is why I think that it works."

Released in 2001, the *Gorillaz* album went on to sell six million copies worldwide and generate more arresting videos for subsequent chart-hitting singles.

"EMI were VERY pleased," laughs Hewlett, "but the album was good and the music was good and the animation was good."

The cutting edge visuals and brilliant music turned the Gorillaz into a phenomenon, such that voice actors were brought in so that the band could do press interviews. Despite being a fictional band, like the Archies before them, the Gorillaz also stepped out into the live arena with a memorable computer-generated performance at the Brit Awards.

"We just sat in the audience and watched our band with great pride," recalls Albarn, "it is more fun that way."

Less fun for Albarn was a small Gorillaz tour, where despite being the lead singer he had to play second fiddle to the animated 2D!

"You really have to accept that you are being removed. It got quite difficult for me towards the end. We were starting to play to 10,000 people from behind a screen and it was odd. I found it very difficult not to get out there in front of the audience. Occasionally the odd leg would come out from behind the screen because I wanted to be out there performing, as it is a very compelling feeling!"

At one stage it looked as if the Gorillaz were heading for the big screen. Negotiations were initiated by Steven Spielberg to turn the characters into a cartoon film but after two years of artistic ping-pong over scripting and storyline, Albarn and Hewlett pulled the plug on the deal, as their vision and the ideas of Dreamworks were too far apart.

"We fell out with Dreamworks," says Albarn. "They were prepared to waste millions and millions on *Spirit* and *Aladdin* when they could have not done either of them and done the Gorillaz album as a movie which might not have been a massive commercial success but would have been really interesting."

As you read this, the new Gorillaz album, *Demon Days*, will have already hit the beaches. When I met Hewlett in the middle of 2004, Albarn had just started work on the music. When I met Albarn in January 2005, he had finished it.

"All the people we have worked with this time around feel very much part of it," he enthused. "It would be very self-conscious walking into a band situation but as this does not really have that, people see it as a club. This time we have got people like Dennis Hopper, Shaun Ryder, Ike Turner (laughs) De La Soul and Neneh Cherry. It is a real mixture of people and that really helps Jamie, as it gives him a cast to work with. It is a really interesting record. Noodle singing to Shaun Ryder, that is going to be great!"

Slaving away with his team to prepare the visuals to go with Albarn's music for first single "Feel Good Inc", Hewlett was also excited by the possibilities offered by the advances of technology. This time round Murdoc, Noodle, 2D and Russel could do interviews in real time as well as tour with a live multi-media show that will make the famed Brit Awards appearance and short tour seem old hat.

Although the Gorillaz have become Hewlett-designed limited-edition Kidrobot toys, despite much kneeling down and begging from EMI, there will not be a computer game.

"We did some Gorillaz music on a Playstation game," recalls Hewlett, "and there was talk of that, but I play an awful lot of computer games. The best computer games are not necessarily games based on characters, but games that are fun to play, like *Resident Evil*, *Halo* and stuff like that. I love playing those. But the *Batman* driving game? So I could not think of a game that could justify having the Gorillaz in it. We did do some on our own website, we did a rip off of *Donkey Kong* and a Gorillaz driving in a jeep game, and we're working on a shooting gallery game. But as for a computer game, I could never come up with something that would make sense if we stuck the Gorillaz in it."

There will be, for now, no Gorillaz comic book either, although Hewlett does confess that he has recently got back to the drawing board. There is demand for new Tank Girl material, although Hewlett will not draw all of the comics.

"I said I would do a five-page strip in each one – me and Alan – and I'll do the covers as well. It is because Alan has written some very funny stuff that might be fun to draw."

He has also contributed a strip to a friend's comic called *Meat 13* of which only 1,000 were printed.

"It is about two gay cowboys who have a gunfight in the nude. One of them gets shot and as he dies he gets a huge erection. The other stands over him and, as he turns away, he has got an even bigger erection!"

Of course as Albarn and Hewlett are swinging high through the trees with the Gorillaz, one imagines that their own cocks are pretty hard as well...

AFTER TWO WEEKS OF TRYING TO TEACH BOOGA TO COOK 'LEAN CUISINE', THE STAFF SEND HIM TO THE WORKSHOP WHERE HE MEETS COLLEGE BAD BOYS PETE DIGGLE AND STEVE SHELLEY. FOR THEIR END OF TERM PROJECT THEY MAKE A PERFECT REPLICA OF A 1963 FENDER TELECASTER.

IT'S FUCKING GREAT, BOOGA, IT'S THE SMOOTHEST GUITAR I'VE EVER SEEN. YOU SHOULD BE PROUD!

CHEERS FELLAS, I COULDN'T HAVE DONE IT WITHOUT YOUR HELP!

C'MON, LET'S GO TO THE COMMON-ROOM AND WE'LL TEACH YOU TO PLAY 'HARMONY IN MY HEAD'!

A YEAR AND A HALF LATER...

HOW DID IT GO, BOOGA? WHAT DID THEY TEACH YOU?

WELL, I LEARNED HOW TO MAKE A POT NOODLE; I'VE GOT KEN HOLM'S ADDRESS; AND I MADE THIS GUITAR AND MY MATES SHOWED ME HOW TO PLAY 'HARMONY IN MY HEAD'.

MOVE OVER DANDO

I'LL GIVE YOU HARMONY IN YOUR FUCKING HEAD!!

EARTH?

SNATCH!

YOU BURK!

CRUNCH!

OW!

HEALTHY EATING WAS STILL AN IMPORTANT FACTOR IN OUR LIVES. WE DECIDED TO FOLLOW UP THE ADDRESS BOOGA HAD BEEN GIVEN. WE GOT ONTO THE DUAL CARRIAGE HIGHWAY INTERSTATE JOURNEY PLANNER ROAD THINGY AND HEADED FOR DUNNSTAIN, A SMALL SEASIDE TOWN ON THE COAST, REKNOWNED FOR IT'S ABUNDANCE OF CELEBRITY RESIDENTS, INCLUDING THE WELL KNOWN AND MUCH LOVED COOKING ACE, KEN!

GO!

16

Allredy, Steady, Go!

Casting an eye over the current rock scene, one of the hottest bands in the business are the White Stripes. Sure, the Strokes, with their New York attitude sparkle like prisms, but Joe, Fab and the boys are more of a screen upon which the image of Tron-like cool are projected by the music press and fans, rather than a TV set pulsing out style instructions. In other words, their excellent music speaks for itself and, unlike say, the Darkness they don't need to resort to cat-suits and pyromania. Then again, I'm crossing the central reservation and straying into the oncoming traffic of another musical genre where such things are expected…

Returning to the White Stripes, putting aside the brother+sister=lovers angle initially whipped up by the English tabloids, the compelling sound generated by Jack and Meg White is vibrant testimony to the power of music. Who would have thought in this modern day and age of sampling, beats and computer generated prowess, that a basic mix of guitar, drums and vocals would be so compelling? The White Stripes hail from Detroit which, as every reform school child is taught on their foster-parent's knee, is the

Red Rocket 7 © Mike Allred. Used with permission.

home of Iggy Pop, the MC5 and Motown records. Inspired by the blues, Jack and Meg have enthralled legions of fans with great songs like "Hotel Yoruba" and "Seven Nation Army", as well as brilliant albums like *Elephant* and their latest offering *Get Behind Me Satan*. Of course, Jack and Meg also have a very strong image. Like the flag of a former Communist state, their wardrobes only fly

the colours of red, white and occasionally black. Thus they would probably also appreciate the cover – if not the electronic music – of Kraftwerk's 1977 opus *The Man Machine* where Ralf, Florian and the boys pose in red shirts and black trousers.

With their strong visual look, and success not only in America but also the UK and Europe, the White Stripes would be ideal to

© Mike Allred.

put into a comic book. Joe Quesada, whose editorial alchemy helped put several new wheels upon the Marvel bandwagon, would not rule it out when we spoke.

"If the White Stripes came to us with a good enough idea for a one-off comic that we felt could be profitable and expand our readership, we would absolutely do it," he purred down the telephone. "No question about it!"

Of course, would such a project get off the ground? Apart from the White Stripes convenient brightly-coloured stage costumes, what sort of plot could you put in the book? Jack meets Wolverine? Jack meets the X-Men? How about Jack's driving accident, broken finger and how he then allegedly tested the healing powers of his hand by spanking Jason Stollsteiner from the Von Blondies? Then again, Jack and Meg swear by ancient equipment and recording techniques, so perhaps they could be sent back to the Sixties in a time machine and indulge in spaced-out adventures with Jimi Hendrix.

Perhaps respected music journalist Charles Shaar Murray, who once scripted a comic about the legendary Purple Haze, could write that one.

Who would draw a White Stripes comic? In an ideal world it would be Robert Crumb. In fact, with his love of old blues records, the legendary underground artist and Jack White would probably hit it off big time, especially if White went out to France and listened to some of Crumb's 78rpm record collection. Sadly, Crumb's fine tastes do not extend to modern musical freemasonary.

"White Stripes?? Never heard of them…" he wrote to me in his letter for this book. So, quoting Pete Townshend, if Crumb can't do it, Who's Next? If it were up to me I would go straight to Mike Allred.

Comics fans reading this book will know that Allred is not only one of the hottest and most stylistically visual artists working in the field today, he is also a mad, rabid, foaming-at-the-chops music fan. Better still, anybody whose eyes have caressed the visual beauty of

Red Rocket 7 © Mike Allred. Used with permission.

Allred's work (check this book's front cover, non-believers!) will know that he has already created a convenient Jack White prototype called Madman. Would Allred entertain pencilling Jack White in a Madman consume?

"Yeah! Let's make it happen," he communicated to me via email. In a strange, but delicious coincidence, like Jack White, Madman wears a costume that is white and red. The occasional black leather jacket also gives him

a cool look. Madman also has a girlfriend who could easily be turned into a sister-like figure called Meg.

Madman is one of many characters that Allred has created. Indeed, as an artist and writer Allred has worked hard to stretch his talents into as many areas as possible. He has not only fermented the Madman universe that extended to hanging out with Superman, but has also taken a step outside the es-

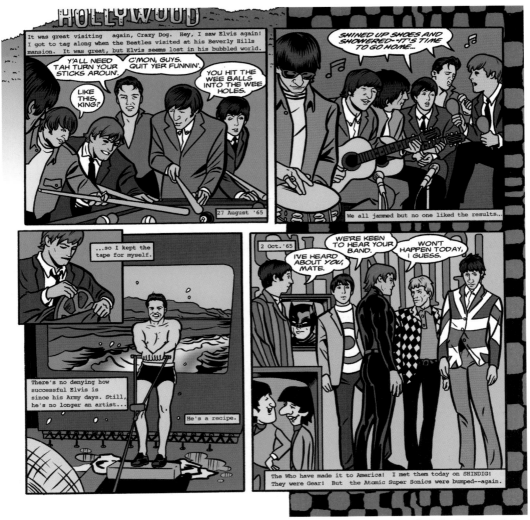

Red Rocket 7 © Mike Allred. Used with permission.

tablished crop circles and published his own comic books about a group of heroes called *The Atomics* under his own AAA (Allred's Atomic Art) Pop Imprint. A possible White Stripes comic aside, Allred has also created the perfect music comic.

Red Rocket 7 was conceived by Allred as part of a wider scheme of things.

"I wanted to make a multimedia project that stretched comics. Music, movies comics. And tie them together."

In many respects his previous work had been leading up to this moment. One of the earliest comics he wrote and illustrated was a series called *Grafik Musik* way back in 1989, published by Slave Labor and Cailber Press. Each issue contained two stories and featured an ongoing guest appearance from former Rolling Stone, Brian Jones, as some kind of instructing angel.

"He's always been the ultimate tragic rock figure in my mind," recalls Allred. "He formed the world's greatest rock band and, though the most innovative member, (the Stones have stuck to straight R&B ever since) was cruelly squeezed out."

Allred worked other less obvious music references into *Grafik Musik* with songs like "All Tomorrow's Parties" and "How Soon Is Now" forming story titles.

Red Rocket was published by Dark Horse comics in seven parts between August 1997 and June 1998. Unlike normal comic books, each issue was the size of an old 10-inch 78rpm record.

"I wanted to play with the format," Allred recalls, "and make it clear that it was music-themed." This album cover template gave Allred more interesting page layouts for the series, which was later compiled into a graphic novel.

The plot revolves around an alien called the Original who crashlands upon Earth and in nearly dying, splits himself into several different clone-selves called Red Rocket two, three, four, five, six and seven. Red 7 is intent on a musical career and, as the Original conveniently arrives in America in the mid-Fifties, goes on to befriend a wide range of artists from Elvis Presley, Little Richard, the Beatles, the Rolling Stones, David Bowie to the Dandy Warhols. Red 7 eventually forms his own band – the Gear – whose career begins to develop, and by 1997 he is a cult artist. Although I don't want to give the entire plot away, the clone brothers are being hunted and eliminated by Norkum Bah, leader of an evil race called the Enfinates. At

the end of the day the guitar-playing Red 7 finds the mythical lost chord on his guitar that literally saves the day. In true heroic fashion, whilst saving everybody else, Red 7 dies and goes to rock and roll Heaven were he is reunited with old friends like Elvis Presley, Jimi Hendrix, Karen Carpenter, Brian Jones and John Lennon.

This summary fails to do justice to the vitality and sheer *élan* of *Red Rocket 7*. Allred's artwork is breathtaking, enhanced by the vibrant colours chosen by his wife and collaborative partner Laura Allred. Although the plot is weaved into the very fabric of rock and roll history, it never strays into being contrived, even if Allred manages to cram a vast number of bands and artists into the pages. For example Suede, Lou Reed, Roxy Music, Oasis, Blur, the Clash, the Prodigy and even *MOJO* magazine are just a few stations where the train stops on this compelling journey.

"The whole British invasion and its ancestry is the epicentre of my musical taste," Allred confessed when asked why so many British bands appear, "Though the Prodigy is not on my own chart, my son digs 'em way too much!"

As the story leads up to its climax, the Dandy Warhols appear as themselves, the most recent musical friends of Red 7.

"I think they are the most underrated band working today," states Allred, "They should be top of the charts! For me, they represent the best elements of all my favourite bands."

Although the Dandys enjoyed seeing themselves in comic book form and "dug it all the way", there were grumbles from other quarters. A Beatles' representative was annoyed that the Fab Four were depicted with-

Finally Break came and we all headed for the Water.

The Originals © Dave Gibbons. Used with pernmission.

out permission, although as they "saw the affection in the book, that there was nothing grotesquely exploitative, let it go."

Someone else who let it go was Gene Simmons from Kiss, who also appeared in *Red Rocket 7*.

"Laura and I actually had breakfast with Gene in San Diego," recalls Allred. "He threatened me in a very friendly way but settled for some original art. He was very cool. If I wasn't so naïve about likeness rights I never would have done it (*Red Rocket 7*). I'm surprised Dark Horse never blinked."

When it was published, *Red Rocket 7* received fantastic reviews, although comic shops grumbled a bit about displaying a 10" comic. Today it remains a compelling read in graphic novel form and is recommended to every reader without reservation. However, *Red Rocket 7* was only one element of a three-

pronged assault by Allred on the senses. Inspired by the example of Robert Rodriguez's *El Mariachi*, Allred also made a low-budget film for $10,000 based on the *Red Rocket* concept called *Astroesque*. Typically Allred recorded the soundtrack with his band The Gear. The album, entitled *Son of Red Rocket 7* featured tracks like "It Was…Anon" and "Subculture Superstar" with Allred singing and playing guitar.

Today, as well as being an in-demand artist from the likes of Marvel and DC, Allred continues to challenge the traditional comic book format. One fascinating outing was entitled *Vertical*, which as the title suggests is a thin, narrow book concerning a young man called Brando Bale who is compelled to jump off buildings by a guilty secret. He actually works in Andy Warhol's famed Factory, although sadly we don't get to see the Velvet Underground and Nico rehearse amidst helium-filled silver balloons. We don't see Andy Warhol's face either, due to the publisher being worried about the image rights issue. This was small beer compared the to the problems Allred and writer Peter Milligan encountered when they wrote Lady Diana into the plot of the dearly departed *X-Statix* comic. But that is another story…

Of course, whether Allred will ever get to draw a White Stripes' comic remains to be seen. But music comics are making something of a comeback. *Watchmen* artist Dave Gibbons recently stepped into the ring with *The Originals*, a graphic novel based on his young days as a Mod in England during the late Sixties.

"My first sighting of a guy on a scooter with all the chrome and mirrors and dressed in really cool clothes made him look like something from another planet. So I treated the entire story to make it seem larger than life to people who would look at it now."

Gibbons took these experiences as the basis for a plot set in an imaginary Sixties England that involves hover scooters, drugs, smart clothes, gang conflict, music, nights out and rites of passage that must be passed when growing up. It is an excellent read and Gibbons could not resist inserting a reference to the modern Modfather himself:

"Paul Weller is someone I always thought had a really good feeling for that culture and that kind of ethos, principle and standards of the Mod way of life. He is someone whose music I have always enjoyed, right up to the latest covers album as well. So he has a name-check in there as the name of a street!"

In England, two graphic novels on the life and times of Kurt Cobain (2003) and Em-

inem (2004) have been published by Omnibus Press and are superb career overviews. *Godspeed* which details the life and times of Cobain, and thus Nirvana, is particularly good. It is illustrated by an artist with the delightful name of Flameboy.

"When I read the script I thought it was brilliant because it was telling the story through Kurt's eyes," he told me "and of course, that is what makes it fiction, because nobody truly knew what Kurt really thought. Even after you read his journals, and they are very disturbing, you still don't know Kurt Cobain."

The script for *Godspeed* was written by Jim McCarthy and Barnaby Legg.

"Kurt Cobain is a subject to be handled with care," Legg told me, "we are taking real people and a real tragedy and bringing our own agenda to a certain extent. In Kurt's first person narrative that takes us through the

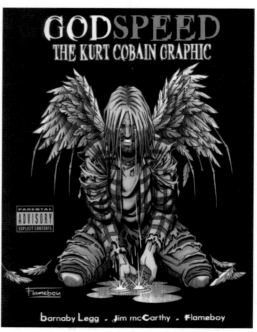

© Art by Flameboy / Omnibus Press.

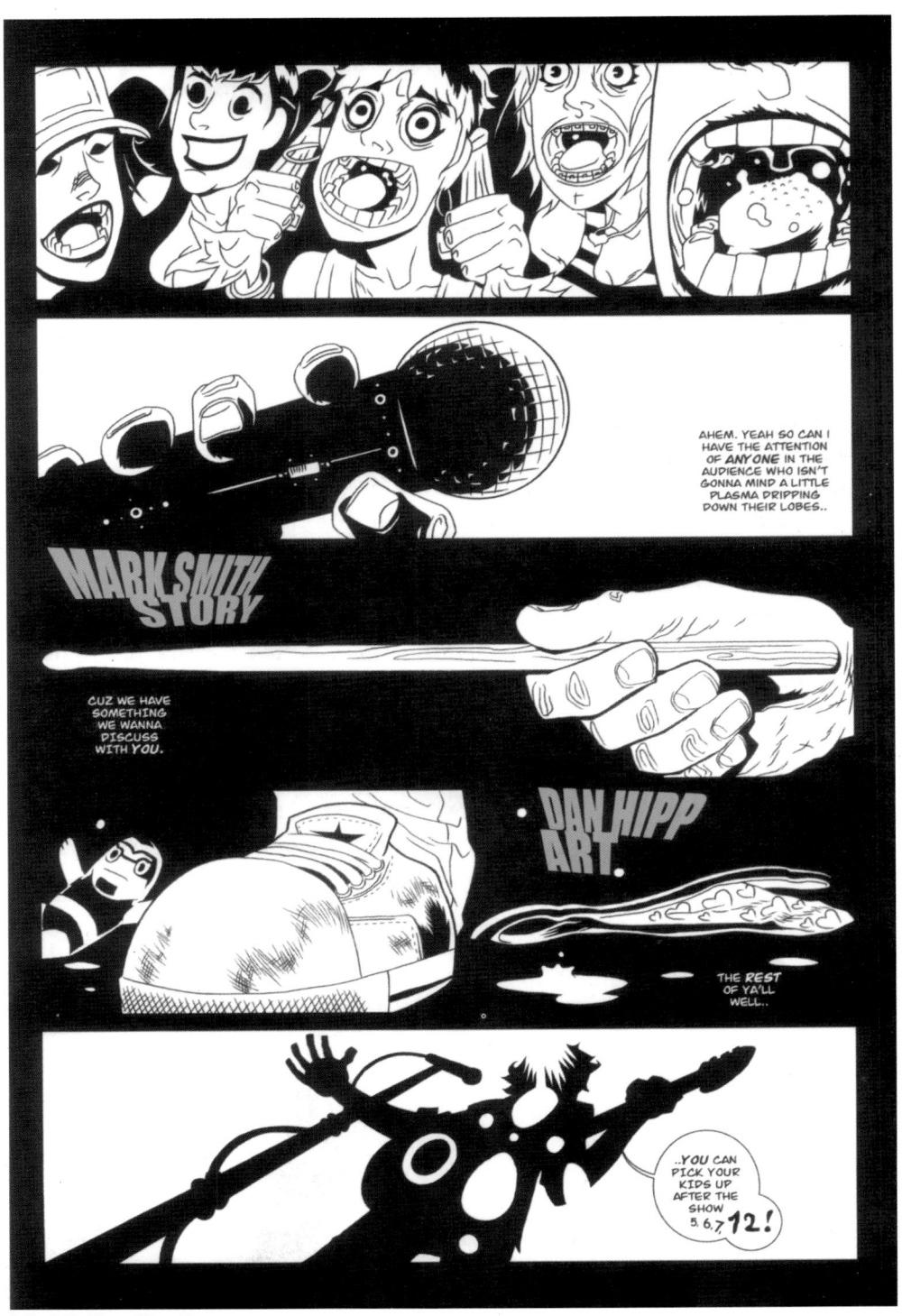

© Mark Smith and Dan Hipp.

book I am not trying to put words into his mouth, but take the reader closer to a sense of who he was. Kurt's narrative that ties together all the pieces of this 'dream' idea, this looking back over the events of his life from the point of his death, has to flow from beginning to end almost like a song."

As McCarthy points out, the graphic novel was also an ideal way to cover Cobain's career:

"I think there is just the right amount of dialogue and pictures that are able to convey things and events on Kurt's life that would be possibly harder in a straight fiction novel. *Godspeed* also adds to the legend, crying Cobain iconic image of a kneeling, crying Cobain with broken angelic wings rising out of his back.

"That was the first image I ever drew of Cobain," Flameboy recalls. "I just did it in pencil and I wrote in quote from his journals,

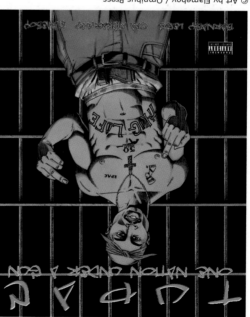

which I think he penned in a moment of desperation which started with 'God Damn, Jesus Fucking Christ Almighty'. And ended with 'I'm so alone. Is there anybody out there?' I read that entry in the journal and thought how bad he must have been feeling to write that. That is where that image came from."

This creative team have now tackled the Tupac story, (*Tupac*, Omnibus Press, October 2005) and from the proofs we have seen it looks superb.

Personally speaking, I'd like to see them wrestle with Oasis next. Not only is it a stonking story of sex, drugs and rock and roll, but the history of brotherly bust-ups between Noel and Liam would also give lovers of fightboy superhero comics something to enjoy as well.

Of course when it comes to fighting, rock bands and comics, there is a new act in town. They are the Amazing Joy Buzzards whose adventures are scripted and drawn by Mark Smith and Dan Hipp.

"The idea came from Sixties television like The Monkees, *Hard Day's Night* Beatles and a mish-mash of foreign cinema," Smith told me, "all that kind of stuff."

Any four-piece that are guarded by a wrestler, have their bass-player turn into a sixty-foot monster and take on killer vampire robots is OK with me.

The last word in the comics and music crossover goes to Stan Lee who, at 84, recently announced the project that will turn Ringo Starr into a superhero. That of course give a new twist to the line from the famed song on *Sgt Pepper's* that asked, "Will you still need me, Will you still feed me, When I'm Sixty Four."

Epilogue

Okay, Okay, Okay…. Some of you have finished the book and are fuming. Old Shirley has missed something of vital importance! The Comics Journal music special from the Summer of 2002, an intricate analysis of Swing With Scooter or Peter Bagge and Jaime Hernandez's brilliant Yeah!, and Steve Lafler's superb tales of jazz Bughouse as illustrated opposite. Where are the interviews with Glenn Danzig, David Mustaine, The Sea And The Cake guy, Grant Morrison and Alice Cooper???

Well, there are some things that I did not have the space to include. I have enough lyrical quotes in comic book to last me a lifetime. When it came to interviews there were some people I just could not get to or – in some cases – did not get back to me even though wheels were set in motion to set up interviews. However, if as the Bride says in Kill Bill 1, "you still feel raw about it" please feel free to drop me an email at ijshirl@hotmail.com. I will be overjoyed to discover appearances by pop stars in comics that I did not know about or be contacted by music and comic book heavyweights who want to be interviewed about music and comics. Robert Smith from the Cure, Axl Rose, Slash, Eminem, Elton John, Ringo Starr, step on down!

Also, if anyone does have that mystical appearance by a member of Duran Duran in a UK girl's comic I want to know about it….

Ian Shirley
ijshirl@hotmail.com

An Illustrated History of Music and Comics

Index

SAF and Firefly Books

Order Online

For the latest on SAF and Firefly titles, or to order books online, check the SAF website. You can also browse the full range of rock, pop, jazz and experimental music books we have available, as well as keeping up with our latest releases. There are also:

Special pre-publication offers
Signed copies
Monthly offers
Book reviews and extracts
Competitions

You can also contact us via email, and request a catalogue.

info@safpublishing.com

www.safpublishing.com

Recent titles:
Morrissey, Devo, Mountain, Alex Harvey, The Pretty Things, Cabaret Voltaire, Coil-Current 93-Nurse With Wound, U2 Encyclopedia (updated), Thin Lizzy, Genesis, Gentle Giant, Nirvana recording sessions, Hawkwind, Suicide

Forthcoming titles:
Soft Machine, Gong, Frank Zappa, Arthur Brown

Backlist titles:
From Frank Zappa to Alice Cooper, From Captain Beefheart to Prince, From Robert Wyatt to The Residents, From Kraftwerk to the Ramones,
and many, many more.....

saf publishing